"Engaging, artful, and moving. I want some of my friends to read it, and soon! May we all learn something about living and suffering for Christ through this heartwarming and infuriating story."

- Amanu Ensis, author of *The Missing Mark*

CALLED TO STAND

CALLED TO STAND

by

PATRICIA FEIJO

CALLED TO STAND

Copyright © 2017 by Patricia Feijo

World Ahead Press is a division of WND Books. The views and opinions expressed in this book are those of the author and do not necessarily reflect the official policy or position or WND Books.

Paperback ISBN: 978-1-944212-96-4
eBook ISBN: 978-1-944212-97-1

Unless otherwise noted, Scripture quotations are taken from the *Proper Name Version of the King James Bible*, Copyright 2015. Name Publishers, LLC. Used by permission.

All Scriptures are based on the Authorized (King James) Version of the Bible, the rights to which are vested in the Crown. Reproduced in the UK by permission of the Crown's patentee, Cambridge University Press.
Author photo by Jennifer Neves Photography.

CONTENTS

DEDICATION

Dedicated to *Yahweh, The Living God, the great I Am*

"I will stand upon my watch, and set me upon the tower, and will watch to see what He will say to me. . ."

Habakkuk 2:1

ACKNOWLEDGMENTS

First and foremost, I must thank all Daniel Chapter One customers, radio listeners, and distributors who trusted us and supported us throughout the years, for your great faith and love. Special thanks to those who have sent donations that helped support us financially, and moreover, with inspiration and cheer.

My deep appreciation to all our fact witnesses and others who were willing to testify on our behalf (most are named in this book) and to those who wrote declarations and character references. I thank Dr. Tedd Koren for being there throughout the ordeal, and for writing a letter to the judge and allowing your letter to be used as the Foreword.

I thank all our incredible lawyers (also named in this book) for believing in us and working so hard for us. It was a hard-fought battle, and one I believe you really cared about. At times you withstood ridicule from the media and the government; thank you for that courage and for your grace in confronting evil injustice.

To those personal friends who helped us get by when things were at their worst: Bert and Claudia Rottach, Doug and Bernadette Coldren, Sue Sullivan, Andrea Hadaya, Edith Malin, Maria Sanchez, Bob Morin and Ben Benevides. I love and thank you for your nonjudgmental friendship and boundless help. Many thanks to David and Evelyn Bertrand for your continued loyal support. And to Dr. Luc De Schepper, my eternal gratefulness for the importance of your teaching and warmth of your friendship.

I thank my beloved brother and sister, Dr. William L. Haith (Larry) and Mary Ann Smith (Mimi), for reading the early manuscript. Your sweet encouragement and comments spurred me on.

Much gratitude to Troy Titus, our dear brother in Christ and friend, for your invaluable editing of the manuscript, insights, patient encouragement and corrections, and to Laura Lisle, my copy editor, for your sensitive technical and artistic polish.

Michael Klassen at World Ahead Press, thank you for all your assistance in bringing this book to print. You've made the arduous task a pleasure.

To my stepchildren, Eric Feijo and Jill Feijo, thank you for being a wonderful part of my life and of this story. You've shown Christlikeness, each in your unique way, by your support, long suffering, forgiveness of our shortcomings, and, in the end, unshakable love.

And I thank my husband, Jim, who had the vision for this book and sacrificed the most in my writing of it. I'm grateful to you for always pushing me to be better and to reach higher. Thanks for loving the Lord as much as you do. I love you most for your love for others, and for your untiring zeal in serving Yahweh. Without you, there would be no *Called To Stand*.

FOREWORD

I was first introduced to Daniel Chapter One and Jim and Tricia Feijo due to a personal tragedy back in 2009. My son, then 17, had just been diagnosed with brain tumors by radiologists from two hospitals. The oncologists told us that unless we began immediate radiation therapy on his brain, he would soon be dead. It was a terrifying experience and we were told we had no other options. The medical journals I began reviewing revealed that radiation therapy is related to, in a surprising number of cases, brain damage and brain cancer years later.

I, my wife, and our son refused to rush into radiation or surgery, telling the doctors it would be our "last resort," not our "first resort." We researched other options. Daniel Chapter One products proved to be one option. Tricia and Jim freely shared their time, thoughts, and experience with me and my son, answered our calls no matter what time of day or night, and hosted us in their home to discuss our concerns. They seemed too good to be true, and I'm sure we are not alone in that experience.

A follow up MRI a year later found no trace of the tumors, and our son remains well. Upon telling the Feijos the good news, their joy was as if it were their own family member that was saved.

Patients need sources of information about alternatives to radiation and chemotherapy of the sort provided by Daniel Chapter One, and the testimonials of those who've used their products. The government should not act to stifle such information and testimonial evidence.

Ignorance can be forgiven, but if combined with arrogance–that only doctors know and can determine what is true–it can lead to misery and death, especially when the power of government and medical boards weigh into personal decisions to demand patient obedience to medical and pharmaceutical interests.

Fortunately, our need for alternative help came before the injunction against Daniel Chapter One for sharing product advice. There are others out there right now like my son who could be helped by Daniel Chapter One, who cannot be helped by them because of the FTC's injunction.

There is a significant interest to the public to keep the channels of communication open about alternative medical care and treatments that the government seeks to close. Rather than condemn Daniel Chapter One for helping people deal with various illnesses, the government should commend the wonderful work that Daniel Chapter One has done to help families like mine.

Tedd Koren, DC, 2017

PROLOGUE

This is the true story of Daniel Chapter One, a Christian house church and healthcare ministry we founded in 1986 to help fund house churches in communist countries. People have asked who we are, how we happened to do all that we did, and why the US government sought to attack and destroy us. This book was written to answer those questions.

The FTC and FDA litigation that afflicted us spanned the entire eight years of President Obama's reign. It was a time of burgeoning government size and power, and growing intolerance toward the Christian faith and freedoms this country was founded upon. Federally mandated health insurance was established, while powerful bureaucracies created more rules and regulations to protect government-approved drugs and to control how Americans take care of their health.

Richard E. Ralston, Executive Director of Americans for Free Choice in Medicine, wrote in a letter to the editor (*Wall Street Journal*, April 14, 2017): *"Internal special interests at the FDA are those whose highest priority is the maintenance of the power of the FDA bureaucracy itself. Their priority is to make sure that no patient obtains effective treatment or survives illness without government permission."*

Our story attests to that point. The Foreword is a letter written by a doctor whose son was healed with the help of Daniel Chapter One. It's a truthful account, one of thousands, and was originally written as a declaration and as a character reference for the court. But it was one of several that our attorneys chose not to submit to the judge, in order that we not look unrepentant.

No longer constrained, we can now say that we are not sorry, for we have done no wrong. We are not sorry for dedicating our lives to helping people in the service of our Lord and Savior; not sorry for speaking the truth in love; and we are not sorry for standing against government tyranny.

I began writing *Called to Stand* in 2014, before our case was over, and finished it in 2016. Some chapters are flashbacks, memoir-like, and some are written in the present as the story is unfolding. I give dates where necessary, for the sake of context and the time of the event. To jog my memory and to be as exact as possible, I used diaries, newspaper articles, and court transcripts. Where it was deemed prudent, some names have been changed or omitted. The names of the professionals involved, such as judges, lawyers, and expert witnesses, have not been changed.

PART ONE

THE FOUNDATION IS LAID

"But seek you first the kingdom of God, and His righteousness; and all these things shall be added unto you."

Matthew 6:33

CHAPTER 1

BEGINNINGS

"It's a raid!!! It's a raid!!!"

Menacing shouts exploded toward my office from the stairwell, over a stampede of heavy, booted feet. Only moments before, I had given two Sesame Street finger puppets a quick spin in the saucer of a baby musical toy, tossing them high into the air to the surprised delight of my 3-year-old granddaughter, Hayden. Our laughter froze as armed agents in black uniforms burst into the room. More agents descended like locusts upon the storefront and office below.

Jim, standing in the doorway watching us play on the floor, was immediately made to relinquish his cell phone with a gun to his head and taken away. Hayden hid behind the blue child's bookcase I bought for her sister, Emma, when she was that age. I made my way to the phone, and was ordered not to touch anything. Nobody explained what was happening, but I noticed the badge on the chest of one of the vested agents: FDA. The only other people in the building, a very pregnant office worker and Hayden's mother, Jill, with her baby, Mya, downstairs, were quickly ushered outside and the door locked behind them. Black government SUVs lined the parking lot, and a state police cruiser and a local police cruiser blocked the driveway.

*   *   *

Late-summer sunlight was beginning to brighten the bedroom, and the rumble and swoosh of traffic could be heard picking up on East Main Road three floors below. I lifted myself, begrudgingly, out of bed.

And morning never came.

Lord, what?! More a thought than audible words, it came not from me but *to* me, in a still, small, and familiar voice.

Shuffling around the room, gathering clothes to take downstairs, I wondered what God was telling me. Might I die soon, in my sleep? Or, perhaps my husband Jim would? Maybe we both would perish before the trial, before the whole ordeal was over.

All day the phrase reechoed, *and morning never came.*

Stop procrastinating, I thought. *That must be it! Don't worry about tomorrow, don't even think about tomorrow or plan for it. 'And morning never came' . . . sounds like the beginning or ending of a story. So, start writing our story? The one my husband and others have urged me to write but I keep waiting until everything is over, thinking I can write it from prison where I'll have more time . . .?*

Start now, I decided, *for the glory of God! Write it now, if ever you are going to. Stop saying tomorrow!*

So I begin. The year is 2014, and it's been four years since the raid. This is our story, a tale of the faithfulness of Yahweh and the wonderful adventure it is to serve Him, no matter how difficult it may become.

✳   ✳   ✳

A heavy woman with dark skin and two young boys walked along the sidewalk the other day, beside where I had just parked my champagne-colored Jaguar behind the Tennis Hall of Fame tennis courts. Good-looking boys, cute, maybe 8 and 9 years old. When I jumped out of the car in tennis whites, shouldering my racket, bag, and purse, the woman glanced and scoffed out loud for the boys' benefit, "Rich people think they're better than everybody else." What?! That was uncalled for! She hurried the boys away before I could smile and say hello.

Such is prejudice; hostile, irrational.

I'm not one of those "rich people" she took me for, and I certainly don't consider myself above anyone else. Jim and I are truly nobodies: sinners saved by grace. We joke between ourselves that the Lord chose a couple of real dummies to stand up to tyranny in the US government, too naive to have any fear, just as He chose us to found Daniel Chapter

One, when we had nothing, so that all credit goes undeniably to Him, lest any man boast.

Born in 1959, I grew up in the suburbs of Shrewsbury, Massachusetts, in a modest, one-floor house with others like it lining the street. Mom was a housewife, dad a teacher. They raised three kids on inexpensive food and clothing, and family vacations we camped. The riches they gave us were principles and values to live by, reinforced by their love for each other, for us, for others, for God and for nature. Gentle and full of kindness, they lived and preached respect for everyone. As a matter of fact, one of my earliest memories from preschool age is of coming home after playing in the neighborhood with other children and innocently telling my mother what I had heard, that a new family just moved in named the Niggers. She told me sternly never to talk that way again. Confused and embarrassed, I didn't understand what I had said that was bad.

Dad taught in an inner-city school in Worcester and cared deeply for all his students. I never heard racial slurs at home. I never heard any denigrating thing about anybody. Honestly, I never heard loud, coarse, or inappropriate words. My mother's response that day was as harsh as it got, which is why I remember it. They taught me to love and not hate. They believed that all men are created equal, a foundational truth they infused into me, my sister, and my brother.

Jim was born in 1947 in Fall River, Mass. His parents worked so many hours they were hardly ever home. His dad toiled in the mills and his mom served as a housekeeper and nanny to various Jewish families. They both continued to work cleaning houses and offices until their late 70s. Jim and his sister were latchkey kids, living in the middle apartment of a three-decker. Love was sure, but discipline tough: the belt. City streets and rowdy groups beckoned young Jimmy, and were it not for a high school coach who took him under his wing, the streets might have destroyed him. Thanks to his coach, Jim channeled his exuberant energy into sports, playing hard and achieving great success, despite sneakers so worn the soles had to be fortified with cardboard inserts. He drank honey for endurance, and set records that remain unbroken in track and football. I think the Lord blessed him for his high moral character, and for honoring his father and mother. Perhaps these were early signs that the Lord does the winning and the choosing.

Jim enjoyed being part of a uniquely extended family that included not only "Voovoo" and "Vovo," his Portuguese grandparents, but also included the Jewish families his parents worked for, his football team, and his family's church. For a time he wanted to be a priest, so he took himself to Sunday mass every week and learned prayers in Latin.

Both our parents were Roman Catholic. My dad was Irish and my mom Polish, born to an immigrant. Their fathers had died at young ages and their mothers had worked in sewing mills. My folks were the first generation in their family to attend college. Jim's parents were both Portuguese, and he was the first one to attend college in his family. He dreamt of going to the College of the Holy Cross to study art, but a scholastic scholarship to Springfield College dictated a different path, and there he majored in Physical Education and Psychology, earning a MEd before beginning his PhD. Jim downplays his education and degrees, calling himself "certified stupid." If there's one thing he detests, its airs about being educated as if it makes one superior. He worked his way through school moving furniture and selling his oil paintings.

A thread common to both our childhoods was a strong work ethic. Hard work pays off; work hard; you must work for what you need and want; don't steal; owe no man! All scriptural principles. Jim remembers his father working three "sweat jobs" in a day, refusing to accept government welfare. I've seen Jim take those principles and go beyond, considering others more important than himself, giving to all who ask, giving to those who cannot pay back and without expecting anything in return. More than once he took our rent money (and did this when we were living hand-to-mouth) and gave it to someone with a greater or more urgent need, like visas for a missionary family, or to a family whose father had cancer.

Several years prior to that, just out of college, he took a cross-country trip with a male friend and ended up in Hawaii after gambling his last $30 in Vegas and winning big enough for airfare to Oahu. While on the island he was unofficially offered a tremendous coaching position at the University of Hawaii, a position later held by Dom Capers. Had he stayed to apply, his life may have turned out very differently, but his father ordered him home to honor his word to another coach who had already hired him for a position in New Jersey. He returned to keep his word.

Jim burst from the starting block in the job he had committed to, as head football coach for The Pennington School. Just 24 years old, he flipped the Red Raiders history of losses that season, leading them to total victory, becoming the youngest undefeated coach in the country. After one major game, a pivotal upset, his jubilant players hoisted him onto their shoulders and carried him high in the air. Exiting the field aloft, he remembers looking up into the sky, shaking his fist at God, and yelling, "I told you I didn't need you!"

He had come to believe that religion was for the weak and not for him, after befriending an atheist in college, and after the church wrote to his parents that they dropped his membership since he failed to send in weekly "offerings." His Philosophy paper entitled, "Fear, The Reason for The Existence of God" got him an A++.

Following two years at Pennington, he next took a coaching and teaching position at Ursinus College, Pennsylvania; however, he was fired after the first year when he refused to help rivals try to bring each other down. The unsettling request was motivated by a power struggle between the athletic director and the dean of men (who was also the head football coach). Each sought Jim privately to join him in defaming the character of the other. Jim would not, and would not take sides. "I refused to bastardize myself," he explains. Consequently, the rivals joined forces to oust Jim, culminating in the chancellor's request that he resign. He refused because he had done nothing wrong. Despite threats that he would be blacklisted forever if he did not resign, he stood firm and was both fired and blacklisted. Some would call his decision admirable, some would say foolish, but the fact is his integrity was not negotiable, despite being married and with a baby on the way. Ending up selling cars, he never taught or coached college again, though eventually he returned to coaching football as well as wrestling at his alma mater, Durfee High School in Fall River.

By the time he was 29, his marriage had become strained. On the surface things looked good: house in scenic Little Compton, Rhode Island, two beautiful healthy children, a boy and a girl, Cadillac in the driveway: the coveted American life! But a battle raged within. Jim was fighting with his wife, fighting with himself, and fighting The One calling him. That's when missionaries and evangelists, John and Eunice Buffam, stopped by one day, visiting whomever they could in the neighborhood to share the gospel, extending invitations to attend the local UCC (congregational) church.

Jim Feijo decided to accept the Lord Jesus Christ on his 30th birthday.

The day before his birthday, as he sat in the back of the UCC church, the Lord appeared to him and said, "I choose you, you don't choose me." That's when he received Jesus and became a new creature, born again by the Holy Spirit. And that's when his life fell apart and he lost everything, although Jim says that is when he gained everything.

His wife deserted with the children and filed for divorce. He relinquished the house they had moved to in Fall River, the car, and full custody of the children to her, "like a lamb in court," according to a friend who accompanied him to the hearing. Jim had challenged the Lord to test him and would stand the test, but cried himself to sleep every night in the Buffam's attic, painfully missing his kids. After months of crying, he heard the Lord say "Stop crying. You're being selfish. Trust Me. What about My sheep?!"

I was born again about five and a half years after Jim, in my second year of college in Dartmouth Mass. I was a late returning student, after graduating from high school a year early and taking several rebellious years off, during which time I worked sorting splits in a leather factory, sanding computer hoods in a plastics factory, and injecting toxic chemicals into mice in a cancer research lab that was like a factory. I had stopped talking to my parents, who disapproved of my living with a boyfriend. My mother eventually reached me with a note, "We'd like to talk to you," and after meeting with them I finally agreed to go to college with their financial help. But soon after I started studies at Southeastern Massachusetts University (now SMU Dartmouth), my parents and I became estranged again. They disapproved of my new boyfriend, rightly so. He was manipulative and used people, a thief who stole from others and from me. I felt bad for him. I didn't want to listen to reason, stubbornly determined "to do my own thing." I stopped talking to them, paid for school myself by waitressing, and moved into a tiny apartment in a seedy part of New Bedford, subsisting on Cream of Wheat cereal.

A young man visiting the university one day stopped me and asked if I knew Jesus. Annoyed, I quickly told him I was all set, knew God, said, "I'm Catholic." I don't remember the exact course of our brief conversation, but at one point I mentioned the Virgin Mary's ascension into heaven (maybe to show I had Bible knowledge), which he corrected, explaining that account is not in the Bible. Soon after, I turned away and headed off across campus.

Could it not be true? According to what the nuns at St. Mary's taught me, I had believed in the ascension of Mary all my life!

But I hadn't read the Bible. It never made sense to me, never held any appeal. That night I began reading it, and while not discovering any of the evidence I sought regarding Mary the mother of Jesus, I did happen upon Ecclesiastes, which begins, "*Vanity, vanity, all is vanity.*" The verse stung true. Then I read Revelation 3:16, "*So then because you are lukewarm, and neither cold nor hot, I will spew you out of My mouth.*" I was not hot, nor cold, towards the Almighty. I was merely lukewarm, and suddenly did not want to be spit from His mouth! I knelt on the hard floor, and in the diffuse light reaching into the room from street lamps, begged the Lord God into my life and to make it right. I confessed my sins and asked His forgiveness.

The weight of my sins lifted, and only then, after Jesus took it from me, did I realize the tremendous burden I'd been carrying. Euphoric, I got up and called my parents! Mom answered as usual, I told her I loved her and that I was sorry for all the pain I had caused them. Her breathe caught in excitement, "Patricia, have you been born again?" "Yes!" I confirmed, surprised by the question. She then called to my dad joyfully, "Bill, Bill, come here! Tricia's been born again!"

I was baptized in a river in North Dartmouth several months later, by the head elder of The First Christian Church of Hixville. My parents both came. I guess Jim was there too, most people from the church were, but he and I had barely met.

CHAPTER 2

NATURAL VERSUS ARTIFICIAL

I'm not usually in our store anymore, but this day in 2014, when Cindy and Liza, two former homeopathy clients, stopped by, I happened to be here. Cindy suffered a head injury in a car accident, and was healed with homeopathic remedies after seeking my help. We originally met about 30 years ago, during the first year of my marriage. In those days I didn't work and spent one day a week with Eunice Buffam. Together we cooked and talked and attended a Bible study with her husband, John, at the Old Stone Church in Little Compton. I met Cindy, who this morning came looking for homeopathic Arsenicum album for the upcoming flu season, at that study. Along with her purchase, Jim and I gifted her with a Names of God Bible, a Bible that uses the Hebrew names and titles of God, like "Yahweh Elohim" (the Lord God).

It was in Israel, years before, camping in Shiloh where the Lord revealed to us His true names. Jim had been praying about using the name Yahshua for Jesus. Several years later, as we finished a live radio broadcast in Albuquerque, New Mexico, an elderly woman came up to us and shared the power of God's real names, explaining that in order to say "Yah," you must drop your jaw and breathe out, as He breathed life into man. We are not legalistic about the names of God because we don't want to ostracize anyone by using unfamiliar words. But we do enjoy the magnificence and meaning of Yahweh's self-appointed names.

Liza, wife of a Rhode Island doctor, came into the store sometime after Cindy left, and was thrilled to see me here so that she might obtain guidance regarding her young son. In the past, we grieved with her and her husband over the tragic death of their firstborn (the baby aspirated meconium in-utero and lived only hours after his birth), and rejoiced with them over the birth of their second son. That child I treated for years for eczema, and later helped the father with Lyme's disease resulting from a tick bite. Both were fully healed.

Can I say healed? I really don't know. But Yahweh Ropheka means "the Lord Who Heals," and He does.

My angst in using the word is because the US government has forbidden us to use certain words, like *treat, cure, prevent* and *mitigate*, unless using the words to sell pharmaceutical drugs approved by the FDA. We are not even allowed to say water can prevent, treat, or cure dehydration! The irony, however, is that no allopathic drug can heal, treat, cure, prevent or mitigate any illness. All pharmaceutical drugs are designed to suppress symptoms; it's mere illusion that they improve health.

Strong's Concordance, under the definition of *sorcery*, reads: "from the Greek *pharmakon*; definition: a drug, spell-giving potion, a druggist or pharmacist, a poisoner." One dictionary definition for the Greek root word *pharma* is "magic charms and potions." Chemical pharmacy is witchcraft, sorcery. The symbol used in pharmacy, big *R* little *x*, is presumably based on the sign of Jupiter and was used to propitiate the god in writing a prescription.

The way of true healing is from the Living God, Yahweh, and is to utilize His creation. As He created man from "the dust of the earth," so He grows plants from the earth that have the same vitamins and minerals in our bodies, nutrients necessary to stay healthy and fight disease. Healing can take place when a need or deficiency of the body is met, and that need is always for a biological, not a synthetic, substance. We do not suffer illness from a lack of chemical drugs, but from nutritional deficiencies.

Homeopathic remedies are energetic, not physical matter, derived from natural substances (plants and other things occurring in nature) that have been diluted beyond measure. Their energy can balance the life energy, or vital force, of a living being, if the remedy taken is the right match. Homeopathy does not treat a disease, it instead treats the whole person, the mental/emotional/physical being. The basic homeopathic constitutional types, the type of person one is, depending on the totality of one's individual characteristics, are all minerals: Calcarea carbonica (calcium), Phosphorus, Sulphur, Silicea . . . stuff of the dust of the earth!

The government sued us because we told the truth about drugs and offered natural alternatives, and threatened to imprison us. Judge Emmett Sullivan called in marshals with handcuffs when we appeared before him on contempt charges, to remand us to a Washington DC jail until we agreed to fully comply with the Federal Trade Commission order to stop our ministry. The order forbade us from sharing health information, and required us to mail our customers a deceptive letter written by the government which stated that only conventional cancer treatments (chemo and radiation) have been "scientifically proven safe and effective in humans."

"It's a matter of coercion" insisted the DOJ lawyer, Jessica Gunder. The judge agreed. "Yes it is, a matter of coercion."

*   *   *

I sit in my second-floor office, outside Providence, Rhode Island, behind a Surface computer perched on a pile of books balanced on one corner of the desk. The desk is a mess. The whole room is a mess; only the pale yellow walls sporting homeopathy posters and children's art look cheery. I gaze out the large front window overlooking the parking lot, to our home. I'm sad to be here in the quiet of space no longer in use. Ever since the Feds stormed this room, taking client files and personal items from my drawers, I no longer work in here. The metal drawers of the file cabinet remain empty. I fear that anything I put in them may without warning be seized again. This manuscript, this computer, could be seized at any moment. It's hard for me to even walk into this room and feel normal.

There's nothing normal about being suddenly and loudly ambushed by men in black uniforms wearing bulletproof vests. It was traumatizing, personally violating. The government agents desecrated this place, this sanctuary where many people came asking for help, came to be cured of their suffering.

But I am not supposed to use the word *cure*, only drug companies can.

To my left and right and behind me are walls lined with bookcases stuffed with books collected over 20 years of study and practice, and where two walls meet to my right hang 14 certificates from homeopathy classes, some signifying 1 to 3 year's work. One absent is from a PhD program nearly completed, for which I had to take an online exam the week we were raided. I managed to take the exam, here in this disheveled room, phone lying broken apart, a pile of papers still heaped on the floor, invisible fingerprints of federal agents on everything.

All praise to Yahshua, I passed the difficult test. Before taking the exam, Brian Fetzer and Jim laid hands on me and prayed. Brian was living with us at the time, after taking a coaching job at Harvard mainly so he could have closer fellowship with us. Serendipitously, through Brian we obtained the California contact to our present legal counsel after the raid.

I can still practice homeopathy. The government has not forbidden it. Not yet anyway. I tried initially to continue helping clients, but my focus was compromised as well as my time by court dates and legal briefs. I closed my practice.

For what reason did government agents aggressively attack us that September day, 2010, and why did they take my files?

In part (from the warrant), their search was for: "any and all correspondence, notes, e-mail, posters, signs, records, both written and electronic, which may be related to the representation, in any manner, expressly or by implication, that any Daniel Chapter One products are articles intended for use in the diagnosis, cure, mitigation, treatment, or prevention of disease in man or other animal." Not only my office but the entire building was turned inside out; every computer and phone was disassembled while videos were taken of the walls and shelves. Daniel Chapter One customers' affidavit testimonies and medical records were seized, along with thousands of citizen signatures on paper petitions supporting health freedom.

Not a single consumer complaint has been made in nearly 30 years of operation that any Daniel Chapter One product has ever harmed anyone, nor any complaint made that we ever misled anyone, let alone the fact that no one has ever died from our products or information. Rather, the Lord has healed thousands through Daniel Chapter One, many after they were sent home to die by their physicians.

FDA-approved pharmaceutical drugs kill over 100,000 people every year.

Our free speech and healthy products threaten a sacred cow: the drug industry. The government's commitment to protecting their monopoly on health care is the reason for such draconian efforts to silence us and stop us from providing alternative treatments.

CHAPTER 3

STARTING LIFE TOGETHER

"**M**ind if I smoke?" I asked Jim, settling into the ride up to Boston in his orange VW bus. I fit right in with its hippie look in my cotton peasant blouse and jeans, bare feet propped up on the dashboard, long feather earrings, soft reddish-brown, matching my hennaed hair.

"No, go ahead," he obliged, hiding his displeasure. He was already apprehensive about this, our first date.

Another couple had planned to join us, but couldn't make it. Jim tried to cancel the outing, but I held him to it, quoting scripture, "*Let your yes be yes and your no, no.*"

We had a blast in the art museum, where Jim was scolded for touching things. We ate sitting on the floor in a Japanese restaurant, laughing and talking comfortably the entire time, instant friends.

After that day Jim gave me rides home from church. Every other weekend we were accompanied by his children, Eric and Jill. We all got along great. One weekend we went camping with a group from the church. Eric noted to his dad that everyone there was married, hinting that he should be too! Before long, Jim proposed to me, if you can call it a proposal. He informed me that he was going to marry me, and I was fine with that: the Lord had brought us together.

In past conversations, we both agreed that diamond engagement rings were overpriced and nothing but a clever business creation. When he later asked if I'd "mind" if he got me a ring, I said "Ok . . . but nothing big." I got a tiny diamond and a formal proposal one starry September night as we sat out on my loft apartment's roof, high on top of an old whaling building in the historic section of New Bedford.

We announced our engagement in church Sunday morning, then drove up to Shrewsbury to tell my parents. They were shocked, but pleased. Mom called our joy infectious. We also visited Fred Bopp, an elderly evangelist whom Jim had befriended in a church in Worcester while away on a wrestling trip. Fred had approached Jim, a visitor sitting in the back pew, and asked, "Is this sinner's row?"

"Yes it is!" answered Jim heartily, making room for Fred to sit beside him.

Reverend Bopp, though he never used the title, laid hands on us and invoked the Lord's blessing upon our union when we visited him with our engagement news.

My parents asked only that we delay the wedding until the school year was over, to give us more time to get to know one another. We didn't think it necessary, but agreed to their request. What a rocky year it turned out to be.

At one point, Jim called off our engagement because, he said, he didn't want to marry a smoker. "I'll quit," I offered. He told me to quit then, for how could he know for sure I'd quit later?

Then he called off the wedding a second time, concerned that I was working toward a degree, saying he didn't want a career woman for a wife. He wanted a helpmate who would be busy at home, as Scripture says a wife should be. He felt I didn't need a degree to be the writer I wished to be for the Lord, so suggested I either drop out of school to marry him, or pursue my degree. I argued that I didn't have to use a degree once I had it, but he said he didn't want to get in the way of my future, and basically, would call the wedding off if I chose to stay in school. As he drove away that night I cried out to God, not sure what to do. The Lord told me that He was changing the direction of my life, and to leave the old path. I told Jim the next day I would quit school at the end of the year.

His last ultimatum was for me to move in with the elder of our church and his wife for the remainder of the school year. That was motivated by the fact that my two roommates' boyfriends stayed over nights in the open space of our loft without doors.

It hurt to tell my parents I would not be finishing school, with just one year to go, and my mother wept. But our plans persisted, and we were married July 2, 1983, in a Baptist church in the woods in Shrewsbury. The building was a mutual consensus: we said no Catholic church, and no church with stage and pews. My mother insisted on some kind of building (versus our beach at sunrise idea). A friend of hers, a Baptist pastor, agreed to let us use his half-built church. My dad and I cut dogwood branches from our yard that morning to decorate the unfinished church interior. Guests sat in folding chairs arranged in a circle, and Jim and I each walked into the church with our mother and father, to signify that God says a man and woman will leave their father and mother and cleave to each other. The song "They Will Know We Are Christians By Our Love," was played on the piano and sung by a teacher from the Christian school where Jim worked. I wore a plain white gown (a $100 prom gown), a wreath of white baby's breath on my head, and carried daisies.

My sister was my maid of honor, and Jim's best man was a friend and deacon from our church in Hixville. Other than that, we had no wedding party, nor did we have a party after. We were under fundamental teaching that forbade wine and dancing. In retrospect, Jim says our wedding reception was boring, and calls fundamentalism burdensome. At the time we didn't know any better.

The theme of our wedding, as printed on the programs made by my sister, was "Seek First the Kingdom of God." For vows, Jim read from 1 Corinthians 13, the love chapter, and I read Psalm 40:2–3: "*He brought me up also out of a horrible pit, out of the miry clay, and set my feet upon a rock, and established my goings. And He has put a new song in my mouth.*" (When I was first saved, my mother sent me a pocket Bible "for reading at the bus stop," and wrote in it, "As you sing a new song to the Lord." When I asked her why she never made me go to the Bible studies she was involved in during my wayward years, she said, "Oh, Trish, that was the job of the Holy Spirit!" and sent me the poem "The Hound of Heaven.") We opened the marriage ceremony to testimonies from others to glorify God, and one man, one of Jim's fellow teachers, rose and shared Joel 2:25, "*And I will restore to you the years that the locust has eaten. . .*"

That is exactly what the Lord had begun to do.

✳   ✳   ✳

We couldn't afford the honeymoon to Peru we wanted, the price of visas alone halted our plans, so Jim chose the next best place as a surprise: Canada. Surprise!!! I had no idea where we were going. We headed up through Maine in the orange VW bus the evening after the wedding, an inflated yellow rubber raft riding on top. Jim had the broken brakes and the steering column fixed before the wedding, but not the side door that kept falling off.

He figured $10 to $30 per day for the trip for gas and everything, so from the first night we slept in the bus, using rolled up clothes as pillows. The next day our money doubled due to the exchange rate, which allowed us to take the Scotia Prince ferry over to Nova Scotia. We slept that second night on the ferry, starting out on its upper deck under open sky until rain started falling, driving us below. We sat in the hallway outside a room where people gambled and drank, not having the money for a cabin. We brought our own food, enjoying my Babci's prune bread, her wedding gift to us, in the morning.

Day two, we drove along the coast. Jim gave me a choice, to take Route 1 or Route 2. I first said 1, then changed my mind and said, "no, 2." He stopped the VW and said forcibly, "You cannot change your mind!" This was a rule established the day before when shopping for groceries. I couldn't decide between apples or oranges, couldn't afford a bag of both, and when it became a belabored decision he put his foot down and told me that he could not, would not, go through life deliberating over every little thing! So we stuck to Route 1.

"For Sale" signs peppered the roadside, so for fun we stopped at a realty office. Nothing back home was affordable, but maybe here, in Canada? We ended up paying $300 for two acres in St Alphonse, South Bear Cove. Continuing up the coast we discovered Kijumkujic National Park and decided to camp there, opting for a lone camping site on an island, the caveat being that we had to get ourselves to it. Boats could be rented, but we had our raft, which we hurried into the water and set out, hoping to beat an impending storm.

Thick seaweed near the shore grabbed at the small motor Jim operated off the back of the raft, soon choking it completely. We began paddling until we couldn't see land any longer. The sky had been darkening until both it and the water was black, and the increasing wind and waves began pushing our little raft backwards.

"Paddle!!" Jim screamed to me. I paddled.

"Paddle harder!!" I paddled harder. We were going in a circle.

"Not that side . . . the other side!!" Jim bellowed.

That's when I placed my paddle across my lap, folded my arms, and said, "That's it! I'm done!!" He had the back, rudder responsibility, our circling was not my fault.

Paddling together was, as yet, unrehearsed and inexperienced.

He next told me to look at the map, but strong wind made it impossible.

"Grab hold of that buoy!" he yelled, referring to one tossing about in the rough waters. I could not! All I could picture was me holding onto that buoy and the raft being pulled out from under me by the waves. I was scared, we both were. Terrified. The storm roared.

I thought of Jesus when He walked on water. Peter walked on water too, by faith, until he looked at the wind and grew afraid, then he began to sink. *Oh Jesus, help us now! Calm our fears!* We both silently prayed. *Lord, save us!*

We kept paddling, again, this time together.

An hour passed before the sea and the sky calmed down. We had traveled about a nautical mile without a map. Our weary arms no longer able to paddle, we landed abruptly. The direction of the water had changed, pushing our raft by currents until we bumped the island's shore. By then all was tranquil.

Supper was miso soup cooked on the Coleman stove, with more prune bread and kasha (buckwheat). That night we lay down to sleep inside our two-man pup tent, imagining ourselves as happy as Adam and Eve in the garden before the fall. . .

Splish splash!

Splashing in the water disturbed the stillness. We next heard thumping on the ground, tearing, and crunching, quickening our heartbeats. It sounded large, and was vigorously eating right outside the tent! Jim felt for the small knife beneath his head and held it up in front of his face, its silhouette visible in the moonlight.

"Why don't you go see what it is," I whispered.

"Why don't you go see what it is" he whispered back, holding out the knife to me. Neither of us moved.

We didn't see the warning until our return to the ranger station on the mainland. "Beware! Black bears! Don't leave food out!" We'd missed the list of instructions due to our haste to beat the storm. The arms of the Almighty had protected us in our oblivion.

We next journeyed up through Newfoundland, and beyond, into Labrador.

Approaching the coast of Newfoundland by ferry, after a night spent in each other's arms, barely fitting on top of the life preserver box, we awoke to a brilliant sky of crimson and peach heralding the dawn. It was very early, and very cold, but in the glory of that morning we were richer than those tucked into their warm cabins below. God was giving us a private show of His splendor, a spectacular panorama in the theater of His creation!

The countryside of Newfoundland looked prehistoric. We drove through Gros Morne National Park, below towering, flat-topped mountains divided by cold, freshwater fjords, navigating winding roads without another visible soul for days. We bathed in bodies of pristine water, slept in the VW, and ate off the land. Although we were only able to muster one meal a day, we enjoyed such varied delicacies as wild strawberry crepes with berries freshly picked, pasta with snails plucked from the sea, and fish freshly caught and poached in sea water. Jim caught the fish from the raft, after a much larger fish pulled him out to sea like Hemingway's great marlin in *The Old Man and The Sea*. Eye on the prize, Jim refused to let go, and disappeared over the horizon. He eventually lost the big one, but caught another that I cooked on the Coleman from the back of the bus. Best fish we ever had!

Labrador was starker still. From the solitary dirt road we travelled, we could see small wooden houses dotting the landscape, each with a teepee of firewood in the yard higher than the house, erected tall enough to poke through deep snow in winter. We saw no people.

The black flies were thick and pesky, at every chance attempting to get into our eyes, noses, ears, and mouths, so we stayed in the vehicle and drove until we ran out of road. Thrill mounting, we thought: we can be missionaries to Labrador! We both wanted to be missionaries, especially somewhere the Word of God had not yet reached. Surely this forsaken place needed missionaries, this foreign land we didn't need visas to visit.

A couple of large billboards appeared on the roadside, dispelling our dream of bringing the gospel to Labrador. One read, "Prepare to Meet Thy God," the other, "How Shall We Escape If We Neglect So Great A Salvation?"

"Know who put those signs up?" Jim asked the middle-aged man who had stopped his truck off to the side in front of us, the very first vehicle we encountered.

Starting with a gulp of air, he replied "Ye, m'fadder-puddemup."

He was difficult to understand, his words ran together. *Newfie*, as the locals in Newfoundland and Labrador call their language, is Newfoundland English spoken rapidly with a Scottish brogue. The affirmative *yeah* is made with inhalation, rather than with exhalation.

The man invited us to accompany him to his parents' house. His father had suffered a stroke, but rose up out of his wheelchair when he began to tell us "'Ow de gospel cam t'Labrador!" It was he, Spoffard Earle, whom the Lord used, from a boat, using a megaphone to preach God's Word to the people onshore.

In the Brethren Assembly worship service we attended that evening, the women all wore dresses and head coverings. I was in dirty jeans, my head uncovered. Jim had been praying for months that the Lord would reveal the truth of head coverings to me, and here the issue presented itself. The women back home at our church, all besides Eunice Buffam (who wore a scarf when she prayed), dismissed the scriptural ordinance in 1 Corinthians 11 for women to cover their head when praying, saying, "That was for back then." (Most Christian women object to a head covering and therefore heatedly argue the scripture, as if it's something oppressive they must resist. But the Lord showed me it's to our advantage, and for the angels to witness. *"Ought the woman to have power on her head because of the angels."*)

I went to the kitchen afterwards to talk to the women, and to apologize if my appearance had offended anyone. They assured me no, they judged not. "De Lord knows de 'art, eh?"

"Why do you cover your heads in worship?" I shyly asked the elderly evangelist's wife.

"De Lord sez to in 'is word, eh? An' ye wantz t'pleaz de Lord, eh?" Simple as that.

*   *   *

It rained for days as we journeyed back through Newfoundland. Passing by a tent meeting, we stopped and there met a family, Herman and Yvonne Matthews, and their two young children, Kimberly and Peter. They invited us back to their home, and Yvonne offered to wash and dry our damp clothes, fed us well, gave us Peter's bed to sleep in, and sent us on our way days later with the best food she could gather from her cupboards, though they had little.

In the time we stayed with the Matthews, they brought us to meet another family whom Jim and Herman helped later that day to pour a house foundation. The young couple lived in an even more remote area, and the man made a living hunting moose and fishing for salmon. Their present house was a drafty shack.

But oh, those people loved the Lord! They treated us royally in service to Him. We sat at a table beside the wood stove, on which the woman not only cooked but washed clothes in a giant pot, and feasted on fresh salmon boiled in salt water, and "Newfie steaks," thick slices of bologna browned in a skillet. Later, the Christian brothers fixed our van door, and lavished us with gifts such as a handmade, wooden lobster trap and moose antlers.

We kept in touch with our new friends and visited them three years later with Jim's daughter, Jill. On that trip, we bought a house for a couple thousand dollars, a diminutive yellow dwelling with brown trim, surrounded by mountains on three sides with a view of cascading fjords on two. We never got to live in our Newfoundland house, but resold it later at a small profit and used the money to share with the believers there, and to start Daniel Chapter One.

At the wedding of Jim and Tricia Feijo, 1983.
Left to right: Fred Bopp, Eunice Buffam, John Buffam.

Honeymooning in Canada. Jim and Tricia with their VW bus and raft.

*Jim and Tricia, far right, at the Gospel Tent in Newfoundland
with the Matthews family. Left to right: Kimberly, Herman, Yvonne, and Peter.*

CHAPTER 4

LEARNING TO LIVE BY FAITH

After our honeymoon we returned to the attic apartment where Jim lived with his cockatiel, Judah, on Thomas Street in Fall River. It was in a high crime area in the city, but Jim liked it for the street ministry the Lord gave him there. Before we were married, he'd walk the streets at night and visit the bars to meet people to share the gospel.

We returned from Canada late, on a hot, humid night, exhausted. Our apartment was waiting for us—full of balloons! Each balloon had a $1 bill inside. When I pulled out drawers, the contents spilled; they were all upside down! I sat on the bed, it collapsed! Jim decided to take a bath, groaning and laughing to find it had been turned into a giant fishbowl! White rocks covered the bottom of the tub which was full of water and swimming goldfish. He got down on his hands and knees, naked, and began chasing the fish with a saucepan.

We had been pranked by several people from our church, to pay Jim back for all the pranks he had pulled on them over the years.

*   *   *

Later that summer we returned to Nova Scotia with Eric and Jill, along with a family from our church, Jack and Claire and their infant son, to revisit many places including the land we owned in South Bear Cove. While camping on our land we were deluged with rain, so a neighboring farmer, Simon, took us all in for the night. He offered us what he could, including whiskey. Jim accepted even though we didn't drink alcohol. It seemed the polite thing to do, and furthered a closer relationship.

*   *   *

Jim taught at The First Christian School of Fall River, making only $10,000 a year. He had to pay child support *and* my student loan payments. I forget how much I borrowed, but do remember that my ex-boyfriend had taken most of it to buy drugs. Jim never complained about paying off my loan, slowly but surely paying off the debt that wasn't his. As part of the budget he devised to make restitution possible, we kept the heat so low that winter we wore hats to bed and could see our breath.

Months into our marriage, Jim told me to cancel his life insurance and health insurance policies. We couldn't afford it; we had to trust the Lord. I didn't call when he first asked. It took me several days and a couple reminders to get up the nerve, holding on to the security those insurance policies promised. In retrospect, that now strikes me as idolatrous. Yahweh promises to be our Provider. He wants to be the only One we trust in.

I was allotted $25 a week, for the Laundromat, groceries, and household needs. *And* my husband told me he wanted to have different people over every Friday night for dinner! Through that, I learned it's prideful to be ashamed to serve nothing but soup to company, or potatoes, and was humbled. I also learned creative ways to stretch $25, joining a food co-op where Eunice Buffam and I would forage in boxes at the end of the Saturday sales and glean edibles such as broccoli tops that had broken off and would be discarded. There I could buy a pound of soybeans for less than $1, and turn it into many meals: cooked beans, soymilk, tofu, and okara (the left-over soy pulp). The Lord was putting me through *His* school.

Jim didn't want me to work outside the home, believing he should provide, so I busied myself mostly with cooking by day, and cleaning, and hauling clothes down the street to the Laundromat on foot. We were waiting for me to become pregnant, expecting that soon I'd be caring for a baby and eventually many children!

He was home by early afternoon, but yearned for us to be together more, to spend more time serving the Lord together. He also wanted to live more by faith. Before his school year was over, he made the decision.

"I quit teaching today" he announced chest out, standing in the kitchen.

"You what?! What are you going to do?"

"I'm going scuba diving for quahogs."

"I didn't know you can scuba dive."

"I can't. I'll take lessons."

He enrolled in diving classes at the YMCA, bought equipment, and put his resignation in to the school, vowing to finish out the year.

Next he told me we couldn't afford the apartment anymore, but not to worry; he found us a new place to live. Sakonnet Oaks was a campground in Tiverton, Rhode Island. Living there was unexpectedly the best, by far the easiest, six months of my life!

Our site was on a manmade pond. I could swim any time, and Jim made a campfire nearly every night. We slept in a tent, and had a wee camping trailer to cook in. Jim was delighted to have different neighbors all the time, plus to have a choice of so many toilets, sinks, and showers, where he'd meet different people every day.

He joined up with another diver who had a boat until we found an old wooden fishing boat for sale in a yard, a "sea dog" (meaning its better days had passed) that looked like Popeye's boat. Named the *Stornoway* after a town in Scotland, it had a hole in the hull and needed a lot of work. Jim bartered for it with the VW bus, and we proceeded to make it seaworthy by fixing the hole and fiber-glassing the foredeck, learning as we worked how to do what needed to be done.

We also acquired an antiquated camper for sale in a driveway, the kind you drive, with a cabin bed over the front seat. That old white "Obile Raveler" gave us a vehicle that we could travel and camp in, basically sleep anywhere in, yet was small enough to use as a car.

Jim dove and fished from the *Stornoway*. During one fishing trip on the Sakonnet River, he and a man from our church, Shorty, were perilously stranded on the boat. There had been gale warnings for later that day, but when they had left the mouth of the river and headed towards the Atlantic, the sea was calm, the sky clear.

Troubles began unexpectedly due to shearing of the alternator shaft. Ever so slowly, power to the supply pump was drained while all attempts to fix the engine failed. Shorty took a lift from another boat, back to shore to try to get help. The sea and sky darkened ominously; the storm was approaching. As water poured through the old boards of the *Stornoway*, Jim began bailing with a 5-gallon bucket. Increasing winds and the pounding of the waves caused the boat to spring a leak just below the water line. He set anchor over the bow and stern and kept bailing, working against winds increasing to gale force.

Waves and wind kept up their tumultuous force as deep night set in. Jim kept on bailing, but felt his energy waning like that of the *Stornoway*. Eventually he, too, was utterly depleted and fell asleep. Because the boat had been anchored, the wind lifted it so that the leak site became lifted above the water line. As Jim slept and the storm raged on, barely another drop from the sea entered the boat.

Shorty came to the door of our trailer at sunrise, telling me Jim said to contact the Coast Guard for rescue but not to send them if it cost anything. At the police station, as the woman on the phone placed the SOS call, I interrupted and asked if there was a charge.

"Twenty five dollars."

"Forget it" I said.

She frowned in puzzlement, then spoke flatly into the phone, "The wife said forget it," and hung up.

We were scheduled to get Jill that day, and had planned to travel up to Shrewsbury for my parents' thirtieth wedding anniversary party and from there journey on to Canada for the month. I picked Jill up by myself, and told her we had to look for her dad at the river.

She and I drove along the river's edge until she spied him spread-eagle on a thin strip of beach, like Jonah regurgitated from the whale's belly. He had caught a tow in that morning, and collapsed on the sand. We drove home to pack, left from there for Shrewsbury, then on to Newfoundland.

Memories are often marked by the food we share, and a highlight of that road trip I remember was my Aunt Liz's turtle candy, homemade with caramel and nuts and chocolate, leftover from the anniversary party. And less delightful: canned moose meat from which one had to pick out the hairs, and moose tongue we were treated to in Newfoundland. *"And into whatsoever city you enter, and they receive you, eat such things as are set before you." Luke 10:8*

As to the *Stornoway*, it served its purpose for a season. When we no longer needed it, we gave it to Shorty.

CHAPTER 5

YET FREE

After a criminal investigation which lasted over three years, involving several Grand Jury hearings with three different prosecutors -- we were indicted, and arraigned by the US Government in May, 2014. Media hysteria followed. Television news ran bogus, hyped stories about us, and newspaper articles reported the government version of the story with boldfaced titles such as: "Indictment: Business Sold Unapproved Cancer Drugs," and after arraignment, "Couple Plead Not Guilty in Cancer-Drug Case." Reporters knocked at our doors and those of Daniel Chapter One, but we refused interviews as our legal team had instructed. Some stayed outside our home until 11 pm, camera lights shining on the front of the house.

Since that time we have been on pre-trial release and cannot leave the states of Rhode Island, Massachusetts, or Florida without permission. The probation officer has come to our Rhode Island home to inspect it, and may drop in any time, and has the power to require urine samples. The first Tuesday of every month we must visit the probation office in Providence, and must call in every Friday. We have not been found guilty of anything at this point, only charged, each of us with several misdemeanors, and Jim with felonies as well. We were "released on our personal recognizance," without a surety bond, but they are keeping watch on us.

It's been a long road since 2008, when we chose to fight an unjust Federal Trade Commission order censoring our free speech and denying us and those in our community religious freedom.

Tom Briody, my criminal defense attorney, called months prior to our indictment to say that an attorney for the DOJ offered "to take all charges off the table" for me, if I pled to one misdemeanor count. "What is it?" I asked.

"Something to do with an FDA count of putting unapproved drugs onto the marketplace."

"I didn't do that." I would not say I did.

It's a word game. The government says that only drugs can heal the body, and therefore, say that if our products are used for healing, they must be drugs. The threat was that I may be facing felony charges and may be found guilty and sentenced to prison, and/or would be put on a no-fly list. That would limit my ministry, suggested my lawyer. I explained that I was not going anywhere without my husband, it was our ministry together as one, but would pray about it and discuss it with Jim.

"*I'm* your lawyer," Briody asserted in frustration, believing I should accept—at least seriously consider—the offer. *But Jim is my head and authority under God,* I thought. I discussed it with Jim, and we decided together I would refuse the deal offered to me.

We found out months later that the government had no felony charges against me after all. I suppose it's also a game of chicken. But we are not playing games. This, to us, is serious spiritual warfare. We are standing for Yahshua our Lord and His truth.

Waiting for a trial date, we now need a well-defined, detailed plan and government clearance to travel. We used to travel freely, unencumbered by any plans. We'd go where and as the Spirit led us.

*   *   *

The third summer we were married we took off for Europe with backpacks and Eurail passes. It was the first time I flew in a plane! Still dazzling my mind's eye is the radiant white light I encountered in pushing up the plastic window shade at daybreak, high above the clouds, as the plane approached Charles de Gaulle airport in Paris. It was the brightest, whitest light I'd ever seen; a searing luminance. To think Yahweh Elohim is brighter than that, the source of all light! He says no one can look at Him and live.

We walked miles throughout Paris. That first day all we had to eat was a baguette purchased in a bakery, with chicken I saved in a napkin from our last Lufthansa airline meal. My backpack, too big for my frame, was pushing my head down as we walked. In addition I was suffering from jet lag, and by nightfall was overwhelmed by the need to lie down. We searched for lodging, but all the youth hostels were full. Finally we found a room, but for a woman; another woman was already in the room. In crowded Europe, and as we'd later find in China, strangers were seated together in restaurants, and housed together in dorm-style rooms.

"You stay here, Trish," Jim offered, "I'll come back for you in the morning."

"No! Don't leave me. . . I'm staying with you!" I'd rather suffer not having a bed with him, than for him to be wandering the streets at night alone.

We walked the streets some more, and ended up sitting on a wall with backpackers and vagrants. We slept that night, eventually, in a train station, something we came to do when all else failed.

Trains took us all over Europe with our rail pass. We'd plan overnight trips so we could sleep on the trains. From the southern tip of Italy, we took a ferry to Greece, sleeping on the main deck with other backpackers. It was freezing, crossing the Adriatic Sea at night. Jim let me have the life preserver box to sleep on, while he curled up on the deck in a thin aluminum space blanket we brought from home.

"Good morning, my little baked potato!" I greeted him in the morning. He actually looked like a giant baked potato. I might have been thinking of food since we had none but a hunk of stale white bread someone on the deck gave us.

Weeks later, four Palestinian terrorists hijacked a cruise ship, the *Achille Lauro*, in the same waters, shooting and killing an elderly disabled Jewish-American passenger, throwing his body overboard. There was a bombing in Paris right after we left the city. Our families feared for us, and didn't understand how we traveled the way we did, or why we did, or how we could afford it.

Greece was brutally hot by day, as is most of Europe in August. One of the first things we did after landing was to buy a watermelon and eat it on the train, tearing it apart without a knife. Arriving in Athens, we rented a room in an elderly woman's house. We walked miles a day to view the Parthenon and other famous places. At some point Jim developed severe back pain, maybe due to carrying my pack at times besides his own. I tried adjusting his back for him amid the ruins at Athens. He laughed as, lying down on a stone wall, a stone head looked right back at him when he looked down at the ground. Many stone heads and headless bodies lay strewn about, like a scene out of a Monty Python film; especially amusing from Jim's ground view! Even in pain, his sense of humor prevails.

Back in Italy, I tried once more to adjust his back, in a dark parking lot near the Vatican. A man jumped out of a truck cab and asked if he could help. He grabbed Jim in a strong bear hug and squeezed him, correcting his spinal dislocation. His pain was much improved after that! The Lord never ceases to amaze us with who and what He sends to help us; with how He provides for our every need.

On to Spain, Germany, Switzerland . . . perhaps not in that order, but going wherever would give us a night's rest on a train. I'd hand wash shirts in the train sink, and pin them onto our backpacks to dry as we hiked. We covered a lot of ground to visit churches and art museums, view architecture and statues, and experience as much history and geography as possible. We slept wherever we could; if not on a train, on a bench, at the station, or anywhere we could take off our packs and lay down for a few hours. We trusted the Lord to lead us and protect us.

In Frankfurt, Germany, we were locked below the airport by security because of a terrorist bomb, and ended up sleeping on the floor by the subway tracks with other backpacking travelers and homeless people. A train rocketing to a metallic, screeching stop beside our heads was our morning alarm!

Some days we walked nearly 30 miles, eating mostly thickly crusted bread with slabs of Swiss cheese or other salty, creamy cheeses, which at times melted in the bread from the afternoon heat. Occasionally we'd stop in a park and enjoy a $1 bottle of sparkling white or rose wine with our bread and cheese, less expensive than a bottle of water or juice.

It was during that trip that we were freed from the legalism of abstinence. Under the fundamental Christian teachings of our Reformed Baptist church at Hixville, as you may recall, we didn't have dancing, nor wine, at our wedding reception. In Munich, Germany we stumbled upon a YMCA, one that was still a true Christian group for young people. The rooms were cared for by Christian youth, it was inexpensive, and we needed to shower, so we stayed a night. While attending a Bible study in the cafeteria that evening, we saw a keg of beer rolled into the room.

"You drink?" Jim queried.

"Sure! But we don't drink to get drunk," replied Helmut, the man he had turned to.

They would have only one stein of beer, and after that a "Radler," a drink of beer and lemonade. The lemonade protects against dehydration, and dilutes the alcohol.

*   *   *

The Lord teaches us continually as we walk with Him. His teaching always leads to greater freedom, and He repeatedly renews the joy of our salvation. Teachings of men can interfere with our relationship to Him and with our spiritual life, burdening a love which should be easy and light, as it was when we were first saved. We were freed from doctrines of men in this matter, for the kingdom of God is not about eating or drinking. *"Not that which goes into the mouth defiles a man; but that which cometh out of the mouth, this defiles a man." Matthew 15:11*

CHAPTER 6

A NEW JOB

In the autumn of 1984, as the Sakonnet Oaks Campground season drew to a close, owner Frank Nightingale told us we had to leave when all the other campers were gone. He refused to heat the restrooms for just two people! When Jim tried to persuade him to let us stay, offering to get us a Porta-Potty, dear Frank found a trailer for us in nearby Portsmouth, in a trailer park behind Johnny O's gas station on East Main Road.

It was a trailer with a hitch to attach to a car, not a mobile home, but larger than what we had been living in. We bought it and moved into it that fall. Before we left the campground, however, Jim's sister arranged a job interview for him at Westport Middle School. She and his parents wanted him to get a "real job" for the winter. The reason he didn't arrange for the interview himself was because he wasn't interested, but he went at the appointed time.

Since most of our clothes were stored in garbage bags in our parents' attics and basements, Jim wore what he had, jeans and a t-shirt, for the interview. His dark hair had grown into long, tight curls that grew out, rather than down, and his beard was full.

"What statement were you trying to make, coming to an interview looking like that?" demanded one of the two men seated at the table, in the second meeting they called him to. Principal and vice principal, both Harvard graduates, were understandably unsure what to make of him.

Little did they know, the day of the first interview, right before going into the building, Jim asked me with measured dread, "What if I get the job?"

"I don't know . . . I guess take it," I reasoned.

He was the most qualified of over 100 applicants. Yet his interviewers had to get past his appearance, which was situational he explained. The fact that he lived in a campground wouldn't help his cause, but he was honest about it. It would be a miracle if he got the job.

"We don't know why we chose to hire you, but we chose you," Jim was told, to which he candidly remarked, "I know why. You had no choice. God is in control. It's like when Jonah was chosen to go to Nineveh. He didn't want to go, but he had to. This is Nineveh!"

He left the men shaking their heads.

His mother embraced me in pleased relief, jumping up and down when we shared the news.

*   *   *

Jim began teaching Phys. Ed. to seventh- and eighth-grade boys in Westport that September. We moved into the trailer by the time winter brought sagging temperatures. We also had the "Obile Raveler," which Jim would drive to school, bringing me with him. I'd cook, or read, or write in the parking lot of the school while Jim taught. He'd tell his pupils to go visit me at recess, in "our living room," and I'd sometimes be interrupted by teenagers knocking on the door or windows, "Hi, Mrs. Feijo!"

The Lord says we are "a peculiar people," and we two surely are! Jim, definitely, is not inhibited by social norms nor worried about proper image. He simply lets the Lord lead, following Him with a fun-loving heart and childlike faith. I follow along and don't mind doing so . . . most of the time.

CHAPTER 7

BORN AGAIN

"I can't do this anymore." Jim pulled over to the side of the road.

"What do you mean, you can't do this?"

"I'm not going to church this morning. You can go. I'll drop you off and pick you up. But I'm not going, can't do it anymore."

"Why? What's the problem?" I started to cry; my class of preschoolers was waiting for me.

"We aren't to hide our light under a bushel basket, and this church has become our bushel basket! We're supposed to go *out*, but we only come here, every Wednesday, every Sunday. Fridays we just have people from the church over. Our light is hidden!"

"I should stay with you," I sniffled.

We turned around and went back home. From there we called the elder in charge and told him we wouldn't be in church service, and to please get a sub for my Sunday school class.

Jim had been preparing to become a deacon, led Bible studies for years, and had preached in the church. Neither he nor I understood this sudden turn, although his unrest had been brewing for some time. He attended a deacon/elder meeting one weekend and came away frustrated that God's Word was not being followed in some things, like with church discipline. He tried raising issues, always based in Scripture, but was repeatedly shot down as "overzealous Jim."

After that morning we spent time in fervent prayer, separately beseeching the Lord to guide us. If it was His Holy Spirit that was moving us away from Hixville, our church family, where exactly did He want us? What did He want us to do?

During the next few days, we both received the same message: *"All scripture is given by inspiration of God, and is profitable for doctrine, for reproof, for correction, for instruction in righteousness. . ." 2 Timothy 3:16– 17.* The Lord says He changes not. There's no modern interpretation. We received similar but different verses, together confirming that we are not to interpret away any of God's Word, but are to read it, believe it, and do it. *"But be you doers of the Word, and not hearers only, deceiving your own selves." James 1:22*

Jim asked the Lord God to use us to meet the lost and to share the gospel. His short request was, "Give us fellowship with those whose names are written in the Book of Life."

No matter the name on the building (as we saw it, all walls of division), on Sundays we began visiting different churches. Every church had differing doctrine; this one loved music and believed it was to be part of worship; that one said no music. This one believed in spiritual gifts; that one said gifts had been done away with. Pre-millenium, post-mill, a-mill, pre-tribulation, mid-trib, post-trib; different teachings, differing opinions, about the end times and return of Jesus. The Lord says not to argue about disputable matters; those not critical to salvation. We asked Him only to give us His Truth. We were thirsty, in a spiritual desert.

We stayed home many Sundays and sought the Lord through scripture and prayer by ourselves, taking whatever we read in His Word literally. No longer did we "study" it, examining the original Greek or Hebrew, no longer did we read commentaries written by scholarly men. We actually burned much of our library in a barrel bonfire. We committed to receive His Word as The Truth whether we understood it or not. He promises that the Holy Spirit will teach and guide us: *"[A]nd you need not that any man teach you." 1 John 2:27*

His Word opened up to us anew. As we followed, more understanding came. Enlightenment is sometimes the reward of obedience, while blessing always is. If one has clear sight first, faith is not needed. We are to believe without seeing, and act without knowing why. Such a walk is the true walk of faith. This, our new walk, grew into exciting, uninhibited freedom and an expression of love. We felt born-again, again!!

*   *   *

"I read today where the Lord says to sell your possessions and give to the poor." Jim entered the trailer after spending the morning outside reading his Bible.

"But we are the poor" I responded, quickly assessing our possessions. We lived in a trailer behind a gas station, for gosh sake!

"We have the brown car."

The camper had to finally be junked, but we had bought an old car from a friend for $200, and later, an old station wagon. The little brown car was dispensable.

Jim sold it for $100 and took the money down to the docks where we used to keep the *Stornoway*.

A tall, bearded man was working on his fishing boat that morning, and Jim gave him the money, saying it was from the Lord.

"I got my Bible right he-ah!" the man pointed to the book in the boat. His name was David, and he recounted how he had accepted the Lord in prison. Recently released, he was trying to make a new start fishing. Jim invited him back to our home for a meal of curry, which begat a sideways glance. Dave showed him his bucket of fish bait, "This is curry!"

He ate with us that evening and many more after that. We still have the rocking chair my mother purchased at a yard sale that he fixed in the trailer by firmly tying the rockers together with rope and fishing knots, expertly tied so as to never let go.

*   *   *

Life was good. We were happy and wanted for nothing. Except children. We both wanted children, yet I had not become pregnant. Weeping about it on occasion, feeling bad about myself and for myself, Jim rebuked me for being selfish. He was right. Tests and procedures were beyond our means, but the Lord says He opens and closes the womb. We were in agreement not to go down that road even if we could.

"Let's ask for spiritual children," he gently urged.

The Lord speaks intimately to us when we're open to hear His voice. At my lowest point of despair about being barren, I cried out to Him and He answered me. He gave me two verses, two gifts to cherish and hold: *"As one whom his mother comforts, so will I comfort you. "* *Isaiah 66:13,* and, *"Yahweh your God . . . will joy over you with singing."* *Zephaniah 3:17*

As promised in the first verse, He comforted me. As a mother would her child, He wrapped me in His loving arms and told me that one day He would sing over me. The Almighty will sing *over me*! What will His voice sound like? With what magnificent tones will He sing over me? I marveled, and in that moment He made His joy, my joy. My painful desire changed to contentment and a desire for His will in my life. We prayed for spiritual children from then on, and the Lord gave us children.

CHAPTER 8

A MISSION AND A MINISTRY

After teaching at Westport Middle School for two years Jim was let go. It may have had to do with his faith, or it may have been political. If he had put in three years, he would have been automatically tenured. Due to his more than 17 years of teaching experience, he was highly paid for the position, so it could be they decided to hire someone else for less.

I say it may have had to do with his faith because he was referred to by other staff as "the Holy Spirit," and not as a compliment. Posters hanging in his office on which he had airbrushed verses like "*What does it profit a man if he gains the whole world yet loses his soul?*" were ripped down at night. "Disgusting," some teachers called his lunch of homemade soup in ball jars. He was strange, uncomfortable to them. The spirits in them hated the Spirit in him.

In addition, while his unorthodox teaching style garnered the enthusiasm of most students, it met with the consternation of administrators and many parents. In the Christian school where he'd taught, Jim had implemented conceptual learning, doing away with desks and books to instead teach hands on, experientially. In math class, they made breakfast for which they had to measure. They made tools. They dissected windowpanes and the schoolyard. He created equality among the students with projects. For example, to teach geometry he gave them the project of making a box. Each student had to make a box, any size. Those considered stupid by classmates were soon helping *A* students with their boxes. His ideas were brilliant, but again, unorthodox, challenging norms and the status quo.

Public school officials considered him an embarrassment. For one thing, he gave gym games names like "The Most Dangerous Game in The World." The boys enjoyed it, but parents complained. So he renamed the same game "Powder Puff." The boys got the joke. They loved him, and he them. He started an after-school weight-lifting program on his own time. To this day, some of the boys have kept in touch, visiting, or as many do, contacting him through Facebook.

Then there was the Name of the Lord of which Jim was not ashamed. He spoke openly of his relationship to Jesus, and therefore was kept away from honorary guests. One such time, Celtics player M. L. Carr was visiting, and Jim was relegated to watching teacher mailboxes, barred from the auditorium where Mr. Carr was speaking. But who walks right by Jim in the hallway as he was praying for the chance to tell him about the Lord and salvation? The man he had been praying to meet! Jim got to personally talk with the basketball great, away from the crowd.

Another time, a scientist from NASA visited the school, whom Jim unabashedly invited home. The man turned out to be a Christian brother, and stayed with us rather than in a hotel. He slept on a futon on our trailer floor, ate my whole wheat cranberry bread made with wild-harvested cranberries, took Niacin (vitamin B3) with us for the physical hot flush it causes, just for fun, and made paper airplanes with Jim, using Jim's innovative designs. Upon departing, he said wistfully, "I wish I had what you have."

*   *   *

Westport Middle let Jim go at the end of the year. When he delivered the news that he'd be out of work at school's end, he gave me a choice. "I can spend the summer looking for a job, or we can go to Europe." That was the summer we backpacked through Europe together. Later that summer we sold our extra car and gave the money to David at the boat dock. Then we thought, with some expectation, *Now! Maybe the Lord will send us out now!*

We wanted to be missionaries, but no mission board would hire us because Jim was divorced and remarried. After our initial disappointment, Jim determined that the Lord didn't need a certified mission board to send us out. We'd go with the Lord. He was all we needed. We had been waiting for the day He would give us a mission.

Yet no door to missions had opened, and we were close to broke. Rent for the trailer park was $75 a month, plus we had utilities, food, and child support. Not much was needed, but we had to do something to live. Besides, we wanted to be able to give to others. In our travels we had met people in house churches who really needed help.

"Let's start a health food store" Jim suggested, knowing it was an interest of mine. A store could provide a way to support ourselves and to help support believers overseas, including and especially those oppressed in Communist countries. The only problem, as everyone but he saw it, is that we had nothing to start one with!

Inquiring about rents in the south end of Fall River was discouraging. Certainly any rent in the town of Portsmouth would be higher. But Jim kept thinking it possible, and answered an advertisement for an office down the street. The owner met us in his office, a couple buildings down from the office for rent. He asked what we wanted to do with it. "Sell health food," we answered. It was zoned for business, no problem there. He told us the rent he was asking; hundreds over what we could pay. We stood up to leave. He asked what we could pay. Straight faced, Jim said, "Thirty dollars a month," in truthful accord with our budget. "I can tell you right now you aren't getting that place for $30!" replied the man, incensed.

After thanking him, we walked out, back down the street to our trailer park.

The following day, while taking a stroll we passed by the front of the same building. A car pulled up, the window went down, and the man who had met with us the day before leaned past his wife in the front seat, calling out with a grin, "Hey, you got any health food? Meet me in my office!"

This time, he had questions for Jim . . . about football. He had been telling the story of how we interviewed to rent from him, to an old high school friend of Jim's. The friend said, if it was *the* Jim Feijo from Fall River, Jim was an outstanding athlete and coach, a legend! Portsmouth Football needed a coach. The real estate owner ended up giving us the space to use for a store, rent-free, for the first three months, and Jim agreed to coach freshmen football that fall.

*　　*　　*

"Daniel Chapter One" Jim proposed for the name.

"Loaves and Fishes" I countered.

"Daniel Chapter One. It has to be Daniel Chapter One." He was adamant.

The first year we were married, we tried a diet similar to that of Daniel and his men in the biblical book of Daniel, chapter one. According to that account, Daniel and his friends had been taken into Babylonian captivity to serve King Nebuchadnezzar. The king appointed for them a daily provision of his rich food and wine, but Daniel determined in his heart not to defile himself, as the king's food both defied his religious dietary laws and had been sacrificed to idols. So he requested permission from the king's eunuchs to be given vegetables and water instead. They feared that the young men would languish on such a diet and the king would have their heads for it. Daniel pleaded, *"Prove your servants, I beseech you, for ten days; and let them give us vegetables to eat, and water to drink. Then let our countenances be looked upon before you . . . and as you see, deal with your servants." Daniel 1:12–13*

After the ten days they looked better than all the men who ate the king's food. They were allowed to continue eating their way, and they continued to grow in knowledge and wisdom. The king ultimately found them *"ten times better than all the magicians and astrologers that were in all his realm." Daniel 1:20*

We experienced renewed energy, clearer eyes, and sharper minds during the ten days we ate only vegetables and drank only water. After our first experiment with Daniel's diet, we'd periodically embark on what we called our "Daniel Chapter One Diet," whenever we felt the need. That was before we knew of any other Christian or church group to use the term, though some have, coincidentally or not, subsequently adopted the term "Daniel Diet". (We do not espouse any "diet" for spiritual means; the kingdom of heaven is not about what one eats or drinks.)

Daniel Chapter One would be the name of our health food store, and of our ministry. Jim answered my protests that people would not understand what it meant with, "They can read it." Daniel Chapter One has stood for almost 30 years now, and the name and its association has taken on a strength of character we never imagined. It's laughable to think of my idea having been used instead. If it had, our petition to the Supreme Court in 2012 would have been lamely saddled with the name Loaves and Fishes. Instead it read, with a degree of sublimity: *Daniel Chapter One, et al. v. Federal Trade Commission.*

The name has become increasingly meaningful to us on several levels since the founding of Daniel Chapter One. We, like Daniel and his men in the biblical book, have been faced with decisions that test our integrity and faith. Do we eat the king's food—that is, partake of the food (medicine) of the worldly government? Do we bow down to the king's idol, in this case "scientism," or risk being burned alive for refusing? Do we fear being thrown in the lions' den, or continue praying to and obeying the God we know, where we can be seen? The baseline dilemma is posed simply in the book of Acts: *"Whether it is right in the sight of God to listen to you more than to God, judge you."* Acts *4:19*

A recurring theme in our namesake, book of Daniel, is that the God of Israel is in complete control and He can be explicitly trusted no matter what circumstances befall us. Therein lies our strength and solace.

CHAPTER 9

DANIEL CHAPTER ONE

"**M**ind if we pray?"

"Not at all!" I answered the Customer Service rep.

He prayed over the phone with me, closing with, "*Eye has not seen, nor ear heard . . . the things which God has prepared for them that love Him.*" 1 Cor. 2:9

Excitedly thanking him, I hung up from placing the first order of natural foods for our store. Despite no money and no references, we had been granted a 30-day credit with Country Life, a natural foods distributor. That's unheard of in business, as it is to have the person on the order line pray with you! Never happened again, but it happened that day.

Our retail space had been the starting law office of Ron Machtley (former US House of Representatives member, current president of Bryant University) and, before that, the town post office. We were working feverishly to turn it into a health food store. The orange curtains with vertical zigzag print came down but the lime green rug had to stay. We covered one of the paneled walls with a life-size mural of a forest to offset the rug, and I washed it the best I could. Jim made free-standing shelves, though he is no carpenter. They were rough and skinny, and tilted rather than standing straight. A man once joked that the Holy Spirit must be in that place, because "that's the only thing that could be keeping those shelves up!" We made a front counter for the first room, and a table in the second small room by placing an old door over two sawhorses. Jim made a one-sided sign for the outside, carved and painted with a depiction of whole foods and the words

DANIEL CHAPTER ONE in calligraphy. The word *Daniel* looked like *Dance*, but it was a handsome work of art. The sign would stand on two posts in the ground, but it wasn't yet finished the day the food arrived.

The summer day was sizzling hot when a truck pulled up to deliver bulk boxes of grains, and beans, nuts, and seeds, pastas, dried fruits, and dairy items like cheese. Other than shelves, the store was empty, unprepared. Just in time, Jim returned from the used restaurant equipment store in Fall River with a huge, stainless-steel cylinder with a curved glass door that looked more like a rocket ship than the refrigerator it was. But thankfully, no food would perish! Later that day, a friend from Hixville stopped by to say hello. He taught refrigeration and air conditioning repair in a trade school, and offered us a couple of free air conditioners from a hotel dumpster that his students had refurbished as a class project. Of industrial size and strength, they were installed in our store windows, one in each of our two rooms. For the duration of our near ten years there, they ran every summer and never quit.

Jim purchased an old, used scale, and my parents came down from Massachusetts the following weekend to help with the weighing and bagging. In a tedious marathon we managed to bag and price all the bulk foods. Many clear plastic bags full of bulk items we then spread out, in an obvious attempt to make the humble table and shelves look full.

My parents were initially against our idea of starting a store, since we had no business background and no money. Jim's family was upset that he left teaching. They were all well-meaning, just scared for us.

"You can't start a store. You have no money, no cushion!" "Jim's close to teaching retirement; a couple more years and you could collect a pension!" "Most businesses fold in the first five years."

No one supported the vision except our friends and mentors, John and Eunice Buffam and Fred Bopp. They graciously encouraged us, believing all things are possible. Faith is learned as it's practiced, and grows as it's tested. Their great faith came from many difficult, miraculous adventures of their own. They understood what drove us, and were not consumed with earthly worries. The Buffams had also been the only people when we attended the Hixville church to encourage another ministry we started, "Growing Seeds." With an old discarded hand printer, another gem from a dumpster, we produced the monthly booklet as a Christian outreach to children. Most everyone, including Christian friends, thought we were crazy.

"How I wish I could be part of the work in Rhode Island!" Fred enthused, when we told him about the store. By then he was living in a nursing home.

"If one person is saved through Daniel Chapter One it will be worth it," Jim told him.

"One?!" Fred smiled, then exhorted, "Pray for hundreds!!!" His eyes shone, seeing what we did not.

Daniel Chapter One was in an unlikely place for a store. The building sat on a busy throughway, East Main Road, with no other stores around it. People generally predicted it would fail, as "location is everything," and since we had done no marketing or other research to ensure success. Besides that, from day one Jim gave things away from our sparse inventory.

We prayed that the Lord would bring people in. We wanted to be missionaries, and here we were; the Lord could bring people to us. I had a dream early on, in which I walked through our trailer park at night. Through the windows, I could see handicapped people in lit rooms. I ran home to Jim exclaiming, "We don't have to go anywhere! The mission field is right here!"

Opening day, the store made about $20 . . . because our parents came in and shopped. It was slow starting and slow going, but we never had a zero-dollar day, and the Lord saw to it that all our bills got paid. The following summer we left again for Europe. The timing was inopportune, the journey difficult, but it turned out to be the most important trip of our spiritual life.

CHAPTER 10

SPIRITUAL GIFTS

Since leaving the church in Hixville and visiting many different churches in our search for fellowship and truth, we ended up regularly attending a Brethren Assembly in Saugus, Massachusetts. The hour commute every Sunday seemed well worth it. We appreciated their adherence to the Word of God, simple a cappella singing of hymns, and the seating arrangement with no elevated stage or platform. Worship was open; not prearranged. As scripture dictates, anyone could offer up prayers or hymns as they felt led by the Spirit. The women covered their heads in worship, and only the men led and taught. Members only were allowed to partake of the breaking of the bread, however, which we didn't agree with.

But after several months we asked to become members. Our request was put off many times, with the explanation that we had to be "interviewed" for acceptance. We kept asking for interviews, which were finally granted to Jim, me, and David, our fisherman friend who had starting coming with us. One by one we were interviewed privately by three men, elders in the church. I was the last, and after the men tested the validity of my having been born-again, I was ultimately told that I could become a member but my husband could not, since he was divorced and remarried. They could accept David, but only as long as he remained single, since he too was divorced. They quoted the book of James, saying that an elder in the church "must be the man of one wife."

I was stunned. A solitary banner that stretched across the front wall of their church interior boldly declared, from 1 John 1:7:

The blood of Jesus Christ cleanses us from all sin. They considered my husband to have two wives? To be in a perpetual state of adultery? After their interrogation, I hurried out to the car where Jim and David waited. With heavy hearts we drove home. More than the rejection, I was shocked by the way they had strung us along for months, never explaining their criteria for membership. They knew Jim was divorced; his daughter sometimes came with us. Their position and the way they handled our request mystified us.

We never went back there. Instead, we asked the Lord to bring us to disciples who walk as He walked, and who know how to worship Him in Spirit and in Truth.

"Truly, truly, I say to you, He that believes on Me, the works that I do shall he do also; and greater works than these shall he do . . ." John 14:12. His Word is true, so why weren't we experiencing that reality, I questioned. How were we to access and manifest the power of the Holy Spirit as evidenced by miracles?

So, soon after starting Daniel Chapter One, in the summer of 1987 we headed back to Europe with backpacks and no plan, this time with Jim's daughter, 11-year-old Jill. Family court had appointed one month visitation rights with the children each summer. Jim's son, Eric, had stopped visiting. I'm sure it was hard for a 12-year-old to live in a trailer, sleep on a futon on the floor, and be away from friends and a comfortable house with his own room. But Jill still came every other weekend and now for the summer month, and Jim wanted to do something special with her. She already had spent many boring weekends in the store while we worked, and he felt compelled to go out, though he didn't know why.

Before the trip, we had taken over the other half of the first floor for the store, expanding the product area and making an office. We also moved in above the store, into an area that used to be upstairs bedrooms. The landlord had it converted to a small apartment by adding a bathroom and kitchen. The two young men living there before us had uncaged pet birds and the place was dirty. When I asked my husband if we could replace the soiled carpet and paint the walls, he referred to the biblical book of Haggai, saying, "We've not been paneling our own house, we aren't going to start now!"

True, and true that the money was better put back into Daniel Chapter One. Soon after, however, Jim worked out a deal with the landlord. We'd do the work, and the cost of materials would be taken off our rent. Everyone benefitted, and I got to pick out new carpeting and fresh paint.

To make our trip possible, my parents once again came to help. They stayed in the apartment, and watched the store the weeks we were gone.

*   *   *

"God told us to speak to you. We're servants of the Lord Jesus Christ."

A bearded, ruddy-cheeked man with grey–and-white hair, and a smaller man with dark hair, approached us as we sipped cocoa at a communal picnic table in a campground in Paris, our first, rainy night there.

"We're His servants too!" Jim replied.

After a short conversation, the men invited us to their house in Udon, Holland.

"If the Lord wants us there, we'll be there," said Jim, "just give us the address."

Jim, Jill, and I managed to fit into our two-man pup tent to sleep that night, on rocky, uneven terrain, other tents so close the tent ropes overlapped. It cost a manageable $5 a night, so we stayed a couple days before moving on.

We journeyed by bus and train as before, looking for any train that would mean an overnight trip so we could sleep and then start the new day in a different country, such as France, Italy, Germany. One long night we slept on the cold marble floor of a train station. In Luxembourg we again slept in "a campground," an open field full of tents and campers. The following morning we packed up and walked to a nearby bus stop.

As Jill and I sat on a stone wall shaking bugs out of our hair, Jim asked a few young men waiting for a bus how to get to Udon, to accept the invitation we'd been given. One of them came over and gave train-by-train directions in detail, explaining the close timing between the trains we'd have to take so we'd know to run in the transfer. To this day, we marvel at his accuracy, and wonder if we met an angel unaware. Jim wrote nothing down, but committed the directions to his memory by faith.

*   *   *

The front door to the house in Udon opened as soon as we knocked, and a man we had never met before invited us in with open arms. "Welcome! The Lord told us you were coming. Bring whatever He has for us (whatever teaching, rebuke, encouragement, et cetera)." From the kitchen and into the main room of the house we met a handful of men and women who lived there from all over the world. Ray, who opened the door, was from America, his wife Magdalena from Poland; Paul from England; Sally from Oklahoma; and another sister whose name I forget but who sang beautifully and played a lap harpsichord. Gary Orr, the bearded man who had approached us in Paris, was from Canada. He and the other man who invited us (from America) lived there, but were not at the house that night.

We ate and talked and were given a room with beds! After Jill turned in for the night, we stayed up until late, blessed with a spontaneous time of worship; songs and prayer, and *prophecy*. People spoke from the Lord, and through prophecy Jim and I had our eyes anointed and received the gift of prophecy. Jim also received the gift of tongues. In the Spirit, we felt we had come home. By the word of the Lord, Jim brought a teaching about head covering, an answer to *their* prayers, and Ray shared the concept of spiritual covering with us. A significant role of the husband is to spiritually cover his wife, the point at which Adam failed and fell in the garden.

We could have stayed longer, but only stayed a few days. Then on to see London, the zoo and museums, and to continue our walk in greater depth and fullness of the Spirit. Spiritual gifts would give us the power we sought, not for ourselves but to better minister to others as we toiled for the Kingdom of God. The value of gifts is in using them to build up His church.

PART TWO

THE HOUSE IS BUILT

*"Commit your works unto Yahweh,
and your thoughts will be established."*

Proverbs 16:3

CHAPTER 11

HONOR BESTOWED

I t is the fall of 2014, and the Federal Trade Commission recently sent us a legal document demanding over $3 million in fines for past violations of the order. We are still waiting for DC Judge Sullivan's decision, and we continue to wait upon the FDA and IRS for a trial date. Meanwhile we visited Jim's son, Eric, in Nashville, Tennessee as planned, with permission from Rhode Island Judge Almond. The day we arrived, Jim received a call from The Pennington School. His 1971 football team was about to be inducted into the Hall of Fame! Yes, Jim answered the caller, he would try to be there in New Jersey to speak.

During our visit, Eric noticed I was limping. The pain in my foot was due to plantar fasciitis, an inflamed ligament, for which I had taken nutrients and homeopathic remedies with only palliative relief. The ligament needed mechanical support in order to rest and heal, and he offered me a brace for that purpose. The next morning I was pain-free for the first time in months, and in just a couple of weeks my foot was completely healed!

By the grace of God and the mercy and assistance of another, I had been freed of my affliction. Eric had the professional knowledge and materials needed. Through him I was blessed with a solution that was surprisingly simple, inexpensive, and did not require a doctor. The Lord says, "*My people are destroyed for lack of knowledge.*" *Hosea 4:6*

That is the issue at the crux of our legal battles with the FTC and the FDA, and why we have fought their censorship. Through prayer and revelation, and years of research and experience, Jim and I have been given solutions to many people's health problems, but government agencies say we cannot share what we know because the solutions are products we developed and sell.

A pine tree in our front yard provides apt analogy. Several of its branches became diseased. We didn't know why, or how to save the tree. Portsmouth has many farms and nurseries, and someone at a local nursery might have the information needed. Imagine if we went to them asking for help, and all they could tell us is that they sell a product that may save the tree, but could not say which product or how to use it. What good would their knowledge be, what good their products to us, if we couldn't access that crucial information?

All we have ever done is answer people's health questions honestly, for almost 30 years, without customer complaint. We didn't advertise, but educated through our radio program and shared true testimonies on the website to glorify God. The FTC charged us with making "claims" we never made, but when we argued that fact, they accused us of having "implied" those alleged claims. They applied the rule that "reasonable basis" is required to make any health claim, saying in court that only "double-blind placebo-controlled studies" suffice as reasonable basis. Such studies are the gold standard for drugs; unattainable, unnecessary, and even unethical for a natural supplement. We were found guilty in an FTC court, a veritable Star Chamber, of "false and misleading advertisement," without evidence of anything false, or misleading, and were ordered to abort our ministry.

Most offensive to us, the FTC also ordered that we print a letter they supplied, on Daniel Chapter One letterhead, and send it to all our customers by name, in a Daniel Chapter One envelope, with no accompanying letter. The letter contained the government message that there is no science behind our products or any ingredient in them (not true), and that if you have cancer you need to seek conventional treatment (chemo and radiation) because only conventional cancer treatment has been "proven safe and effective in humans," another lie. That letter, and how they ordered it be sent, was deceptive and misleading. We could not sign and send it, our conscience wouldn't allow it. We would not bear false witness.

The government letter also directed the recipient to the National Cancer Institute, including the contact. We would not advertise for them, how could they make us? We were threatened with incarceration unless it was sent, and we faced backbreaking fines for all the days we did not send it.

*   *   *

Jim was honored at the induction of the 1971 Pennington football team into the Hall of Fame on October 11, 2014. We had to ask Probation for permission to travel, and explain the purpose of the trip. *"You prepare a table before me in the presence of my enemies: You anoint my head with oil; my cup runs over." Psalm 23:5*

I met men who played for Jim as boys at the banquet in New Jersey. Many told me he was their greatest inspiration in life, and that they talk about him still to their children. The Pennington Red Raiders were the underdog team who went undefeated because Coach Feijo made them work hard, believed in them, and made them believe in themselves. "He always stayed positive," said the team captain.

"Coach told me: You never quit! Never quit! Never quit!" one less athletic man told me. He wanted to quit the team. "I couldn't run" he admitted. But he didn't quit.

"Coach used to give us chewable vitamin C," he added, for endurance energy and health.

A news article from that time reported: "*Feijo stayed up until 2 am for three straight weeks planning his offense . . . and all season opposing coaches have spent sleepless nights trying to defend it.*" For pre-season practices, he conducted triple sessions, while other schools conducted double sessions. By the end of the season, the Red Raiders ranked top 10 in the country, and Jim was named Coach of the Year. He was the youngest undefeated coach in the country. The team other teams used to laugh at, had become the one to beat. Applauded once again, the success of Jim Feijo and his Red Raiders has been carved indelibly into the prestigious history of Pennington.

CHAPTER 12

BIOMOLECULAR NUTRITION

Back when Daniel Chapter One was newly up and running, in the fall of 1986, football season was underway in Portsmouth, and Jim was away most of the time coaching. I ran the store, which was so quiet some afternoons I'd lock the doors and run the mile down to the school to watch a game. Jim was tough on the boys, but they knew it was for their good and they loved and respected him. He spent many evenings with his assistant Greg Engle working out plays and viewing tapes. Of the small sum he was paid, he invested back into the team, buying a video camera to tape all the games.

A popular product we sold was an all-natural energy and hydration drink that contained minerals called electrolytes. Some of the parents bought it by the case to provide to the players because it kept the boys from cramping.

The Portsmouth Patriots had a great season, and Daniel Chapter One was standing on its feet by season's end.

* * *

Jim and I were quickly learning a lot from research and books we read for hours each morning, from people coming into the store, by divine inspiration, and from personal experience. Motivated by the desire to solve problems for ourselves and others, we were being led by the Lord in answer to our prayers for knowledge and the gift of healing. *"He causes the grass to grow for the cattle, and herb for the service of man."*

Psalm 104:14. We asked Him for insight into the use of His creation for health and healing.

When Jim needed surgery for an anterior cruciate ligament he tore playing baseball in his final year teaching Phys. Ed. in Westport, we had opportunity to test some of our new-found knowledge. An excellent doctor was recommended, Dr. Tozlowski in Boston, and Jim chose an experimental GORE-TEX® ligament over reconstruction to minimize healing time. Dr. Tozlowski graciously allowed him the nutrients he wanted to take for pain and healing, prescribing them so the nurses would allow them in his room. Surgery and post-op went well; no painkillers were needed after surgery; and he was walking the hall with crutches and visiting other patients within days. By the second week, he was stationary cycling at the gym. His doctor carefully wrote down the list of nutrients Jim was taking, commenting, "This could help other patients." He mentioned a female patient down the hall who was packed in ice because she was allergic to painkilling drugs, a case where natural alternatives would be helpful.

We sent a friend who needed the same surgery to Dr. Tozlowski the following year. Helen took the exact same products Jim had, and experienced the same positive results. Anecdotal, but true, to the glory of our Creator.

Another situation that propelled our learning curve occurred when Fred Bopp developed pneumonia in the nursing home and almost died. We knew from previous visits that he was hardly eating the food served, which was meat, white starch, and Jell-O or pudding. We brought in a nutrient powder from our store and asked a nurse to make a shake and give it to him several times a day. As if by miracle, he survived. We thought more about the need for additional, better nutrition for the elderly or infirmed.

I was growing in the ministry of teaching others how to cook with natural, vegetarian foods and how to use food for healing, while Jim was growing in his knowledge of biochemistry and sports nutrition. Teaching himself how to use a computer, he wrote a computer program to assess the exact nutritional needs of an individual based on energy demands. Inspired by the Holy Spirit, he stayed up all one night working on it, at one point losing his work and having to rewrite the entire program. He says he could never do it again. My husband began to insist that our store have a few shelves of sports supplements. Those I relegated to one dark corner, unconvinced that anything could be better than whole foods!

That winter he coached wrestling at Portsmouth Abbey, a private boarding and day school. His team started out weak, the underdog, but he was primarily concerned about the boys' health. It disturbed him that young athletes jeopardize their health to make a weight class. Wrestlers notoriously starve and dehydrate by consuming inadequate calories and water, and in addition "walk and spit" before weigh-in. Too many get colds and flu during season, and often, the dreaded mono.

"Any good coach can teach skill; the difference in making winners will be their nutrition" Jim told me.

With informed consent from the parents, his wrestlers took vitamins, energy supplements, and supplement powders as Jim directed, and won the Championship that year. The other coaches approached him after the Abbey's final, victorious upset, wanting to know, "What'd you do to those guys?!"

Again, his main objective was to keep the boys healthy, but an additional benefit of fortifying their nutrition was that their performance went through the roof. It confirmed what he believed to be true about nutritional support, applied through the new science he discovered and called Biomolecular Nutrition. The body's nutrient needs can be and must be met at the molecular level.

The principles of Biomolecular Nutrition proved effective again when our landlord brought his teenage son and daughter to Jim for help. His son was a star football player who had just been told he'd be out for the rest of the season due to mono. Jim suggested nutrients and nutritional powders to support his immune system, and the boy was back playing in two weeks. He would be named Most Valuable Player that year.

His sister was a runner and a dancer. She "hit the wall" one day while running track, slumping to the ground suddenly when her body ran out of fuel. The doctor said she was doing too much and had to curtail activities. Jim suggested instead she increase nutrients, including more protein and carbohydrates in supplement form to meet the great energy demands of her activities. She never hit the wall again, shone in track and dance, and went on to become an outstanding athlete for the Naval Academy, as did her brother.

Many people came into the store with chronic illness. Jim began to apply the science of Biomolecular Nutrition to those people in the same way as he did with athletes. The result, when they followed his suggested supplement plan, was improved strength and energy. One woman with multiple sclerosis went from a wheelchair to walking with a cane. Her breakfast before Biomolecular Nutrition consisted of tea and white toast, insufficient nutrition for healing.

The problem with whole food is not everyone can digest it, it does no good if not assimilated, and it takes energy from the body to break it down into usable form. That's why Biomolecular Nutrition is optimal for those sick, weak, or involved in sports or other high-demand physical activities. It requires no digestion as it is pre-digested with enzymes, and it retains the osmolality of water when mixed into water, meaning it is ionic and isotonic; as readily and easily assimilated as water.

Biomolecular Nutrition and Jim's computer program would eventually get the attention of China and Russia, and launched Daniel Chapter One's success.

*   *   *

In December, 1987, Gary Orr, whom we met in Paris the previous summer, and his new wife, Rhonda, came by from Canada for a surprise visit, on their way–they hoped–to Africa. They stayed through Christmas. That was the year we stopped celebrating Christmas. We stayed home that evening and sang to my amateur electronic keyboard playing, enjoying fellowship in Christ our Savior.

My mother was hurt and angry. Originally we had planned to spend that Christmas Eve with Jim's parents, which my mom accepted, but she couldn't understand why we neither visited them nor her and my dad. I wasn't happy about it either. It was my husband's decision, one he had wrestled with for a while. He'd grown increasingly uncomfortable with the materialism associated with Christmas, and besides that, said the Lord tells us to remember his death and resurrection, not His birth. He was personally convicted not to partake in the world's celebration. He did not put that on anyone else, saying only, *"but as for me and my house. . ." Joshua 24:15*

We later came to celebrate Jewish feast days like Passover, because they were appointed by God, not man. But then we came to see that despite their significant meaning, there is no command from Jesus to keep them as under the law. He tells us to do all things by His Spirit.

Jim did as he felt led by the Holy Spirit to do. Who's to say, "It's no big deal," when the Lord convicts? After all, the serpent said to Eve, "Surely God didn't mean that," to convince her to eat from the tree He told them not to. People are free to do what they want, as each sees fit, *"but as for me and my house . . ."* Jim chose not to observe the holiday. About observing special days, holidays, the Lord says, *"But now, after that you have known God, or rather are known of God, how turn you again to the weak and beggarly elements, whereunto you desire again to be in bondage? You observe days, and months, and times, and years." Galatians 4:9, 10*

Again, it was a matter of personal conviction, and for Jim, obedience. There have been times since then when we *have* gathered with family on Christmas, because the Holy Spirit led us to. One time was to be with my dad after mom passed away. There is freedom in all things.

Jesus angered people because He always did the Father's will, and that often meant going against the acceptable social norms or religious laws, for example befriending prostitutes and healing people on the Sabbath. Jim had no intent other than to try to do what Jesus would do.

*   *   *

Before the Orrs left, I was invited to a birthday party for a woman from our old church in Hixville. Although we no longer attended that church, we kept in touch with several of its members. A close friend, Judy, was hosting the party. Jim heard by the Spirit that I was to go with Rhonda. We prayed before leaving and one of the men brought a prophecy that Rhonda or I had a word from the Lord for someone at the party.

We prayed together in the car before entering the house, with trembling. We had no idea how a prophetic word, or we, would be received. I remember nothing of the party but Judy's house full of chatting women. Praying silently at the kitchen table where several women sat, I was suddenly moved to say, "I believe I have a word for you," to one woman. She seized upon what I had just blurted out, saying, "What? For me?!"

As I spoke the word prompted by the Spirit, her countenance changed from unhappiness to one full of joy, and she cried "Amen! Thank you! Praise the Lord!"

Rhonda and I left soon after that, with many hugs goodbye and thanks and well wishes. But not all there that day felt the love.

*　　*　　*

Couples from Hixville were now coming to our home above the store in a steady stream, uninvited but heartily welcomed. Some may have come out of curiosity, but most came spiritually hungry. They wanted more of Yahshua and His Spirit. We'd break bread as Jesus did with His disciples, sitting around a low wooden table, sharing bread and wine, sometimes "sop" (bread dipped into broth), and sometimes a full meal. At times we brought words from the Lord, as the Spirit moved. We worshipped freely. The gatherings were small and simple, but believers were being filled. His sheep were being fed.

"Let's go visit the Hennellys," Jim suggested one afternoon. It had been a long time since we had seen our friends, the head elder and his wife from Hixville.

"Ok! Why don't we bring some treats from our store. We have things their boys can eat." I knew from living with them that both children were on a special diet and couldn't have any food with chemical additives. Health-food store treats were expensive, hard for them to afford. It was the least we could do, they had been good to me and Jim. I packed a brown bag of healthy cookies and other treats for them, and we set out for their house beside the church. No one was home. Jim drew one of his signature cartoons on the paper bag, sure they'd recognize it as from him, and tucked it between the screen-door. *Won't they be delighted*, we thought!

In response, the elder sent a letter to all members in the church warning them about us, telling them to have nothing to do with us. He accused us of working our way into homes with bribery, and cited the bag we left in his door as an example of "an anonymous gift." Sternly he cautioned: beware Jim and Trish, they are heretics.

He sent a copy of his letter to us, so we'd know his position.

The letter charged that we had left the truth by believing in spiritual gifts, and admonished the congregation that spiritual gifts—all except the gifts of "pastor" and "teacher" —were given only for the early church, "until the superstructure of the church was underway." Since then, he wrote, gifts of the Spirit have been done away with.

We were aghast. Our present of cookies for his boys was not an attempt to bribe him! Our visit was made in love. It wasn't out of the ordinary for Jim Feijo to visit others spontaneously, nor to leave his comical 'calling card' of cartoon pictures. He had always done that, he was known for it, the Hennellys knew that! We knew they'd recognize it, it was hardly "anonymous."

We would do nothing but wait on the Lord, and in His time would try to revisit the elder at the church.

His letter created confusion and division. I don't know if it came first, or the gossip. Jack and Claire told us that a woman in the church accused me of throwing my arms up in the air and declaring myself a prophetess at a birthday party. I didn't do that; I've never used the term. The insight they shared is that the woman was bitter towards us for leaving the church as we did, "with no apology." They heard her complain about it firsthand; the woman was Claire's mother. I don't remember seeing her at the party. Perhaps she was there, or perhaps she just heard of the incident through the evil vine of gossip. No matter how, what happened that day became overdramatized, distorted.

CHAPTER 13

PAINS AND FRUIT OF OBEDIENCE

We never made it to Peru as we had hoped, but our hearts were still in mission work abroad as well as at home. China kept coming up in different ways, and it became clear that we were to go to China. The son of a pastor came by selling water filters one day, and in conversation told us he could get inexpensive, open-ended plane tickets for us from an aunt who worked for a travel agency. We gave him money long saved for the purpose, about $800. He never procured tickets. After some pressure from us, he wrote a fraudulent check to us to refund the money; funds in the account were withdrawn by him the day before.

I was so upset that he stole our mission money, I called his parents' house where he lived. His mother answered that her son was not home, so I vented my anger by telling her about the check, calling it a felony. Jim did not agree with how I handled it. He called back later that day, and got to talk to the son. He spoke calmly, "Brother, if you needed money, you should have asked. We would've helped you." He invited the young man to our house for a meal and to break bread, more concerned about the man's soul than the money. Still believing we were to go to China, he then told me, "We have nothing more saved; now we have to take it from where it'll hurt."

Worse than that, to me, two weeks before my sister's wedding Jim declared, "I believe we're supposed to go to China now." My only sister was getting married at the end of April, I was to be her maid of honor, and my husband decided we had to go to China *then*! Mind you, we had no idea what we were going to do once we got there.

"Why can't we wait until after the wedding?" I wailed.

"You can stay here and go to the wedding. I'm leaving for China." Jim left the house.

I prayed. I cried, upset by Jim's apparent insensitivity, feeling that he didn't care about me or my family. His decision seemed mean and selfish.

In my distress I opened God's Word, and He gave me Isaiah 45:2, 3, 6: "*I will go before you, and make the crooked places straight: I will break in pieces the gates of brass, and cut down the bars of iron . . . that you may know that I, Yahweh, which call you by your name, am the God of Israel. . . I am Yahweh, and there is none else.*"

Through that scripture, by His Spirit, the Lord assured me that He was about to glorify Himself *and bless my family* with truth, if I obeyed. It wasn't just about me; through my obedience He would reveal Himself to my family, whom I had prayed would have a closer relationship to Him.

He impressed upon me a couple of things that night. First, I assumed that I wouldn't be dying any time soon, but what if I was going to die soon? What if I only had two more weeks to live, what choice would I make then? Spend my last couple of weeks on Earth waiting for a wedding, or go serve the Lord in China? And secondly, He honors those who honor Him. I could trust Him to answer my prayers, including those for my family, *if* I obeyed Him. I had to entrust them to Him, and have enough faith to not worry about how my obedience would affect them. I decided to honor Him by following my husband. "I'll go to China with you," I told Jim when he came home that evening.

My mother was heartbroken when we told her, and accused tearfully, "You never did feel part of this family." She thought we didn't want to go to the wedding because the service was to take place in a Catholic church, but that wasn't true.

The truth was, God was calling.

"Go with my blessing," my dad phoned to say the day we departed. "I love you honey. I'll be praying for you."

I tried to explain. "I don't know why we have to go, or what we're going to do there . . . we have to go, to obey God. Abraham went out, not knowing where he was going, by faith . . . we may never know why we had to go . . ."

We left the next day, without visas, next to no money, and with no place to stay, bound first for Hong Kong.

A mistake we made was in getting shots to travel, and taking preventive malaria medication, both a waste of money and ill-advised since neither is mandatory and, literally, made us sick. That was the last time. We would never be vaccinated again, since learning it is not required or necessary.

A young believer, Matt, whom we met through Daniel Chapter One was living with us at the time, and he minded the store while we were gone. Recently discharged from the army, he needed a place to stay, so we gave him a couch in the room at the top of the stairs above the store, clearing out a small half-closet for his belongings. Matt moved in with his snowboard and guitar and dreams of playing in a Christian rock band. (We've been told that electric guitar was often heard from an open upstairs window while we were gone!) He is now a police officer, and still a beloved friend and supporter of Daniel Chapter One.

*　　*　　*

Maneuvering by taxi and on foot through the crowded streets of Hong Kong our first night, we found a cheap room and paid for a single night's stay. To obtain a room without a reservation is nearly impossible in Hong Kong! The Chinese innkeeper gave us plastic sandals to wear, and Jim and I sat outside until quite late, in a back alley in the dark, drinking Jasmine tea from a Thermos®.

Next day we set out with no place to go. Breakfast somewhere seemed like a good idea. As we walked along, we spotted a lanky white man in the distance walking towards us, dressed in a wool sweater despite the oppressive heat, wearing a green army hat with the red Chinese star above its brim.

"God wants me to talk to you" he grinned, nearing us.

"Allll right!!" Jim grinned back. He invited the man, Mark, along for breakfast.

There was no paucity of places to eat, so we randomly picked one. Few people eat breakfast at home in Hong Kong, as evidenced by the many diners crowded together at tables in countless nondescript little rooms. Even children in the city eat out on their way to school: soup, noodles, rice, and dim sum.

Over breakfast, Mark explained that he had just returned from mainland China. Since he was traveling back to his home in London the next day, he generously gave us all the Chinese money he had left, three different kinds of currency: RNB, FEC, and Hong Kong money. He also gifted us with a book on how to get around China. Then he asked if we'd like to join him to visit the sister of a woman he met in the mainland. "Sure!" we replied.

Tina opened her front door and greeted us in Chinese. Mark knew enough of the language to respond in kind. He gave her a package from her sister, and she invited us in. We sat together, Mark and Tina talking in Chinese and hand gestures. All of a sudden, Tina turned to us and asked a question, making a tent with her hands.

"She wants to know if you need a place to stay," Mark interpreted.

We nodded and uttered the one Chinese word we knew. "Xiexie!!" (Thanks!)

Tina and her husband ran Pilgrim's Home, a house for missionaries on their way in and out of mainland China. Mark communicated to her that we had been sent by God to do His work. She gave us a room for as long as we needed, free of charge. The following day, with a temperature of 100 degrees and 98 percent humidity, we came back to find a new ceiling fan installed in our room.

The next morning we set out walking, happening upon the Revival Church. Not a typical church building standing alone, it looked more like a warehouse sandwiched between other buildings. Because of the name on the building, we knocked at a door at the top of a few steps.

"We'd like to help here," we told the man who answered. "We'll do anything you need: push a broom, lick stamps. . . " He ushered us inside, into a large room with tables and people busy with bags and boxes and books.

"We need donkeys, non-Chinese people to carry Bibles and song books across the border. We'll train you if you're interested."

We agreed to work as donkeys.

We needed multiple-entrance business visas, he told us. The church would buy them, but we had to hurry to the visa office to obtain them before noon closing time. Jim would need to replace his t-shirt with a button-down shirt, to look more business-like. We could buy one on our way there. Buy an extra-large shirt, we wondered, in China?

No time to waste! We stopped at a store, Da-Da Fat, on our way. Jim found a shirt that fit, for one dollar. He switched shirts as quickly as we were walking. The clock was ticking; it was almost noon! We made it to the visa office, a few minutes to 12:00, and left within minutes, visas in hand, our first mission accomplished.

We had to report early the next morning for our next assignment.

Revival Church workers gave us and several people from an American church group bags of clothes and Bibles, and briefed us on the task. Bibles are illegal in China for the Chinese. If Chinese people are caught with Bibles they may be imprisoned, or worse. Believers depend on non-Chinese people to get Bibles to them. Foreigners are allowed to possess one personal Bible. If caught with more than one, all others will be confiscated.

We were to wrap the Bibles in the clothes. When we got off the train at the border, we were to split up. Some may get caught, but some may make it through. We were told how to fill out the paperwork at the border. For destination, write Shenzhen. Head for the exit after the paperwork is completed and submitted. Bypass the X-ray machine, it will detect books. Hurry. Look at no one. If a guard or policeman tries to stop a woman, they are not permitted to touch her, and they will avoid any public embarrassment.

We hastily packed bags, and left for the long train ride.

Hours later, our train screeched to a halt at the border. Into the noisy stampede pouring out of the doors, I allowed myself to be swept up so as not to get trampled, and then lost sight of Jim. Nervous, I filled out the required paperwork inside border security, then rapidly walked by the X-ray machine with my bag.

"Ah-lo! Ah-lo!" A police officer called out in my direction. *Don't look, he can't touch you.* I walked faster and faster, determined not to look his way.

"Ah-lo! Ah-lo!" he raised his voice, demanding I stop. *No! You can't touch me!* I was afraid to stop, and only walked faster.

I tore out of the train station, running by then, down the street, and stopped at a tree a good distance away. *What now? Wait*, I guessed, sitting down on the curb. I waited a long time.

A couple from the American church group eventually appeared, reporting that their Bibles had been taken. Then Jim arrived, relieved to see me, and happier still to hear I got my Bibles through! He had been stopped and questioned, and all but his personal Bible had been seized. At least we had some Bibles to deliver to the mainland church!

A bus brought us to the drop-off point, an old warehouse of sorts that had been converted to a mission home. Sheets hanging from the ceiling created walls for make-shift bedrooms, and a large cafeteria table surrounded by chairs made the central room a living and dining room. Bobby Watts, from the States, oversaw this house church. Part of its mission was packing Bibles into walnut crates and shipping them deep into China to waiting Chinese believers.

"Got any money?" Bobby asked Jim, leaning back in his chair after a brief introduction, his round, pale face shiny with sweat. He was a heavy man, and although he was about ten years younger than Jim, his brown hair was turning gray and he was missing a few teeth.

Jim handed his entire wallet over without hesitation.

"Stay here," Bobby smiled with an approving nod, "There's something different about you."

Without a change of clothes, not even underwear, toothbrush, or comb, we stayed for days. The visiting church group left that same day, surprised that we weren't going back with them.

Bobby, his pretty Filipino wife Ruth, their three young children, and several Chinese believers who had been ousted from their family homes for being Christian, all lived there. Other missionaries and Chinese people began to arrive unexpectedly, and we enjoyed powerful times of worship and fellowship together. To break bread in remembrance of the Lord, we used what was available; pretzels and Coke one time. Ruth and the Chinese women living there made meals such as fish-head soup, with the fish eyes still in the heads.

*   *   *

At the exact same time my sister's wedding service began, 11:00 pm in Shenzhen, China, 11:00 am US Eastern time, I was standing in a shower baptizing a young Chinese woman with a pail of water. She heard about Jesus for the first time in her life from us, and received Him. She was our first spiritual child, to our knowledge; one of the children Jim and I had been praying for!

A young deaf man was also baptized that day. People were prayed over and prayed over others. I received the gift of tongues through the laying on of hands. By then, we were at least 20 disciples gathered together. Bobby told us there hadn't been such spiritual activity in that church in a long time. They hadn't had a baptism in two years.

*   *   *

We left about a week later to return to Pilgrim's Home. It was the beginning of monsoon season, and since we had no jackets or umbrellas, we were soaked by the heavy rain. Wet, shivering in the air-conditioned train ride back into Kowloon, I felt every bone in my body ache and couldn't get comfortable in the hard plastic seat.

It had been a tremendous time in Shenzhen, but how refreshing it would be to get back to our own room, to shower, and to rest! Yet there would be no rest. When we returned that night, we were introduced to a missionary staying at Pilgrim's Home and several other people. We talked, prayed, and worshipped together for hours. By the Spirit, Jim baptized three young Chinese men in a bathtub. We would later hear that one of those men went on to become a powerful church leader in Mongolia.

*   *   *

We made many more trips into mainland China, each a mission impossible. We broke bread in secret behind bushes at the border secured by armed border guards. The secret police kept watch on Bobby's house and were often there.

Then we were sent to Beijing, to deliver 200 pounds of Bibles in two suitcases, during the Tiananmen Square protest of 1989. We first had to pick up the Bibles in a hotel in Guangzhou in southern China, after which we had to take a three day train ride to the drop-off point, the Somalian embassy near Tiananmen Square.

In Guangzhou, we handed the ticket for the suitcases to a hotel steward, and stood by with trepidation while he retrieved the heavy bags and handed them over to us. We then had to wait with the bags in a crowded train station that smelled like an animal stall, due to the heat, inadequate ventilation, and inadequate bathroom facilities. Jim passed the time by teaching a few Chinese men how to play tic-tac-toe.

Once on the train, we quickly shoved the suitcases under our seats in the passenger class cabin. After the train pulled away and headed down the tracks, we settled in for the three days and two night's journey. The air was stifling, but our Chinese cabin mates insisted on closed windows. Most smoked, and trash piled up as it was thrown to the floor. Mice ran by our heads at night searching for crumbs. The water on the train ran out and the toilet stopped flushing.

For three days the train chugged through rice patties.

To break the monotony we played with a red plastic clown nose, taking turns wearing it with a young man named Andy, and a woman, both of whom were traveling around the world alone. We accepted cigarettes offered to us, Marlboros, and smoked them with the Chinese who offered them, to bridge the language barrier and rather than fight the fact that there was no fresh air to breathe.

When we arrived in Beijing, we hoisted the suitcases out a window with Andy's help. He joined us as we walked, and after some time the three of us were picked up by a scrawny, elderly man riding a bicycle for hire. He motioned for us to jump onto the wooden platform on the back of his bike with our bags, and carried us for miles, laboring to pump up and down the hilly streets of the city overfilled with cars and buses and bicycles. He stopped only when we signaled him to, in front of a hotel.

In Chinese and broken English, and by pointing at clocks, the desk clerk at the hotel told us "the Russians are coming," and that we couldn't stay more than one night. President Gorbachev, Margaret Thatcher, and President Bush were coming to town. We had to get the Bibles to the embassy, so found other lodging the following day and set off through Tiananmen Square.

Our white faces, my bright yellow pants and pink shirt, and our squeaky, overburdened suitcases screamed for attention while we tried to blend into the thick crowd at the Square. Several police officers walked over to us as we waited for an opportunity to cross the street, then held up the deluge of demonstrators and motioned us across! The God of Moses parted the sea, and we successfully delivered the suitcases to a woman waiting at the embassy.

✳   ✳   ✳

Tina had asked that we look for her sister Elli in Beijing and bring a letter to her. We found Doctor Elli, and she later came to our hotel room with another young woman, Dream, the daughter of the third highest-ranked Communist official. Dream desired to be baptized. Christian missionaries told her she had to learn doctrine first, but the Bible is clear: believe and be baptized. Would we baptize her, Elli asked.

Elli, Dream, Andy, and Jim and I locked ourselves in a men's room in the hotel at Tiananmen Square, and baptized Dream by pouring a bucket of water over her head as she sat on a stool in the shower. I lent her my yellow pants and a shirt for the occasion, so she could change back into dry clothes.

She was elated, as pictures that Andy took show. Back in the room, we broke bread and worshipped. As we prayed, three men walked into the room, pretended to look at the air conditioner, and walked out. Dream would soon disappear during the chaos of the demonstrations, never to be seen or heard from again. Some Chinese believers manage to stay underground, and some flee to Canada or other countries for religious freedom. Some meet unknown fate in their homeland.

Not knowing the Tiananmen Square protests would become historically famous, nor knowing the danger, Jim and I marched with the students. Ironically, the goal of the demonstrators was to demand a Communist party without corruption, freedom of the press, and freedom of speech. Come June 3, the enforcement of martial law was executed by force to suppress the protestors. The tanks were about to roll in.

CHAPTER 14

LIVING IN COMMUNITY

Missionaries often get sick from the change in climate and food, and also face fear and discouragement. We met some so sick they couldn't work and had to be taken care of, rather than being able to care for others. Knowledge about natural healing, and possession of spiritual gifts are invaluable assets in the mission field as in life.

When I developed a sore throat in China, I purchased a lemon in a street market and used the juice as an antiseptic. For a vaginal yeast infection, I found and used a clove of garlic as a suppository. We suffered no bowel problems as most travelers do, because we took supplemental, beneficial bacteria weeks before the trip to strengthen our gut, and we took supplemental enzymes we brought with us, with meals.

Proof that "the terrain is everything, the germ nothing"—(Pasteur recanted his germ theory on his deathbed; germs are opportunistic and don't cause illness any more than rats cause garbage.)—we were protected from lice at Bobby's, despite sleeping in an unwashed bed a woman with lice slept in previously. And although there were no screens in the windows, we seldom suffered from mosquito bites.

Gifts of prophecy and tongues afforded us spiritual strength. Prophecy mobilized us the night we were sent on two separate missions: I was assigned to go out with Ruth and the children to lead some New Zealand missionaries back to Hong Kong the next day, while Jim was to deliver Bibles with another man. Before leaving the house in Shenzhen, he was gripped by a spirit of fear. I had never seen Jim fearful. Praying in tongues because I knew not what to pray, the Lord gave me a word for him that supernaturally restored his courage. We then departed, knowing we may never see each other again.

I brought the mission group back to Revival Church in Hong Kong, an amazing feat since I have no sense of direction. Jim, with the other brother carrying Bibles, made it to the plane going to Kunming, after jumping a high fence in the dark and nearly breaking his ankle. We reunited late the following night in Kowloon.

When the Spirit moved us to return to America, we managed to promptly acquire plane tickets; however, Bobby had told Jim he believed we were to return to China.

✳   ✳   ✳

"Thank God you left when you did!" proclaimed my mother, answering my phone call to say we were back. Images of tanks in Tiananmen Square filled television news. Jim and I didn't plan to get out of there, hadn't grasped what was going on. The Lord just sent us back as suddenly as He had sent us. Timing is everything. We had to go when we did. If we had gone later, we would not have met Mark, or Andy, or Tina, or Elli. We would not have birthed a handful of spiritual children. It was all orchestrated by Yahweh Elohim, who demands, besides love, obedience to Him.

I've come to appreciate the critical importance of obedience, and why He says that one who follows Him *"must hate his father, his mother, his homeland, yay his own life."* Other voices, if we let them, pull us away from Him. Knowing about Him, and knowing Him, are two different things, and knowing Him, and truly following Him, are different things altogether. Attending church is not the same as following Him. He called His disciples with, *"Come, follow Me,"* and they dropped everything to follow Him.

"Do not forsake gathering together," He instructs, but never commanded that be in a religious building. He met and ate with sinners and tax collectors, prostitutes, and His disciples, in their homes.

To be His disciples we must walk as He walked. He upset people. The religious people, even his own family, didn't understand Him. *"I always do My Father's will,"* Yahshua said. Not that we can ever attain such perfect obedience, but He is our example. Political authorities, religious authorities, family, are never to usurp the authority of our Father in heaven. We're to heed *His* voice.

"*Woe unto you, when all men shall speak well of you!*" *Luke 6:26* "*Blessed are you, when men shall revile you, and persecute you, and shall say all manner of evil against you falsely, for My sake.*" *Matthew 5:11*

We can only enter His kingdom through the narrow gate, and He is that gate. He alone is the Way, the Truth, and the Life. Our walk with Him had become increasingly narrow, but at the same time more joyous, more fulfilled, more free. "*Because narrow is the gate, and troubled is the way, which leads unto life, and few there be that find it.*" *Matthew 7:14*

There was no going back, we didn't want to. But our walk was about to become increasingly difficult.

* * *

After we returned from China, in frequent fellowship with Jack and Claire, we heard a mutual call to come together as the early believers did, and to have all things in common. Convinced they were to leave their house, and Jack his teaching job, they moved in with us above the store. We gave their children our bedroom, and gave Jack and Claire Jill's room. Claire came with some reluctance. The day they arrived, I opened the front door to find her, fish bowl with pet goldfish in hand, smiling feebly.

* * *

Our friend David joined us next to live above the store and to work in the Daniel Chapter One ministry, with his new wife, Kat. He fought the Lord's call to join our ministry three times, and finally capitulated after the Lord sunk his boat, then his truck, and then struck him on the head with a 2 x 4, knocking him off scaffolding and to the ground. David had told the Lord that's what it would take for him to ever work indoors again, to be struck on the head with a 2 x 4, and when it happened literally, he surrendered.

Awhile later, Claire's brother visited one night as we were breaking bread. Her children were with us and allowed to partake (the Lord showed us that He casts out none, saying specifically, *"Let the little children come to Me."*) Breaking bread was always a special event for them, and this night we were joined by their Uncle Rodney!

He was stoned, as usual. We invited him to the table, and as the bread was broken and passed around in remembrance of the body of our crucified and risen Lord, he was not bypassed. Tearing off a piece of bread, he began to cry. The cup of wine was passed; we each sipped from it to remember Christ's shed blood. He stood up, tears streaming from his bloodshot eyes, and blurted out, "Thank you for sharing Jesus with me!"

Raised in a Christian home, he had always been treated as an outcast by his parents. Jesus accepts us as we are; we don't have to change or do anything for His love. That truth, fleshed out, changed a life forever. He accepted the Lord in that moment, and was baptized in the bathtub by Jack that night. He was instantly freed from alcohol, marijuana, and cigarette addiction, and received spiritual gifts the next day.

Then Rodney moved in with us also. He continued his bicycle repair business, and worked in our ministry. Eventually he met and married a young woman from work, and she joined us as well. Dave and Kat slept on the couch in the main room, Rodney and May slept on the floor downstairs in the store, and Jim and I slept on the floor of a small back room of the store, beside a refrigerator and a washing machine.

Yes, it was cramped. Yes, it was uncomfortable. But in forsaking creature comforts and selfish privacy, we received spiritual blessings and joy beyond description! *"Consider others more important than yourself"* is a command that was, of necessity, tested daily. But as obedience to the Lord is never without reward, He gave us abundant riches in His Spirit in those days.

*   *   *

Before David and Rodney and their wives moved in, Jim and I had opened a second Daniel Chapter One store in what used to be a mill in Fall River. Some of us, including Jack's children who were homeschooled, worked in the Portsmouth store, while others worked in the Fall River store. The food we ate came almost entirely from our stores; packaged things that went past expiration date, rice that had become buggy. A trip to the grocery store was hardly ever needed. We ground wheat berries in a Vitamix to make flour, from which we made fresh bread several days a week, and we made our own soy milk from soaked soybeans.

The entire backyard Jim turned over for a garden, and we grew enough organic fruit and vegetables and herbs to feed us all, with plenty to share with customers. We used bales of hay for mulch, so the garden never needed watering. Corn, broccoli, cucumbers, squash, beets, carrots, cauliflower, tomatoes, and cantaloupe grew colossal in size and immense in flavor, right in our backyard! Eventually, apple and pear trees were planted along the perimeter.

The farmer across the street offered us milk from his daughter's 4H cows, which we turned into yogurt. We made butter with the cream by shaking it in a jar. He also allowed us to glean in his field after the potato harvest, and we picked hundreds of pounds of small potatoes that had escaped the harvester equipment. He left baskets of apples on our doorstep. Most astonishing, is that we lived this farm life on the busiest main road in town, not out in the country.

*   *   *

Jim was, in 1989, still head coach of the Portsmouth freshmen football team, and they were close to making the playoffs. They just had to win one more game, then on to the Championship!

I call My watchmen now to stand in Shiloh, he heard the Lord say one night. Or, did he read it in Scripture? He asked me. I could have sworn I read it too, it sounded familiar. Neither of us could find it anywhere in the Bible however. What could it mean?

Days later, we received a telegram from Israel: "*I call My watchmen now to stand in Shiloh.*" We purchased one-way tickets to Israel, on the soonest possible flight. We'd be gone by the Championships. From the bleachers where I sat watching their last game, I saw a plane fly over the field and knew that although they were winning, they would not win this game. We had to go. They lost by a single field goal.

Afterwards, Jim congratulated the team for fighting hard and doing well, and explained to them the sovereignty of God. To this day, some of those boys keep in touch and reminisce about the game they lost "because Coach had to go to Israel for God!"

We soon were on a plane bound for Israel.

CHAPTER 15

DEEPER INTO THE WATERS

*F*ace *Jerusalem, and do not say peace, peace, but that there will be wars and destruction,* the Lord told Jim during the flight. He later delivered the word while standing on Shiloh, facing Jerusalem.

Ray, from the house in Holland, and his friend Robert, had sent the telegram we received from Israel, "*I call My watchmen now to stand in Shiloh,*" the exact words they had heard. They picked us up at Tel Aviv airport and we spent the first night at Robert and his wife's apartment, American believers who settled in Israel on the Mount of Olives. The following day we journeyed out to the desert, to Shiloh. We rode with Ray and Magdalena, and their toddler son and baby, pulling a camper. Sally from Oklahoma, and Paul from England, went with Robert and his wife. The eight of us who had heeded the call to Shiloh, gathered where the mishkan (tabernacle) of Moses had once rested, now an area of desert between Arab territory and a Jewish kibbutz. The desert met us with sun and high, dry heat, the plaintive timber of Middle Eastern music floating over it from miles away. We explored and set up camp, a thick layer of broken pottery pieces (remains from ancient sacrifices) crunching beneath our feet. A young shepherd boy herded his sheep and goats past our campsite one day, and on another day we were visited by Jewish soldiers curious to find us there.

Nights were so cold I wore a big wool sweater even in the sleeping bag. Moonlight lit the sky sufficiently to see without flashlights, and Jim and I decided to place our pup tent high onto the side of the mountain. To relieve ourselves discreetly, we'd take turns disappearing behind large rocks, bringing a small army shovel to bury our excrement.

We used water collected from a fire-emergency pipe nearby to brush our teeth and to sponge bathe, and cooked on a Coleman camp stove and ate together.

Rain started to pour midweek, and it poured for days; cold, damp rain that forced us to seek shelter in what had been a Muslim tomb. For light in the darkness of the stone tomb we made bottle lamps using oil and rope wicks, and hung them on the walls. Everyone spent the days praying, reading their Bibles, and communing together in fellowship. The Lord then called us all to a three-day fast.

After it stopped raining, Jim and I set out into the desert with baby Jesse, infant formula, and diapers. Through a prophetic word the Lord had established Ray and Magdalena's second son, Jesse, as our godchild. We walked for a day, then slept and stayed in the mouth of a cave for the duration of the fast, without food and water for three days, to pray and hear from the Lord. Jim slept across the back of the cave entrance to protect the baby and me, in front of a tunnel which ran from the cave under and through the mountain.

When we returned to camp after completing the fast, we all once again gathered in fellowship. Jim and I had prayed about what to bring the Lord as an offering, as we had been told to do through a word received before we left Rhode Island. Jim brought money for the house church in Israel.

I had secretly vowed to Yahweh to sing praise to Him, in accordance with King David's expression in 2 Samuel 24:24, *"neither will I offer burnt offerings unto Yahweh my God of that which does cost me nothing."* I'm shy and don't sing well, so it was the most valuable thing I could think to offer Him. Maybe it was the Holy Spirit that led me to offer songs. At any rate, I sang, unashamedly, loudly, from my heart during times of our worship there in Shiloh. From that time on, the Lord has given me extemporaneous spiritual songs.

At Shiloh He began to teach us about spiritual warfare, and ministered to us through each other. Deliverances freed us from bondage to evil spirits, one by one. We broke agreement first with the spirit of condemnation/self-condemnation, then with the controlling spirit of Jezebel who seeks to be her own authority, and of Tammuz, the spirit of death and of fear. Some were freed of the spirit of Saul, who wants to be king. With impassioned, tearful confessions, we broke agreement with those spirits at work in the world and in us. God says in Ephesians 6:12, *"For we wrestle not against flesh and blood, but against principalities, against powers, against the rulers of the darkness of this world, against spiritual wickedness in high places."*

The spiritual fruit of that experience would prove its validity. We returned from the desert in greater freedom and power, less fettered by thoughts and behaviors hindering us from full submission to the Father. Once again, our life, our walk, would never be the same. We had been brought deeper into the waters of Yahweh's Holy Spirit.

*   *   *

Robert was the only one who actually drank from the collected fire-water, and he became deathly ill. It's possible the Ezekiel oil (melaleuca oil) Jim gave him saved his life, but his suffering was so great he had to leave. Unrelenting vomiting, diarrhea, and inability to eat left him too weak and debilitated to remain in the desert. He, his wife, Sally, and Paul packed up and left.

Jim and I stayed another week at Shiloh with Ray's family, and then journeyed into Bethlehem with them. To exit Shiloh we had to drive past blazing fires set in the roads, and in Bethlehem our car was stoned. It was the time of the Intifada, the Palestinian uprising against Israel, and violence in the streets was rampant. We slept that night in a school that friends of Ray granted us access to. On the Mount of Olives the following day we visited other friends, an Arab family converted to Christianity in Bethlehem. The woman served us a thin, watered-down chicken soup, and as we ate, told us about a young man in the other room who was too fearful to come out. His legs had been broken by Palestinian Arabs for not joining their army, and he was suffering severe emotional trauma.

We visited others the next day, then drove on, seeking direction from the Lord. At nightfall, Ray pulled the car over to pray about where to sleep, and said, "Jim, I believe your wife has the word of direction for us." *Oh no! Not my wife,* thought Jim, because I have no sense of direction. But he prayerfully agreed that I had a word for us, and encouraged me to begin speaking from the Lord by faith.

"Continue driving straight. Do not turn to the left or the right." I spoke the word as I heard it. "There will be a house in Bethlehem where a righteous man will extend kindness. Accept whatever is given you as from My hand."

"Amen," all assented. The problem was, driving straight would take us out of Bethlehem in no time, back to Jerusalem. Ray drove a short way, stopped just before the border line, exited the car, and walked up a street to the right.

A man answered Ray's door knock. He did not invite us in, but said we could use a side alley to park the car and caravan. Ray returned to the car. Meanwhile, an Arab man from the house we had stopped in front of came out and invited us in for dinner with his family! We dined with them, enjoying a feast of Arabian dishes, drinks, and desserts. Afterward we drove to the alley, where we slept behind a building demolished by bombs, Jim and I in the car and Ray's family in the caravan. In the morning, we woke up to a silver tray on the car hood, holding coffee and cream and sugar and cookies, left there by people who lived in a house nearby and who worked for the United Nations.

* * *

After more time spent in Jerusalem and Bethlehem, we were suddenly called by God to return to the States.

Our first flight was delayed a day, so the airline put us up in a hotel. Electrical lights! Running water! Beds, a toilet, and a shower! At the airport the next day *we* were delayed, searched for three hours, and nearly missed our flight. Israeli security is thorough anyway, but when Jim emptied his pockets and a bullet casing he found in the desert spilled out, they wanted to know who we were and what we had been doing in Israel.

"Camping in Shiloh," Jim told the officers.

"There is no campground in Shiloh," said one suspiciously. "Come this way."

* * *

We arrived back in Rhode Island in time to attend a banquet dinner for Jim's Portsmouth freshmen football team. In his absence, the mothers had planned the banquet. Jim hurriedly made cartoon sketches of each player, and displayed them with an overhead projector during the dinner as he commended each boy. (Some of them still have their cherished caricature!) The team mothers gave Jim a trophy of a metal football, with the inscription on the front plaque, "Captain Cave Man," their endearing nickname for him.

He was a fanatical and unconventional coach. During the season, he made black t-shirts for the team with a gold lion on the front, and gold lettering on the back that read *"A sword, a sword, sharpened and polished – sharpened for the slaughter, polished to flash like lightning!"* from Ezekiel 21:9, NIV. The boys wore the shirts to school every game day, but an administrator complained that Jim could not give away shirts bearing his business logo. The boys could buy them, however. So Jim charged them 10 cents apiece.

*   *   *

We received other, wonderful news when we returned from Israel: Eunice Buffam's sister had been healed of her leg ulcer! Her doctor had told her that a chronic ulcer in an elderly, diabetic person would never heal, instructing "Just wash it with Dial soap." We suggested instead a wash from the 1939 herb book by Jethro Kloss, made of goldenseal root tea, and to cover it with powdered goldenseal root and myrrh, as Kloss directed, and to take specific vitamins to assist circulation. The Great Physician, Yahweh Ropheka, healed her in just two weeks of an affliction she had suffered with for over a year!

CHAPTER 16

THE ESSENCE OF TYRANNY
AND GLORY

Autism. Cancer. Depression; anxiety. I currently am helping people with these conditions, energetic disturbances according to homeopathic philosophy and that of Traditional Chinese Medicine. It's the early winter of 2015, and we're pressing on best we can. We've been able to continue to help people despite the politics of Big Pharma and the government agencies that serve it harassing us, and in some cases, because of them.

Because of the FTC lawsuit against us in 2008, we later met a doctor who was similarly harassed for sharing health information. His case was over, but we had the same legal counsel, Jim Turner. When Dr. Koren's son was diagnosed with brain tumors, Attorney Turner suggested he speak with us. Children's Hospital of Pennsylvania threatened to have state officials take the boy away and force radiation on his brain. He turned 18 before they could do that, and was fully well a year later due to the supportive power of homeopathy, Daniel Chapter One supplements, and the governance of Yahweh. During the agonizing time of decision for the parents, the Lord gave me a word to share with the father, from 2 Kings 16: 2–3 *"He did not that which was right in the sight of Yahweh his God . . . But he walked in the ways of the kings . . . and made his son to pass through the fire."*

It was not my decision nor my words, but the Lord answered prayer for direction by telling us that the fire of radiation is not right in His eyes. It is the way of the world, "of kings," not His way.

Dr. Koren found through research that radiation would have reduced his son's IQ, at the very least. His son is not only healthy today, but has undergraduate degrees in both math and physics, and a master's degree in physics.

"Selfishly, I'm glad you were sued by the FTC! Otherwise we wouldn't have met," his father has said to us.

For one saved, all our tribulations have been worth it. The Lord says, *"But as for you, you thought evil against me; but God meant it unto good, to bring to pass, as it is this day, to save many people alive."* Genesis 50:20

We've met lawyers, doctors, and politicians because of our case, and some have sought and benefitted from our help. The fact that God has brought good out of evil as He promises to, is a comfort in the hell we've been put through.

Our frustration, however, is that the free flow of information to the public has been impeded. While every individual should have access to all choices in matters of health, the US government limits choice by censoring information, thereby limiting individual freedom. The hypocrisy of the FTC is that it is supposed to be working to control monopoly in the marketplace, but it works to ensure that the monopoly of the pharmaceutical industry remains unchallenged by any competition, and strikes down those who dare get in its way.

"Withholding information is the essence of tyranny. Control of the flow of information is the tool of dictatorship." (Bruce Coville)

"Those who are capable of tyranny are capable of perjury to sustain it." (Lysander Spooner)

Permit me to repeat the issues revealing the government's stony prejudice against us. The FTC blocked all our fact witnesses in court, disregarded our expert witnesses, and twisted everything about Daniel Chapter One in order to bear false witness against our ministry. They ordered us to mail a letter to all our customers, which deceptively stated that there is no science behind our products nor any ingredient in them, and that only chemotherapy and radiation have been scientifically proven safe and effective in humans.

When I read the latter point to a group of professionals at a homeopathy seminar, it caused a hundred or so people to erupt into laughter at the suggestion of such a preposterous lie. If chemotherapy and radiation were "safe" and "effective," cancer diagnoses would not cause the terror they do in patients who receive them. Nor would billions of dollars continue to be spent on cancer research.

The founding fathers had a vision that a free society had to allow for the free flow of information. "*The weapon of the dictator is not so much propaganda as censorship.*" (Terence H. Qualter. Introduction to *Propaganda and Psychological Warfare,* 1962) The Constitution was intended to protect our freedom of speech, freedom of the press, religious freedom, and freedom to assemble: each equally important to one's freedom to access information.

C. S. Lewis wrote in *The Four Loves,* "*The little pockets of early Christianity survived because they cared exclusively for the love of 'the brethren' and stopped their ears to the opinions of the Pagan society all around them.*" Their fellowship resulted from their obedience to commands of God, and was ultimately the reason for their survival.

The Lord exhorts us, "*Do not forsake the gathering together,*" which, while church leaders today use to encourage attending Saturday or Sunday worship, was a daily gathering in the early persecuted church. Our heavenly Father tells us to "*Break bread daily, and even more as you see the day approaching.*" It's what keeps us strong, grounded in the truth we have received.

The government has censored our speech, censored our written material, forbidden us to share our religious belief that Yahweh is the Supreme Healer who has given us "*herbs for the service of man,*" and has forbidden our right to assemble. According to the FTC order, upheld by the federal court in Washington, DC, we cannot share our health information in any way, shape, or form. Not in physical meetings, not on the internet, not on radio. For what reason other than to weaken us, render our knowledge impotent, to limit the choice of those who might hear and receive our message?

For 18 years we hosted a daily, nationwide radio program, *Daniel Chapter One Health Watch,* on which we answered an average of 100 health questions a week, besides praying with people and sharing the Word of God. The radio program generated community, and it was largely a spiritual community. The government shut it down without a single "consumer" complaint. Rather, thousands expressed gratitude for the knowledge and fellowship we offered, yet in an act both unrighteous and unconstitutional, Federal Judge Emmett Sullivan bowed to the FTC, who bow to special interest groups, and pulled the plug on our free speech.

The Lord says we are all parts of a body, His body, no man is an island and when one is weak another is strong. At times in our spiritual walk, we need the encouragement and exhortation of each other, and in our physical journey (not that the two can be separated) we need it also. Most people who used to call in to our show and continue to try to contact us are simply looking for the validation or support of what they already believe to be true. Those who seek to walk the narrow way instead of following the mainstream, seek like-minded others because we need each other to help us withstand the attacks of the deceiver, Satan. In moments of temptation or physical weakness, we need others to help us through, and are to help others in turn. It is what our Creator commands, a system of help that AA has successfully adopted, and yet the US government has intervened so that not all people can access who they want to talk to, when they want. Through censorship and propaganda, the FTC and FDA decide the voice people hear in illness, and that is the way of tyrants.

As Abraham Lincoln said, "*The truth need not fear open discourse; only lies do.*"

*   *   *

David picked us up at the airport when we returned from Israel, and hit Jim up with a serious question. He said he believed he had a word from the Lord for someone, and that the Lord told him Jim would know who it was for, as confirmation. Who did Jim hear the word was for? Over a meal of spaghetti in Boston, Jim prayed, then answered: he believed the word was for President George H. W. Bush, that he was not going to be re-elected as president.

"Yes. That is who."

*   *   *

David and Jack set out for Washington DC, word in hand for the president. The night before, and that morning, we prayed together, laid hands on them, and sent them out in the Spirit of the Lord. The Lord told them to go with empty pockets; they had, roughly, just enough money to travel by train to the capital city. It was to be a faith walk.

A woman who was a new believer, named Bethany, came by the store very early in the morning, breathless. She had received visions and a word to share with the men, "You will pass under a trestle. Flee the man in red! Go to the man in black, he will help you!"

David wrote out the word he received for the President, three pages worth. It contained a warning that fire would be brought upon this nation if it did not repent and turn back to God. The Lord said that He would burn Bush like grass and his name would not be remembered, if he did not seek to obey the Lord God. We took that to mean that he would not be re-elected, which he was not. He did not remove Saddam Hussein, and did not re-establish America as a God-fearing nation.

No one but the Lord saw the fires of 9/11 coming. Today when the name President Bush is mentioned, people think first of the son, not the father. The elder President Bush has practically been forgotten.

*   *   *

I received a call from the Secret Service while David and Jack were in Washington. Security was holding our brothers since they found them walking around the White House praying.

"Has your husband or anyone there ever threatened the President of the United States?"

"Oh, no," I answered truthfully, "They pray for him!"

Eventually they were released, with a promise from the Secret Servicemen to deliver the word to the president. David and Jack returned the following week, with stories of how the Lord provided for them, and of fulfilled visions and prophecy. They had suffered freezing temperatures in DC, and gave their thin sleeping bags to some homeless people. A public bathroom near the White House, usually locked at night but that night left open, provided them with shelter and a floor to sleep on.

They had just enough money for a train ride to New York, but not enough to return to Rhode Island, so after delivering the word they headed to New York City. Off the train, Jack attempted to buy crackers from a vending machine. The machine spit back his dollar. A stranded family approached them asking for money to help them get home. Once again, Jack pushed his dollar bill into the machine, once again it was spit back out. After a third failed attempt, Jack turned to the family and handed the man the bill, "I guess I'm supposed to give this to you."

He later revealed to David that he had brought a credit card too, in disobedience to the Lord's direction. David told him not to use it.

After walking a ways, they passed under a trestle, and there spotted the man in red, dressed as Santa Clause, ringing a Salvation Army bell. They turned from him, and saw a man in a black coat, preaching, holding an open Bible over his head. The man in black!

"I'm armed too," said David as he approached him.

"With what?" the preacher asked.

"With the Word of God!"

The man brought them to an empty apartment, and Jack and David stayed there and fasted for three days as the Lord told them to. The preacher then picked them up, bought them a meal, and later drove them to the train station and bought tickets to Rhode Island for them.

*   *   *

Daniel Chapter One continued to grow, and the Holy Spirit within our fellowship grew. His power was manifested as it was in His early church, and we broke bread and worshipped often, anytime, with anyone the Lord brought by. As the Lord led, there was laying on of hands, deliverances, baptisms; spiritual acts done in obedience, setting captives free to the glory of God. It was a glorious time for us disciples.

CHAPTER 17

TRIALS, BETRAYAL,
AND BLESSINGS

Bethany's husband Brett had her locked up in a mental hospital that year. "This is a case of religious persecution," said our friend, Attorney Eric Chappell. We asked for his help when she asked for ours. Held against her will and forced to take drugs she didn't want to take, she called us from the hospital to tell us where she was, what happened, and to ask for help. Eric understood the situation, he told us, because he had a brother who was born again also, and it had been hard for his family to understand the change in him.

Brett flew for a major airline and was away from home a lot. Bethany was a stay-at-home mom raising two children, and used to shop at Daniel Chapter One. We would often discuss spiritual things at the front counter, and I'd encourage her to read the Bible for answers to her questions.

After her conversion she was light-hearted, no longer the stressed out mother and wife she had been. She read her Bible and prayed often. Brett came home to find a new woman in her, and suspected that someone had influenced her. But her change was not, as he thought, from human influence. She asked the Lord to open her eyes one night, He did, and she was born again. She came twirling into our store the day after, calling out merrily, "I can see! I can see!" We baptized her later *at her request*, and she received gifts of the Holy Spirit.

Brett became furious. He tore her head covering off once while she was praying. They were Catholic, but he didn't like her reading the

Bible. When she shared her tribulation with me, I spoke God's word, "*Win him over without a word.*" Love him, be a good wife.

Brett had his own plan. He came home soon after, to his wife dressed nicely to please him, to a meal lovingly prepared to please him, ripped the phone out of the wall, and pulled her out of the house and into his car. His parents were waiting in the car. They drove to New York and made her sign herself into the hospital where her father-in-law worked as a psychiatrist. There she could be deprogrammed.

We would have stayed out of it completely had she not called us begging for help. We couldn't forsake a sister asking for help. Jim told me then, if it took to sell Daniel Chapter One for the money to help her, he'd do it. Her release from the hospital should be easy enough, explained Attorney Chappell, as long as she was not a danger to herself or anyone else.

Jim, Jack, Claire, Rodney, and I made the four-hour car ride to New York to visit her. The staff wouldn't allow us to see her, so we walked around the building praying, then drove back home. When we returned, we found a note stuffed in our front door threatening to burn the house and store down.

Bethany disappeared.

We got a call from her early one morning, from a pay phone down the street from her in-laws' house. Brett's father had moved her from the hospital to his home after our lawyer placed an initial call. The family was holding her hostage. She managed to escape while everyone was still sleeping in order to call us.

"They want me to denounce you!"

My last words to her were, "Denounce us then! We don't matter. Just don't denounce the Lord!"

We never heard from her again.

*   *   *

Committed disciples will be blindly hated and persecuted in this world. The Lord tells us, "*Woe unto you, when all men shall speak well of you!*" *Luke 6:26*

"Blessed are you, when men shall revile you, and persecute you, and shall say all manner of evil against you falsely, for My sake. Rejoice, and be exceedingly glad: for great is your reward in heaven: for so persecuted they the prophets which were before you."
Matthew 5:11–12

"If they have persecuted Me, they will also persecute you . . . these things will they do to you for My name's sake, because they know not Him that sent Me. . . They hated Me without a cause."
John 15:20, 21, 25

*   *   *

The Lord continued to bless Daniel Chapter One, both the store and the house church. Jim and I heard by the Spirit that we were to go out again, believing we were to return to China to live and work. Jim turned Daniel Chapter One over to Jack. Jack and his wife knew that was always a possibility, we had discussed it. Could be why they were willing to give up everything they had, to come. At any rate, we agreed it was time.

Jim felt led to first visit Poland, Ray and his wife, and the house church there. We would then take the Trans-Siberian railroad into China. Bobby said we'd need a "ticket" in, something of value to the Chinese so they would allow us to stay. He suggested a computer, and told us of an orphanage needing workers. As explained to us, in China, the church needs money, but more than money it needs disciples willing to live among the people.

I could only bring what I could fit in a back pack. The rest of my belongings I'd give away. I didn't have much, but handmade baskets (a birthday gift from Jim), excess clothes, and special bread pans for making different shaped loaves, would all have to be left behind. I rolled my favorite clothes into tight logs and bound them with rubber bands, to fit the most I possibly could into that bag. My flute, couldn't part with that, and several jars of face cream went in as well.

We bought inexpensive but warm jackets for the train ride through Siberia. Jim had us test the jackets by driving into Newport with the windows down one freezing December night. We sat on rocks down by the ocean's edge, and decided they'd be good enough.

My parents silently grieved over my final goodbye, saying little to me, trying to stay positive. However, I sent a box of my things to my sister and mother, and my sister later told me, "Mom cried, Trish, she said it was like you died."

Leaving them that way was the hardest thing I've ever had to do. *"Set your face like flint and don't look back,"* the Lord told me.

Jim had to leave his children. We hadn't seen or talked to Eric for a couple of years, since he chose to not have anything to do with us. Jim never pushed the issue. Jesus doesn't force Himself on us. *"Charity suffers long, and is kind." 1 Cor. 13:4.* Jill had stopped spending weekends with us, busy with her friends, coupled with the fact that our house was full of people and she no longer had a room of her own. Since we didn't see that much of her anyway, we thought it wouldn't be a big deal to her that we were moving. Hard for *Jim* to leave *them,* but we assumed, it would not be that hard for them, which turned out to be wrong. Most sad to us to this day is the regrettable way Jim told his daughter he was leaving. He stopped by her school, had her called out of class, and delivered the news to her in the hallway.

The Spirit was moving quickly, and perhaps there was no way around the pain for any of us at that time. Besides being busy with travel plans and things that had to be taken care of with the ministry, Jim and I did not go about it with the sensitivity we should have, we now see, because we were trying so hard to steel ourselves with the Word of God in order to follow Him and not back down.

> *"If any man comes to Me, and hates not his father, and mother, and wife, and children, and brothers, and sisters, yes, and his own life also, he cannot be My disciple." Luke 14:26*

> *"And every one that has forsaken houses, or brothers, or sisters, or father, or mother, or wife, or children, or lands, for My name's sake,*

shall receive a hundred times, and shall inherit everlasting life."
Matthew 19:29

". . . No man, having put his hand to the plough, and looking back,
is fit for the Kingdom of God." Luke 9:62

We had no doubt we were being called. That we were sure of.
Knowing exactly *how* to leave everyone and everything to follow
was difficult. It was an intense time, and overwhelming. We couldn't
adequately explain any specifics to those we loved; our China plans
were vague even to us.

"People disappear in China!" My mother whispered sadly, in saying
farewell. "I'll miss you."

*   *   *

David took us to the airport. Before we parted, he shared four
visions with us that he had received. The first was a symbol, a curvy line
resembling a sideways G clef. He drew it for us saying, "At this sign, a
man will betray you."

The second vision was of a white spider to beware.

The third was of a man in black, with a cane, sitting on a bench.
We were to be wary of him also.

The fourth was of a woman holding a wreath. Near her, someone
would help us.

My backpack felt too heavy to manage as I walked through the
airport, straining my back. I didn't dare say anything to Jim, ashamed
that its weight meant I didn't leave enough behind. A pair of soft
leather ski gloves, a birthday gift from my parents, got lost along the
way, depressing me.

CHAPTER 18

MORE HARDSHIP

We stepped out of the airport in Belgium into an ebony sky swirling with snowflakes. Reaching for each other's hand, we began walking. In the morning we would take a ferry over to London to visit Mark, the brother we had met in China, but we had the night to get through in Belgium. We stopped at a hotel pub to get a bite to eat. As often happens, we met a stranger there who befriended us. He was staying at the hotel, and offered to buy us a meal. He charged the tab to his room, and got us a room as well! We were grateful, but not surprised. Many times the Lord had used others to bless us.

I retired to the room while the guys were still talking. The next morning, Jim told me the man would take me to the ferry to purchase tickets, since he knew where it was, while Jim packed up and secured our bags at the hotel. No need to lug everything we owned to and from London for one or two days. I returned with the tickets, and by late morning we were on the ferry to London.

*   *   *

We enjoyed tea and cookies with Mark and his landlady, an elegant, white-haired older woman. He then took us to see a magnificent Anglican church. The architecture, the works of art within, and the Gothic, stained-glass windows of the centuries-old church building were awesome; designed to inspire awe. Despite its beauty, and others like it, Jim calls such churches the "wood, hay, and stubble" they are, that will not withstand the final fire. The real church is spiritual, built of the "living stones" of believers (1 Peter 2:5).

After a full day spent in London, on the ferry ride back to Oostende Jim turned to me and said, "That guy stole our stuff."

"Oh, no! I don't think so." I couldn't believe it, and didn't want it to be true.

He showed me the ferry ticket. The logo on it was like the symbol David had drawn.

How could we not have seen that?! How could we not have prevented something the Lord warned us about?!

Jim said he knew when we left, but couldn't stop it. I hoped he was wrong.

Back at the ferry dock, we clearly saw the symbol on the sign above the entrance. We retrieved our backpacks at the hotel. They had been emptied. The man had told the front desk person he needed to check the bags of his friends for something, and stole the computer, my flute, and a watch a Chinese man in Providence gave us to deliver to his brother in China. All we had left were some clothes.

The hotel manager told us we had a bill to pay; we owed for two rooms and three dinners. Jim paid it out of the little we had.

A vision is something that has to happen, we now understand. David's first vision had been fulfilled: we had been betrayed.

We began walking, initially in silence.

"Hey, our load's been lightened!" Jim said to cheer me up. "We must not need those things! The Lord lightened our load."

But, the computer was our way into China! The watch was a gift somebody entrusted us with! And he stole my silver flute! I found it hard to give thanks.

We walked a long way, until nightfall, and stopped when we saw a light on in a church. A welcome sign outside invited us to join a Bible study. We followed signs which led us down into a basement, and joined a group of about a dozen adults sitting at a long table. After the study, some of the people asked who we were, what we were doing in Belgium, and where we were going from there.

"We don't have any place to go," we told them.

A young man invited us home with him. At his apartment, he made us boiled milk on a single-burner unit placed on the floor. The hot milk was good, with skin on top, like his mother used to make for him before bed he said. There we slept, and the next day went with him to his university where he was setting up a table for Christian outreach. He was the son of Christian missionaries, and when Jim heard that, he told him his parents would be proud of him for showing us such hospitality.

We were next on a train to Poland.

* * *

Ray gave us prior warning that a foreigner had to pay a head tax of $30 for each day in Poland. We couldn't afford that, but figured the Lord would work it out some way, even if it meant a very short stay. I woke up as the train barreled into the station. Poland! I was excited, eager to see my ancestral country. My Babci left Poland when she was only 17 years old. Alone, she came to America for freedom, and to where, she had been told, "the streets are paved with gold."

I jumped up to see out the window, and surveyed a drab, gray sky and gray, leafless trees. Men without facial expression, dressed in dingy clothes, were standing around drinking bottles of Coke and smoking cigarettes near a couple of dilapidated wooden apple carts that held piles of dull, greenish-red apples. Poland was a dreary place, resembling an old black-and-white movie in which no one smiles. The air was always sooty with coal dust, as in China, affecting our breathing and soiling our clothes.

We departed that morning into the cold grayness, picking our way through figures bent and solemn. Most people never looked up. The oppression Poland had existed under for so long still affected the demeanor of most Poles.

We found a phone to call Magdalena's father, as she told us to. A retired professor, he picked us up and took us to his home, where we visited for hours with him and his wife. He told us he might be able to find a flute for me. Weeks later, he did manage to get one, a rarity in Poland at that time. Under communism, goods were scarce. Stores were limited, and many items were restricted. Musical instruments were reserved for professional musicians and music students.

That afternoon Ray and Magdalena, along with their two boys, picked us up and drove us to their home. They lived on the third, top floor of a brick house in Wielka Wies (meaning "Little Village"), in the country. We drove long roads to get there, passing through barren fields of grass and dirt stretched out like patchwork that rose and fell into hills and valleys. It was too soon for any crops to be growing in what otherwise appeared to be farmland. Behind their house was a room they gave us to use, a humble guest house made of gray cement that had a coal stove, wooden table, and a bed. It had no bathroom, and no running water.

On the ground floor below the main house was a post office. I had promised my bereaved parents I'd write to them if I could, and was quietly relieved at how the Lord made that possible.

It was late February. Spring was around the corner, but nights still left frost, and sometimes snow, for the morning. We had no heating system in the house but the coal stove. While it was still dark, Jim would gather coal from a bin outside, below us, and start the coal burning in the stove before I got up. We had an outhouse to use, but at night I used a bucket that he would empty in the morning. We lived there for several months.

The Polish government was in flux. Soon after we arrived, communism collapsed, and the head tax for visitors was removed. We could then stay as long as we wanted to without threat of penalties. But we had our sights on China. This was to be only a through-visit. We wanted to obtain visas as soon as possible. A friend of Ray and Magdalena's, Kasia, accompanied us on the hours-long train ride into Warsaw for visas. The young woman knew no English and we knew no Polish, but she could at least get us there.

In the Chinese embassy, a man scrutinized the accordion pages of our passports, stamped in and out of China, and slid them aggressively back to us, across the table. "Ni visa!"

It was 1990, just one year after the Tiananmen Square protest and bloody government crackdown, and China had cracked down on foreign visitors. We tried to plead, but he quickly turned from us to the next person waiting.

Kasia was distraught. "Ni visa" meant "no visa." That much we understood.

*　　*　　*

After going to see the remains of the Warsaw ghetto, we headed back to Wielka Wies, on the train home. Kasia was seated across from us, looking distraught.

"Ni visa, Hallelujah!" Jim shrugged, smiling. When she didn't smile back, he repeated with greater vigor, "Ni visa, Hallelujah!!!"

He kept coaxing her to concede happily that God is to be praised, no matter what, until finally she laughed, "Ni visa; hallelujah!!" It was all we could communicate on the trip back to Krakow.

*　　*　　*

Ray and Magda felt led to visit the Daniel Chapter One house church in Rhode Island. They left 10-month-old Jesse, our godchild, with us and invited us to move into their apartment until they returned. The day after they left, the baby suffered a burn in an accident with me in the bathroom. After lifting the big, heavy baby from the bathtub, for a moment I leaned with him on the washing machine next to the tub. I didn't know that, unlike American washing machines, the *outside* of the Polish machines became hot after running and stayed hot. The accident happened in the blink of an eye, due to my ignorance of unfamiliar surroundings. But it also felt somehow out of my control. Like being betrayed by the stranger.

I was devastated. That morning Jim and I had a disagreement. I don't even remember what about, but he left angry and I was angry at him. After the accident, I grieved that maybe it happened because I was spiritually uncovered, vulnerable to spiritual attack that day, deceived. Even though it felt out of my control, my guilt was crushing. I never had a baby or child hurt in my care, never, how could this happen? The whole mission trip so far seemed to be nothing but battles. Why?

Where was God?! Why did He tell us we'd be betrayed, and then just let it happen? Why did He allow us to be ripped-off? Why did He call us to China, and then block us from getting into China? I felt isolated and horrible. The baby's skin healed, but I continued to wonder why we were stranded in Poland, and why we had so much travail.

Before we left for China the first time, and the money for tickets was stolen, a Christian sister pointed out to me that when God is about to do a great work, the enemy's attacks often feel like hurdles placed before us. Before Jesus began His ministry, He went out into the desert to fast and pray for 40 days. During that time, Satan appeared to Him and tempted Him. Jesus came back from His desert trials, "*in the power of the Holy Spirit,*" and then began His ministry.

David's second and third visions would soon manifest.

Magdalena's parents visited the following day. We told them about the mishap in the bathroom, and they took Jesse. Later it was revealed that her mother, Henryka, was angry and jealous that he was left with us to begin with. The burn on his buttock cheek gave her cause to seize him, but I can't say I blame them.

Ray ordered them over the phone to return him to us. It was up to him as the spiritual head of his family, and up to Magdalena (who was in agreement with Ray), *who* would watch their son until they returned. It didn't matter to us. The grandparents bitterly brought him back. We cared for him for weeks afterwards without a problem, but for the remainder of our time in Poland, they tried to divide us and Ray and his wife in resentment.

Henryka cornered me one time in our kitchen and tried to get me to remove my head covering, which I wore more often than not in those days. Another time, she lured me into the bedroom to talk, and then attempted to come between me and my husband by closing the door on him and urging me not to submit to his headship. We understand this behavior to be from the spirit of Jezebel who hates the prophets of God and seeks to devour them. "Beware the white spider," the Lord had warned through David's vision.

Magdalena's father, Bolek, used to sit outside on a bench in the driveway, dressed in black, holding his cane. His spirit also opposed us, and he tried to destroy our relationship with Ray and Magdalena.

David's third vision was of a man in black with a cane, of whom we were also to beware.

*　　*　　*

Winter passed, and the trees and earth sprang to life. Hyacinth burst out in yellow blaze, and the delicate, white blossoms of cherry trees graced the land, brightening the yards. Crocuses cropped up in the city parks. We hiked through the national forest, which was only 30 minutes away, where the air was clearer, the woods full of wildlife.

Other disciples began coming to us. Expecting to find Ray and Magda, first Piotr and Danuta came knocking, and stayed. Then Pawel and Ewa came, not yet married because his Catholic parents and her Communist parents did not approve. They also stayed, as did Kasia. Some just came to visit, like Grzeg and Bogdana. She was a chiropractor, and blind, and worked in a hospital treating babies born with birth defects. (Since the nuclear leak at Chernobyl, 50 percent of the babies born in her hospital had defects.) He worked in hotel service. They were yet to be married, because his parents did not approve of her.

No one else worked or had any money, except a friend of Kasia who visited for fellowship. Jobs were hard to come by, as were apartments and food. The public grumbled, "We were better off under communism!" We stood in long bread lines for a loaf of bread. With so many mouths to feed in our house, we had to portion bread to one piece per person, per day. One meal, often soup, and one piece of bread is all we had daily (except for the baby, who was fed on a schedule left by his mother). White fat (lard) was used as a sandwich spread.

We bought eggs from a farmer down the street, eggs with dried blood and feathers stuck to them, and milk still warm from the cow. Our housemates would leave the milk on the counter to curdle, which at first Jim and I were fearful to eat. But sour milk that has not been homogenized turns sweet/sour, like yogurt, since the good bacteria in it has not been destroyed. It's safe to eat, and really good!

The Polish people were resourceful, and wasted and disposed of next to nothing. Every glass jar or bottle, and even thin plastic bags, would be washed and reused over and over.

When Ewa had menstrual cramps, Pawel went out to the roadside and picked stinging nettle. He set up a meat grinder on the edge of the kitchen table, and laboriously ground the spiked leaves to extract a couple ounces of juice. After drinking it, Ewa was up out of bed.

We shopped at the open-air market, mostly for root crops like potatoes and carrots to make soup. Rotten parts we'd cut out. The day Kasia's friend brought over a pound of lentils mailed to her from the States, and the time Grzeg and Bogdana brought chocolate and oranges, we all danced. The chocolate was gritty and sugary, but a special treat, and I couldn't remember the last piece of fruit I had!

To minister to these young believers who came to us was the reason we were brought to Poland. Besides mundane activities and duties of life, as in the house church in Rhode Island, there was intense spiritual ministry and activity ongoing. It was an anointed time of deliverances, spiritual gifts, and a wedding.

Pawel and Ewa desired to be married, and we heard by the Spirit that they were to be married and not put it off any longer. We all prayed and sought the Lord's direction for the ceremony, waited upon Him, and He appointed the day. Ewa had a white dress given to her, way too long for her tiny frame but we pinned it up. Kasia's friend brought a lamb leg from a neighboring farmer, and with just flour and water we women made unleavened bread, and, somehow, something of a dessert. We bought wine for the occasion, which we had to stand in a long line for, like we did for bread.

There would be a wedding feast!

I played the flute. The bridegroom blew Ray's shofar (ram's horn) to signal his bride when it was time to enter the room. The ceremony was a picture of Christ, the bridegroom, uniting with His beloved church. I thought our loud praise would raise the roof! Worship that day was like none other we had experienced, similar perhaps to what the early disciples experienced at Pentecost when onlookers thought them to be drunk. They were not, and we were not, drunk; just Spirit-filled.

In the weeks to come, the Lord sent people out. Piotr and Danuta were sent out with a word for the Pope, who was visiting nearby Czechoslovakia. They managed to bring a forbidden Bible on a train, because the guards didn't see it. With almost no money, they traveled, ate, brought the word, and then returned.

Two sisters came knocking at our door one day, saying they were friends of Ray and Magda. They stayed, but in days to follow, their bizarre words and actions made us uncomfortable. Witches, literally, the demons in them rose up when asked to leave. In prayers calling upon Satan, chanting, and wielding imaginary swords, they tried to intimidate Jim, and me, and separate us and all in the house. They tried to steal extra food. When Jim ordered them to leave, they refused.

The men locked the toilet paper and food in a closet in an attempt to drive them away. They lived without either for days. Jim was tempted to physically remove them from the house, but didn't want cause for police to come to Ray's house. After we endured a tense week of their evil chanting, they fled at night after stealing a picture out of its frame that hung on the wall in the living room. The picture, a water color of the horsemen in the biblical book of Revelation, had been a wedding gift to Ray and Magda.

*   *   *

Poland was fraught with hardships from the beginning. But we had good times, strong spiritual times, and times of refreshing. Grzeg and Bogdana took us to tour the salt mines, and to hike the Tatry Mountains. Though blind, she climbed the dangerously steep mountain trail able as a mountain goat.

David and his wife, Kat, came to visit us in Poland. We welcomed the visit, familiar faces from home! Yet a spirit of confusion was about to infect the fellowship. Kat had a strong Jezebel spirit, and wanted the authority of her husband. She sought headship through manipulative "words from the Lord," which were in actuality her words. You may wonder how one knows the difference. The Holy Spirit within confirms a word or not. Sometimes it's not clear. But a word from the Lord will come true. If it's not from Him, the falseness of it will come to light. We spent many hours in fellowship and worship, all of us in the house, and trusted the Lord to reveal the lying spirit and clear the spirit of confusion. But it got worse.

Ray and Magda returned, and Ray didn't want to believe us about the sisters. He questioned many things, apparently jealous of the spiritual activity that had taken place in his house in his absence. We later learned he had come back from Rhode Island with a spirit of Saul (who wants to be king.) Years later, he came to us in repentance.

Their first night back, we stayed up all night, seeking the Lord over a word that David or Kat had spoken. Ray and everyone else said "amen" to it, but Jim could not. He knew, and David knew, that there was a lie in the word. This was hard for Ray, because he was the head of the house and a spiritual elder. Long after fatigue and hunger set in the group, Ray would still not allow the meeting to end. That's when Jim excused himself and me, and told me it was time for us to leave. We packed our bags and left at daybreak.

Grzeg took us in, to his parents' two room flat in Krakow. They slept in one room with his brother, we three slept in the other. Soon after, Grzeg and Bogdana were married in a church service. We attended, but his parents did not. They were Catholic, Bogdana was Protestant, and she was blind; therefore the marriage was unacceptable to them. After the wedding, Grzeg returned to his parent's flat, and his wife to the women's housing unit where she lived, because there was no apartment available to them. They put their name on a waiting list, and had to wait a year or more before they had a place of their own.

*   *   *

While in Poland, Jim and I made several sojourns into surrounding countries; short faith walks. Demolition had begun on the Berlin Wall, the symbol of divide between freedom and totalitarianism, and we traveled to see it, on a train so crowded we had to stand for hours. Jim vividly remembers the rubble and dirt at the wall, the wooden planks we had to walk over, and the border guards with German shepherds at the train station. My memory of it is not as keen, but I do remember Jim's concern when our money suddenly lost its value. The money system, the East German and West German mark (deutsche mark), crashed along with the political structure, leaving us with useless pieces of paper. Fortunately, we had some Polish zloty, and used it to buy seats on the train back to Poland.

We also visited the haunting Auschwitz concentration camp. With no desire to see it, we went at the urging of Polish friends. Incidentally, there's a link between Auschwitz and the cancer industry. The I. G. Farben cartel was the world's largest chemical and drug cartel, and it controlled the Nazi state and secretly funded Hitler. Farben operated Auschwitz. The name doesn't function today, but the branches of the chemical conglomerate are the same, and it is they who operate the "science" and politics of cancer therapy today. (see *World Without Cancer,* G. Edward Griffin)

Back in Krakow, life for us quieted down. Grzeg's parents were very kind, though his father was rarely home. Matka (mother) would make us sandwiches of butter, or lard, and sliced sausages, and serve us smiling, but could speak no English.

Jim and I prayed about what we were to do next. The brethren from the house in Wielka Wies had all left. We spent time researching the possibility of helping Polish believers open Daniel Chapter One stores, and looked into raw materials available to develop supplements, but Poland had strict laws on vitamin potency. One could only purchase vitamin C in 25 mcg, for instance; not nearly enough for a therapeutic level.

No money was ever sent to us during that year away. The church in Rhode Island sent nothing. Jim had only asked Jack to continue to pay his child support obligation, $50 a week, from the store income, which Jack did and for which we were grateful. But we had almost nothing left of the funds we had brought.

David's fourth vision was then fulfilled in downtown Krakow. As we sat one afternoon near a large statue of a woman, into the hand of which someone had placed a fresh wreath, a stranger came over to us and handed us money. Neither of us remember the dollar amount we were given, but with it the Lord met our needs. "Near a woman holding a wreath, someone will help you," David had told us.

*   *   *

Still seeking a plan or vision, one Sunday morning we felt led to attend a church service. There, an old man sitting in the pew behind us dropped a note in Jim's lap. With our limited understanding of Polish, we could make out the reference scribbled on it from the book of John. The verse the note directed us to assured us that the Lord had not abandoned us! The choir broke into a glorious song of praise as we read the note.

The next day mail arrived for Jim from America, two letters from his children. He sat quietly on the couch after reading them, and handed me the letters to read.

"*I'm glad you're doing God's work,*" Jill had written, but shared also how she had been hurt since we left.

"*Dad, please come home for Jill, she needs you,*" wrote Eric.

"God said to set our face like flint and not to look back!" I cautioned Jim. "Satan knows the kids are your heart . . . he's trying to get to you!"

He didn't say a word as he fought back tears.

CHAPTER 19

CALLED BACK

"*And Satan would not let his captives go home.*"

I left Jim in the living room and went to the kitchen to pray. My Bible lay open on the Formica table, and I flipped through it desperately until being stopped by the Lord at that verse in the book of Isaiah: *"[A]nd (Satan) would not let his captives go home." Isaiah 14:17 NIV*

Could it be that the very Word of God He used to send us out, Satan was now using to keep us captive? It could be. Satan knows the Word of God; he used it to tempt Jesus in the desert.

Suddenly I was not so sure about keeping our faces set like flint, about not looking back. "Lord, show me what you want us to do!!!" I implored.

He answered by giving me a vision of Abraham about to sacrifice his son Isaac on the altar, as Yahweh had commanded. Yahweh stopped Abraham at the last second.

God wants our obedience, but He also is full of mercy and grace!

I ran back to Jim, crying, exclaiming with great cheer and surety, "God is letting us go home! He's calling us home!! God is merciful!"

With tears of joy we wept, and then prepared to head home. Yahweh was restoring Jim's son Eric to him, and we would return to Jill.

*   *   *

Buses and trains got us quickly to Amsterdam. Disheveled, packs on our backs, we walked a ways until finding ourselves facing a high-rise building with giant letters lit up across the top that read: Jesus Loves You. A middle-aged woman responded to our knock on the door by opening it just a crack, hissing "Go away!" and slamming it shut.

We walked on until we came to a travel agency where Jim purchased plane tickets to LaGuardia Airport, New York.

* * *

The airport in New York was immense, and strikingly bright. We were back in America! I had never been so happy, so in love with my country. I bought a soda that came in a giant plastic cup with a picture of the Statue of Liberty on it, and saved that cup until the picture wore off from use. Praise God for America! I loved the people here, the places, the light of it, its colors! It felt good to be home.

Jim called the house church in Rhode Island. Jack said he and Claire would come get us. How wonderful it would be to be reunited! They questioned our decision to return, but we would explain in detail how the Lord led us. There was so much to talk about!

We sat outside on a bench and waited. Hour after hour, we waited. A man working the night shift called out, "Hey! Did someone forget about you?!" We couldn't imagine what was taking so long. In the wee hours of morning they finally arrived. That's all right, I thought, we're going home!

Jim and I had discussed on the flight back that we were returning only temporarily, and not to resume authority at Daniel Chapter One but as servants. Jack and Claire seemed glad to see us. We would much later learn that they procrastinated picking us up that night, insisting on finishing dinner and then bathing the children and putting them to bed, even though other women in the house could have done it. I wouldn't have cared had I known that then. Heck, we were home!

When we arrived at the house, David took our bags from us, dropped them at the top of the stairs, and indicated that we could sleep on the couch in the living room. I was asked to make dinner for everyone, so I did. Their reception of us was perplexing; perhaps it would take time for the group to adjust. After all, they expected to never see us again. David's wife, Kat, had redecorated, and it didn't look like our home anymore. But I didn't mind, really. It looked great!

Days passed, and things seemed normal enough. But the store shelves were not full. Jim found out that the finances he left in the black were for the first time in the red. Daniel Chapter One was dangerously in debt.

*   *   *

Kat was the first to see the problem with the baby. Claire had given birth to a baby boy, in the house the previous year, before we left. The Lord said not to call a midwife but Jack had anyway, only for the midwife to get stuck in traffic and miss the birth completely. Jack delivered his son, Samuel.

Now, a year later, Jim and I were back in Rhode Island, discovering serious financial trouble that Daniel Chapter One was in, and then discovering a more serious problem within the fellowship. That problem involved baby Samuel, and the Lord exposed the problem, which was his parents' sin, through Samuel's disease.

On a day soon after our return, Kat happened to walk into the bedroom where Claire was changing Samuel, and saw his skin covered in boils, which Claire had been hiding. Horrified, Kat alerted us all to the problem. The men called a meeting of everyone in the house, and we gathered together to talk and pray about the situation.

It was revealed that Claire did not want Jim and me to come back. She admitted despising our presence in the house. This was because her mother, who had never forgiven us for leaving the Hixville church, said she would not set foot inside the house if Jim and I were there. We had sought reconciliation with her and her husband years before, but they refused to talk to us. They became more angry when their daughter, Claire, and son-in-law left Hixville to join us, and even angrier when their son, Rodney, was born again under our roof. Theirs was an unreasonable, selfish anger.

Rather than confront the sinful situation according to scriptural principles, Claire submitted to her mother's demands that the grandchildren, including Samuel, be brought to her house. Jack and

Claire acknowledged to us that they had been sneaking over to visit Claire's mother at her house, not wanting any of us to know. In fear now for their baby, they repented of their agreement with a spirit opposed to us and to Christ. Through prayer, one of us brought a prophetic word that nothing in creation would heal Samuel. He was to be dipped in the river seven times.

Only after several days of applying natural remedies that did not help, Jack finally obeyed the word of the Lord and brought his family down to the river. He walked into the water holding his infant son, and submerged him quickly seven times. Samuel never cried through it, and within hours his skin began to heal. Jack, Claire, and their children returned to the house with joy. That night, the twelve of us in the house danced with tambourines to Messianic praise music in boisterous, jubilant praise. We were living in unity once again, and peace had been restored. The business aspect of our ministry was failing, but we had faith that the Lord would restore it, too.

⚹   ⚹   ⚹

Not long after Samuel was healed, tension grew high in the fellowship once again. Kat had become bitter towards her husband David because she wanted the headship in their relationship. She rebelled against his authority, and left him to go live with her adult daughter. David and Kat divorced. Soon Rodney and May left also, grumbling, tired of communal living. Then Jack turned on Jim.

Jim had taken back the reins of overseer of Daniel Chapter One after discovering its sorry financial state. He had no choice. Whether due to selfishness or gross mismanagement of funds, Jack had not been a wise steward, and the ministry was about to go under. Distributors would not fill new orders because accounts with them were outstanding. Shelves were bare. People coming in with needs could not get what they came for because the store was out of stock.

Not one to hurl accusations, Jim quietly went about the business of restoring order and paying off the debts. He tightened the belt on spending in the house. Jack didn't appreciate it. He opposed everything Jim was trying to do, and accused Jim of having a spirit of Saul. He began to act irrationally, making false accusations and walking in complete disobedience. He couldn't be reasoned with. At first his wife saw he was wrong, but eventually she sided with him. Daniel Chapter One suffered in the chaos, and Jim and David made the difficult decision to tell Jack that he and his family had to leave.

Remaining in the house to run Daniel Chapter One was Jim and myself, David, and Carol. Carol was a believer whom Bethany met in the mental hospital. Though we didn't succeed in getting Bethany out of the ward, we did help with Carol's release, and brought her into our home with the consent of her parents. She had been institutionalized since her early teens, after intentionally driving her car into a tree. Carol was schizophrenic and suicidal. In the time she lived with us, over a year off all medication, her father told us that she was better than she had been anywhere else. When she decided to try living back home with her parents, we drove her to their home in New York. When she asked to return, we took her back in. When she started wandering off unsupervised, we felt we had to call her father. He came for her, once again expressing gratitude.

I didn't know homeopathy then, so was limited in the help we could offer her. Since then I've been able to help people suffering from schizophrenia, bipolar moods, depression, anxiety, and suicidal ideation, with homeopathy. Dr. Samuel Hahnemann, founder of the Science of Homeopathy, was the first doctor to call for the humane treatment of the mentally ill, and he successfully cured many patients.

After Carol left us the first time and it was just me, Jim, and David running the stores and working to restore financial footing, a female customer and friend told us that her boyfriend, Rob, was liquidating his health food store, and offered us his stock. He owned the Golden Sheaf in Providence, started by his mother, a hip, popular store that many of our customers bragged to us about. It was much nicer and better stocked than our humble store. Health food store owners began calling him as soon as word got out that his store was closing. But their greed offended him, and he refused to sell anything to them. He'd rather give his stock away!

David drove his pickup truck up to Providence with us. At the urging of Rob and his girlfriend, we filled the truck to the brim with roughly $10,000 worth of health foods, supplements, and herbs. We gave him several hundred dollars, all we could afford, a pittance for the valuable amount of goods we obtained. There was so much that our store shelves couldn't contain it all, so we filled an upstairs bedroom with the excess. The room ended up looking like a pirate's treasure chest, its bounty heaps of health food and supplements instead of gold!

We didn't want the perishables to go bad, so we ran ridiculous sales on things like pine nuts from our 50-pound tin. When people with needs we were aware of came in, we'd bring them upstairs to help themselves. The incredible gift from the Golden Sheaf enabled Daniel Chapter One to get back on its feet.

Jim called our suppliers and made deals to keep getting product, telling them we would repay every last cent and we did. Unwise headship had gotten us into a debt of about $60,000, but the Lord helped Jim to dig us out.

CHAPTER 20

A FAREWELL

Daniel Chapter One was saved. If we hadn't come back from Poland, it would not have survived.

We were reunited with Jim's children, through whom the Lord had called us back.

And we were home to support my mother through cancer.

Mom wouldn't have told me about it while we were away, but soon after returning, she confided that she had a small lump under her jaw and was scheduled for a biopsy. The biopsy was positive for squamous cell carcinoma, mouth cancer.

The news was hard to believe. She had always been healthy and took good care of herself. The doctors kept asking if she smoked or drank. She did neither. They acted puzzled, since she was otherwise vibrant, and only 58 years old. Mom told them she suspected her dentures, which didn't fit properly and abraded the inside of her cheek, were the cause. Her doctors dismissed the notion.

My parents had been fulfilling my mother's dream of traveling in Europe, staying in elder hostels. When she first noticed the lump, Dad had recently retired (at Jim's urging), and they were truly enjoying themselves. She and my father ate healthy and exercised regularly (they hiked, swam, and skied many times with us). Surely this was rectifiable. She felt fine!

Prior to going to college, I worked for a few years as a lab tech in experimental oncology (cancer research), at Mason Research in Worcester, Massachusetts. My experience there left me disillusioned with the whole sham cancer industry. One evening a colleague and I attended a seminar in the city held by a group out of California, about a dentist's natural treatment for cancer, the persecution he endured, and the politics of the cancer business. His name was Dr. William Kelley, and I took notes that night.

Now my mom had cancer. I dug up those notes, and reread them. *"Modern cancer therapies are, at best, uncertain."* I turned to my favorite herb book, *Back to Eden*, in which the author says the cure to cancer is fresh air, sunshine, specific herbs, and clean water. I was familiar with chemotherapy and radiation from my years at Mason Research, and knew those treatments to be dangerous and torturous. The Mason Research lab was affiliated with UMass Hospital, and we worked directly with patients' tumor samples, testing chemical agents against them to see which worked best.

I had worked my way up to head of surgery, where a tumor sample would be cut up and pieces of it implanted with a trocar under the renal membranes of nude mice. Nudes are bred for this purpose: they have no thymus, and thus no immune system. That makes them ideal for growing tumors. In a week, we'd contact UMass to report which agent worked best in delaying the growth of a particular patient's cancer. The patients were dying despite this "science."

I now turned to the Lord and begged Him for His guidance regarding my mother's illness. He gave me a dream in which I was riding in a car, my mom in the back seat. I turned to talk to her, but her face was not hers. It was disfigured. When I woke up, He gave me a word for her that said, in part, "Do not trust in the arms of men." I wrote it out, about two pages long, and Jim and I brought it to her and my father. My mother received the word, and said, "I believe you are prophets of God! I'll do what He says."

We gave her herbs recommended in *Back to Eden*. I laid hands on her and prayed. The Lord gave me a song by His Spirit to sing to her, in which He called her to Himself, and called Himself her husband. *"I prepare you now for Me"* was a line in the song.

Weeks went by. She stayed active and cheerful, laughing at the fact she had cancer, saying she didn't feel sick.

"She's wasting precious time," the doctor sternly told my father.

"That's not from God!" I blurted out when mom told me that.

"But he's a very godly man," she defended.

"Peter was too, and Jesus said 'get behind Me Satan' to him because he didn't have the will of the Father in mind!"

I left it at that, and when mom informed me she was scheduled for surgery, I said nothing more. It was her and my father's decision. She asked me to take her place babysitting my sister's two-year-old that week, so I stayed at my parent's house, and visited my mother in the hospital right after surgery. Strange, she said, the doctor came in her room afterwards chuckling, "That was the funniest looking tumor I ever saw. It was all shriveled up!"

Oh Mom, I thought. *It wasn't threatening. It just needed time to be broken down by your body.*

Despite the oncologist's claim "we got it all," she consented to radiation, "for any stray cells." Radiation began without much trouble, but each treatment was harsher than the last, and her neck was eventually burned. She held her head high and kept any fear to herself, enduring it nobly, as most patients of allopathic cancer treatment feel they must.

Within months the cancer returned with a vengeance. Initially a doctor diagnosed the swelling as jaw necrosis from radiation, but soon tumors were visible on her neck and jaw. Surgeons removed one quarter of her face, replacing it with a piece of her back and shoulder blade. They prided themselves on their handiwork in front of my parents and medical students.

My mother lay twisted in the hospital bed, a foot length of metal sutures in her back. They were the same kind I used on the lab rats. Her face was puffed, swollen, and big black stitches marked a large circle around her entire cheek area, extending down under the jaw, like those of Dr. Frankenstein's monster. She could hardly talk, her speech was slurred, and a tracheostomy tube implanted in her windpipe stuck out from the center of her neck.

She wrote with pen and paper, "The service here stinks." It took a kind cleaning woman who noticed my mother's hair, bloody and dirty after surgery, to wash it with the hand soap in the room.

*   *   *

"They can only cut so much" my brother sighed when chemotherapy was suggested. Within months after her major surgery, tumors had cropped up along the suture lines on her face, and on the front and back of her neck. Her skin was burned. Her immune system had been destroyed, and the cancer was spreading like wildfire.

I sat with my dad in the hospital through her chemotherapy treatments, while she vomited until she had nothing left to vomit, her body heaving with effort still. She told me she wanted to throw the IV out the window, and I wanted to do it for her. "Hazardous Poison" signs were posted in her room, and above the toilet it warned, "Flush Twice." She never wanted to take chemotherapy, but couldn't say no. She did it because, she said, she'd kick herself if she didn't and the cancer worsened, and in large part she did it for my dad.

Mom was dying, and in the midst of it we received an invitation to China. The Beijing Research Institute of Sports Science wanted Jim to lead research in Biomolecular Nutrition.

✳   ✳   ✳

My mother's ordeal spanned a two-year period, in and out of the hospital with brief rest periods after treatments when the cancer would be temporarily suppressed. We continued to run Daniel Chapter One, Jim and me in the Portsmouth store, David in the Fall River store.

Jim had been developing our own nutritional products, with formulas based on extensive research, divine inspiration, and personal experience. He wasn't satisfied with what was currently available, and knew that many supplement companies overhyped, and overcharged, for their products.

During that time we were in contact with world-renowned German oncologist Dr. Hans Nieper. We exchanged ideas and knowledge, with the common goal to better help people with serious chronic illness like cancer and multiple sclerosis. Jim not only had worked with MS patients using his computer program, but he had started to experience symptoms of MS. We were driven to help ourselves, our loved ones, and anyone suffering whom the Lord brought to us.

Our first product Jim named Metabolic Optimizer. He made it in response to pleas from parents with athletes in college (many of them the boys Jim had coached years before) for an "everything in one" powder, in a one-month supply container for shipping purposes.

Daniel Chapter One's Metabolic Optimizer, later renamed AM*PM, was the first sports nutrition supplement sold in 10-pound buckets. We also were the first to use whey protein besides soy and egg, and to emphasize the need to take carbohydrates before, during, and after a workout. Jim based the concept on God's Word in which He says, "*You shall not muzzle the ox when he treads out the corn.*" *Deuteronomy 25:4,* one of the verses he used to formulate his concepts of Biomolecular Nutrition. The idea for AM*PM he derived from 1 Kings 17:6, when the prophet was fed by the raven every morning and every night.

Jim's 15-year-old son, Eric, had moved in with us after we returned from Poland, and wanted to gain muscle and lose body fat to be a stronger, faster football player. He had always been a picky eater, but Jim told him as long as he got proper nutrition he didn't care if he ate solid food. The challenge for Jim was to make a high-quality protein and nutrient shake that tasted great. Eric was an ideal taste-tester, and became a successful football player and world champion power lifter, placing second, totally drug-free.

Jim requested protein and carbohydrate samples from Archer Daniels Midland and Protein Technology International, and received a wide spectrum of both. The samples varied in taste, texture, quality, and price. Sparing no expense, he opted to use the highest-quality, best-tasting, and most soluble ingredients, which happened to cost the most.

Nutritionists look at whole foods, but not all food is perfectly digested and assimilated by all people. Jim considered how to maximize nutrient efficiency at the molecular level, and used enzyme enhanced proteins and carbohydrates for immediate absorption and maximum assimilation. This new science he called Biomolecular Nutrition, and the foundational products, when mixed in water, retain the same osmolality as water: ionic and isotonic in property. No energy is used by the body to digest biomolecular shakes, since no digestion is required. The nutrients are immediately assimilated.

Biomolecular Nutrition revolutionized our work with both athletes and sick people, and would revolutionize Daniel Chapter One.

✻ ✻ ✻

Pre*Post was developed from AM*PM, and is a shake powder with higher carbohydrates for the person with greater caloric needs. With Pre*Post, AM*PM, and Mega Carbs, and the use of Jim's computer program to properly guide one in how much to take and when, results of improved health skyrocketed.

When my mother could no longer eat, and couldn't keep down the supplement from the hospital, AM*PM became her sole source of nutrition. She lived on it for six months.

Many athletes sought Jim out after word spread about "the guy whose products work better than steroids." That's how he came to work with wheelchair athletes. He was hired by two male paraplegics (paralyzed from car accidents), and one young woman born with spina bifida, to help nutritionally with their training as they prepared for world competition.

With the day of competition approaching, Elli called, the doctor we met in Beijing! She was in one of the Carolina states doing research. Jim invited her to visit us in Rhode Island, and she arrived the weekend of the World Wheelchair Powerlifting Competition and accompanied us to the event. All three of Jim's athletes broke records that day, and all three won the World Championship.

Elli afterwards contacted her colleague Dr. Li Cheng-zhi, who was vice chairman of the Chinese Athletic Association and of the Beijing Municipal Government for Physical Culture and Sports, and resident professor and director of the Beijing Research Institute of Sports Science (BRISS). He became very interested in Biomolecular Nutrition from Dr. Elli's verbal report, and sent a formal invitation to Jim to lead research at BRISS. We would soon be guests of the Chinese government.

✻ ✻ ✻

It was 1991, and the Portsmouth Patriots made it to the Super Bowl. The game was played in snow on a December evening. I sat numb in the bleachers watching Eric and the boys that had played for Jim as freshmen. A woman we knew came up to me and said, "Wow! You're going to China! You must be excited."

"Not really" I mumbled, adding politely, "It'll be hard." *I may never see my mother again*, I thought to myself.

"I wish you didn't have to travel in winter" Mom said, but forced a smile when we visited days before to say goodbye. She encouraged me, "Go, for me!" not wanting to hold me back.

We laid hands on her, prayed together with her and my father, and broke bread. It was bittersweet, a time of close fellowship in the Holy Spirit, with Jim suffering increasing symptoms of MS, and mom dying of cancer. Together we cried, and together we praised.

"Good bye my darling!" She waved to me bravely from where she sat on the couch, beside my father, her shrunken body small and weighted with sadness, as we stepped outside to leave.

CHAPTER 21

WORLD SPORTS NUTRITION

Jim asked the Lord to give him one last walk of faith. He was unsteady and stumbled a lot. His chest felt like he was being sawed in half. He either couldn't feel his feet, or felt like he was walking on jellyfish. In great pain one night, he sat outside in the car while Eric and I slept, and prayed to die.

Now he prayed to be able to walk in China, if never again.

The night before we left, we came home from the Super Bowl game to find a stranger waiting in our parking lot. He stepped out of the car and greeted us. Eyeing Jim's worn out Bible, he said, "That's an idol to you." (Jim never was without his Bible, and used as a reference, "*it* says," rather than "the Lord says.") He invited the man in. Upstairs in the house, the stranger prayed with us, for our trip and for Jim, spoke from the Lord, then vanished into the night. We never saw him again, and still don't know who he was.

*   *   *

Several Chinese scientists met us in the airport, one tall and waving to us above the crowd of heads. They ushered us past the security line, preferential treatment for honorary guests. The red carpet was being rolled out to us in China! The men spoke with excitement as they drove us to our Beijing hotel in two white cars, transporting five adults and our luggage, including Daniel Chapter One products for the month-long studies.

The men who met us were Liu Xing Zhong, president and chief editor of Sports Vision Magazine, and Zhang Lu, vice director of BRISS and deputy secretary general of the Beijing Sports Science Society, and Chen An, vice director of the BRISS Sports Science Laboratory. Chen An worked in the Department of Biochemistry, and would be the man assisting Jim.

They brought us to the Temple of Heaven Hotel, came into the room to inspect it, ran the water in the bathroom, and announced we'd have hot water until midnight; for another 20 minutes. That first night the hotel lost power, a regular occurrence in China. Jim went out to search for a flashlight, leaving me with a candle stub and matches.

Chen An visited the next day with the assistant professor of the Division of Nutrition and Biochemistry at the Nutrition and Recovery Center of the National Research Institute of Sports Medicine. Jim introduced his computer program to them, which they took great interest in, especially with regard to weight control for wrestlers.

Other scientists came the following day and questioned Jim extensively about his program and products. Their interrogation lasted many grueling hours, until they were satisfied. This went on for days; every day new people would come to question Jim. Some, we suspect, were police. Eventually the authorities were appeased, and 11 days later our lodging was moved to a nice, modern room on a top floor of the high-rise hotel that houses the Chinese Opera. The hotel did our laundry for the month at no charge, and we were exquisitely and generously fed by our hosts.

Chen An gave us a tour of his lab at BRISS, showing us its sophisticated, computerized equipment. Dr. Li later told Jim, "The laboratory is yours to use!" Chen An asked if we were Christians. Jim said "Yes, but we don't go to church. We read the Bible in our home." At that, the room got quiet. It's illegal to do so in China.

A government-appointed driver would, on occasion, bring us places after work, such as to see the Great Wall, and we were issued bicycles for getting ourselves to work at the Institute every day. One morning we awoke to deep, freshly fallen snow. Many floors below us, we could see an elderly woman in a blue coat and a white cotton, fitted hat, sweeping the snow from the hotel driveway with a wide, fan-like brush. Bicycles were out as usual. Chen An came by on a bike to lead the way.

"We can't bike today, there's snow and ice on the roads!" Jim objected.

"Why not, boss? You just go slower."

And so we did. Bicyclists were slip-sliding all over the roads, picking themselves and their fallen bikes up out of the snow, laughing. The conditions made it fun, if you looked at it that way, and we joined in the laughter when we, too, fell! Chen An carried the camera for us, and did not fall.

We had brought black down jackets to wear, lined in red, with World Sports Nutrition embroidered on the back in gold. Bobby cautioned us that the name Daniel Chapter One would close the door to China, so we went as World Sports Nutrition, another company Jim had started years before to separate the sports nutrition ministry from the health ministry of Daniel Chapter One. We gave Dr. Li a similar jacket as a gift.

He was fascinated by our Christian faith. Jim cannot help but talk about the Lord, and Dr. Li wanted to hear more. He sincerely asked about what we believe and practice. That's what I most remember about our early days at BRISS, sharing and answering questions about Jesus. It made me a bit anxious at first, not sure what motive the doctor had, but Jim spoke candidly to him. As it turned out, many of the Chinese scientists wanted us to share our faith with them! Their eagerness to hear about our Christian beliefs was explained to us by fellow missionaries in China as being due to "a spiritual vacuum."

After coming to power in 1949, Chairman Mao Tse-tung forbade the practice of any religion, in an effort to coerce the masses into serving the Communist Party before God. All religions were attacked as "superstitious" by reform officials and intellectuals, and by 1958, the atheistic government had closed all visible churches. But the hollow in the heart of a man is one that only God can fill. We are created to *yearn to know* our heavenly Father. The spiritual vacuum forced upon the Chinese people created a crisis of longing within their souls.

China presently has a pretense of religious freedom, as long as one's "religious activities" take place within government-sanctioned organizations and registered places of worship. The Three Self Church and the China Christian Council together form the state-sanctioned Protestant church in mainland China. Attendees are monitored and watched by government agents. Christians unwilling to submit to the state's control and supervision go underground. They meet in homes, referred to as "the house church," to worship freely. They continue to be persecuted by the government.

Not that different from America today! Most US Christian churches have 501(c) (3) status: nonprofit, controlled by the government. Pastors are told what they cannot say. For instance, they've been forbidden to preach about political issues, according to the 1954 Johnson Amendment. Jim organized Daniel Chapter One as a corporation sole, filed with the IRS as a 508, in order to retain the sovereignty of Yahshua. Jesus Christ is the head of our church, not the government. We are vicegerents (officers) of Jesus, Yahshua, our God and King, not of the government. We're law-abiding citizens who work for the Almighty God. As overseer of our church and ministry, Jim has to answer to Yahweh and will be judged by Him one day.

*   *   *

We biked miles every day to BRISS and back, to measure body fat and lean muscle mass percentage of the athletes on the powerlifting, wrestling, and judo teams in the study. Over lunches of rice, fried frogs, toasted maggots, eel, and other Chinese delicacies, always with Jasmine tea to drink, we had tremendous opportunity to talk more about the Lord to our inquisitive, spiritually hungry comrades. One time Chen An and another scientist, Miss Pung, asked us to pray before a meal in a public restaurant, a bold request in China!

Besides the scientists we worked with daily and top Chinese doctors who had us in their homes, we met many Chinese believers and fellowshipped with them in their homes and in our hotel room. Those meetings mostly took place at night, and had to be in secret for the sake of the Chinese believers. Some elderly Chinese believers told us about the persecution they suffered under Mao. Families were ripped apart and sent to different work camps. We were meeting the children, now old, who never saw their parents again.

No matter what people have been through, those who know the Lord and love Him have His peace and joy, and desire nothing more than to share their faith and worship together. Fellowship between Christian brothers and sisters is a spiritual gift the Lord tells us, in Romans 1. He brought us to China to work for Him, and also to gift us and believers there.

Through obedience to His command to "go out," I've learned its importance. The Lord sends His disciples out, partly because "*a prophet is without honor in his home town.*" A prophet is more likely to be listened to when he or she is a foreigner. Familiarity makes it hard for people to see past the person they know well, hard to see and hear the Holy Spirit speaking through them. Those who grew up with Jesus had difficulty accepting His deity and believing that His was a divine mission.

*　　*　　*

Jai and his wife are Chinese believers we met who became close friends. He told us that God gives him messages, dreams, and visions, and he had a dream before we arrived by which the Lord told him we were coming, and told him to prepare for our visit. In the dream he saw "a couple of white people climbing a mountain by the east gate of the Temple of Heaven," the location of our first hotel, and heard God say, "Learn English." His wife had no knowledge of it, nor did anyone else. He secretly learned English, and the day we met she was surprised when he could speak to us. He said, "You are the people I saw in my dream!"

They entertained us in their home. Jai prepared a multi-course meal, and after dinner asked me to read the Bible into a tape recorder so they could listen later, to better learn English. His wife and 6-year-old daughter knew no English, but his was very good because he had obeyed the Lord. He worked restoring traditional Chinese buildings, and was involved in the creation of Chinatown in San Francisco. The couple cherished our fellowship, and longed to have as much time with us as possible. On Christmas Eve, the family rode hours on a single bicycle, the father peddling, mother on the back, and their daughter on the handlebars, without gloves or mittens, to meet outside the city in a secret room where we fellowshipped past midnight. Beijing is frigid in winter, and the streets are not well lit. At great sacrifice they came and stayed late, even though the little girl had school in the morning.

*   *   *

Sporadically, power would be lost in Beijing at night, extinguishing the lights. One night, we had to burn paper torches to see our way down an unlit stairwell, at the home of another family. We followed in the darkness, running down 14 flights of stairs, Jim and the other brother relighting the newspaper torches on the way.

Evenings there was no hot water. Toilets, even at BRISS, were just a hole in the concrete floor. I got used to squatting beside other people when nature called. The female scientists would talk to me as we squatted. "Merry Christmas!" one smiled on Christmas morning, turning to me from where she squatted beside me. I laughed back, "Merry Christmas!"

Three top Russian scientists were at the Institute when we were there, and we spent time together after work. One showed us his inventions for bettering athletes: a swimmer's cable, computerized testing of skills of reflex and shooting, and physical therapy for the handicapped. Another was head of the biomechanical lab of the Research Institute of Moscow, and used to coach the national team in track. The third doctor had been a decathlete. With a formal letter, they invited Jim to Moscow to lead research on Biomolecular Nutrition.

We happened to watch the news of the collapse of the USSR with them, in real time, on our hotel television. "Ah, home will not be the same when we get back!" they exclaimed.

*   *   *

Twice, we received honor in Beijing. The first time was at a New Year's party held at the Institute. That day, Jim presented the study results, explaining the biochemistry involved. There were many questions from the audience of over 100 scientists packed in the room; intelligent questions, genuine and not contentious. He did a scholarly job answering. Tired from the rigors of interpreting two hours of presentation, at the end of the seminar Chen An sat down and smiled with thumbs up, "Great, boss, great!"

That evening we were the honored guests at a banquet party. The room erupted in applause as we were escorted in, at which we clapped too because I had read that is the Chinese custom. There was a meal but no alcohol, and I explain that because the party was so hilarious, you might think it due to the punch! The life of the party was the entertainment provided *by* the party goers, and their ability to laugh at themselves. One by one, each scientist got up on stage to perform an act; singing, or playing a musical instrument.

We were told it was our turn.

"Oh, no! We can't sing!" we protested.

The crowd heartily insisted.

"Trish, we have to," Jim ordered me under his breath.

We picked a song hastily out of a karaoke book, John Lennon's "Yesterday."

There on stage, for all the BRISS world to enjoy, we sang best we could, but horribly out of tune. "*Yesss-terday, all my troubles seemed sooo far away. . .*"

The crowd went crazy! Cheering loudly, they didn't let us stop, and after "Yesterday" was finished, they began to chant, "Jingle Bells! Jingle Bells!"

So we sang "Jingle Bells," to the exhilarated delight of our audience.

Once again we went to exit the stage, but again the audience began chanting, this time, "Disco dance! Disco dance!"

"Oh, no! Do I have to?!" I whispered to Jim.

"Yes! Just do it!" he said, 'getting down' with dance moves.

Oh, my God! I danced too, embarrassed beyond belief that we were doing so, and soon we were joined by the whole room in disco dancing. The Chinese relish most things American, and they were absolutely thrilled by this.

We had hours to bike back to our hotel that night, on roads dark and rough, and were still laughing so hard we could hardly keep balanced on our bikes or see straight.

Our last night in China we were treated to a meal of Peking Duck. We ate in a private, ornate hotel room called the Emperor's Room. The window dressings and tablecloth were bright golden yellow, the carpet and walls detailed on a background of golden yellow. Yellow had been the emperor's color, and no one else in China had been allowed to use it. They seated Jim in a large, masterfully carved wooden chair, the head scientist to his left. Jim was the honored guest.

We had what they called "a 100-course meal" of everything duck, beginning with duck tongue soup and ending with duck brains. It was extravagant, "the Emperor's meal," to demonstrate their respect for Jim and his achievements. Said Dr. Li, raising a tiny glass of wine, "Thank you for coming to China. Yesterday you were new friends. Today you are old friends. Tomorrow we begin working together for something new."

Jim's computer program was brought to the attention of the chief negotiator for Sports in China, who was trying to get the 2000 Olympics held in China (which eventually happened in 2008). There was serious interest in Biomolecular Nutrition and for us to return. Jim gifted BRISS with a computer.

Chen An and Miss Pung rode with us the next day to the airport, together in the back seat, and wanted only to talk more about our faith. Miss Pung said, "I want to know your God! God blesses you. Your God is good. He likes you."

Tricia smuggling Bibles into mainland China.

Ministry to Tricia in China with laying on of hands.

Tricia marching with demonstrators in Tiananmen Square, China, 1989.

*Jim and Tricia baptizing a woman in a bathroom
at Tiananmen Square during the protest.*

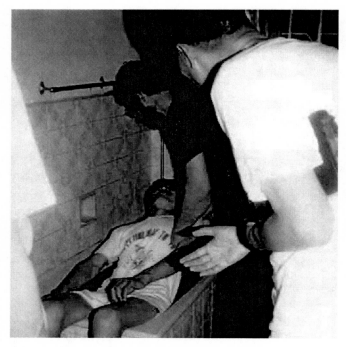

Jim baptizing a man in Hong Kong.

Tricia in the desert at Shiloh, Israel.

Tricia with Arab Christians in Bethlehem.

Tricia at the open market in Poland.

Tricia, front and far right, and Jim, far right, second row, next to last man, with scientists at the Beijing Research Institute of Sports Science.

Jim with a Russian scientist, traveling to the Great Wall, China.

*   *   *

We stopped in Hong Kong to visit Bobby on our way back to the States. He had been kicked out of China after being tried in a court of law and found guilty of being a Christian. He and his family were living in a high-rise, Chun King Mansion, with many Chinese believers, and with rats who poked their noses out of the floorboards. I asked to use his phone to call my dad.

Mom was still alive and on hospice care at home. I knew that meant my mother had been sent home to die, and was visited daily by hospice care workers for palliative care only. The doctors, he said, called off any more chemotherapy, saying "it's like fertilizer to her cancer," calling the cancer very aggressive.

Squamous-cell carcinoma tends to be slow growing, and her cancer was not aggressive until the treatments destroyed her immune system. I said nothing about that, just that I hoped to be home soon, and gave him the date.

Hawaii was next on our itinerary, where we stopped and stayed with friends of Bobby, a family of five. We attended church with them and helped out in a soup kitchen. The family would later join us in Rhode Island to live and work at Daniel Chapter One.

After a week in Hawaii we flew to California to visit Theodore Stapp at the mission home where he worked for World Missions Far Corners (a group that had also made us ministers for them.) There, Ted, and Jim and Gloria Portias, "Mom" and "Dad" to the people they took in, had a street ministry to the homeless and drug addicts. They fed, clothed, and taught Bible to all they housed.

We spent several days there in ministry and fellowship before flying back to Rhode Island. On our last night, Ted woke up in the middle of the night compelled to worship. He woke everybody in the house, and all, including children, gathered in the kitchen. We prayed and worshipped. Many prayers were lifted up for my mother. The Lord gave me a song, and I sang it with a full heart, hopeful and appreciative of our great God, believing that He could still heal her as He did the lepers, the blind, and the lame.

The first night we were home, Eric had a football banquet we attended. My father called the next day to ask if we were back yet. He and mom had marked the date. My mother was waiting for me, dad said, asking every day what the date was. It's what kept her hanging on, he believed. I know it was the Lord's grace and mercy that had kept her alive.

*　　*　　*

Kneeling beside the bed she couldn't sit up in, I hugged my mother in grateful reunion. Mom wanted to hear about the trip, and remarked on what a miracle it had been, noting its success on two levels, both business and spiritual. We then talked about her situation. Perhaps her lack of faith was preventing her cure, she lamented. She had been sent religious cards, some suggesting that.

"Oh no, Mom! It's not up to us. And you still have faith, you trust in Him?"

"Yes!" She believed and trusted the Lord with all her heart and soul. She told me He had given her the gift of tongues. "Don't feel bad Trish, I've had 60 wonderful years! I'm not afraid to die."

When we returned home, Jim told me to pack my bags and stay with my folks as long as they needed me. He brought me back to them right away. My sister lived in nearby Worcester, but had a toddler and a newborn, and my brother was in medical school in Maine. My schedule was the most flexible.

Dad and I cared for Mom together for two weeks. When she developed a pressure sore on her ear from lying on the one side she could lie on, I remembered the earache pillows sold in China and made her one like it by cutting the center out of a piece of foam. I gave her fenugreek tea for the thick mucus filling her throat, and used it instead of water for AM*PM shakes, her sole source of nutrition. She never needed a feeding tube, and did not choke to death as the doctors predicted. Hospice nurses said, "She's lucky to have you, with what you know!" They were amazed she needed no painkillers or other drugs.

My father and I took turns sitting by her side, day and night. At one point she turned to me, noting regrettably, "Hippocrates said never cut a cancer." (Surgery for cancer does not cure the fundamental, systemic disease, and also, can spread cancer cells.) Then, to be certain

I would not, she said, "Don't be angry with anyone, Trish. Everyone spoke out of love," referring to family who pushed for the chemo and radiation when Jim and I opposed it. She added, "If my story will help anyone, you share it."

She played with my hair, twirling it in her fingers. "You're a wonderful daughter."

I hung my head in shame and said, "No, I wasn't always."

"I don't even remember" she replied, the love of Yahshua on her lips.

*   *   *

Jim drove up often from Rhode Island to visit us. One evening he arrived, she was in a state of high anxiety, her pulse and breathing rapid. He laid hands on her and prayed, "Thus says the Lord. . ." Immediately she calmed down after the word, fell asleep, and slept through the night.

She asked me three different times, "What's that sound?" When I told her I heard nothing, she smiled and answered, "Oh! It's the wind." Another time she asked, then said, "Oh, it's a flock of birds!" The third time she asked, she answered the question saying, "Oh, it's raining." I believe she was hearing the Holy Spirit.

Her final night, she cried out and I climbed into the bed and held her. Dad called family to come the next day. My aunt was in the room when suddenly mom looked up and smiled broadly. "Rose, do you see God?" asked Aunt Liz. "Yes!" my mother breathed out her last, her soul at rest with the Lord. He did answer our prayers, healing her in the most profound way.

My brother considered becoming an oncologist (cancer doctor), but chose emergency medicine instead, and gave me his oncology medical books. In one textbook by the American Cancer Society, in the chapter on squamous-cell carcinoma, causes are listed: smoking, drinking, and *ill-fitting dentures*. Mom was right! The book also states, "*Present methods of treatment need to be reevaluated.*"

✳   ✳   ✳

People with natural solutions to cancer have been persecuted for decades. Why? Because there's no money in herbs and nutrients that cannot be patented, for one. In terms of spiritual warfare, it's more sinister than that. Satan is behind it, to deceive and destroy, the enemy of truth and adversary of the Creator and His creation. *"The thief comes not, but for to steal and kill and destroy: I have come that they might have life, and that they might have it more abundantly." John 10:10*

"If my story will help anyone, you share it," my mother had told me.

In that, I heard the Lord. I have shared her story many times. I chose to fight the government lawsuit against us to fight for the right to do so, as well as to stand for the truth of Yahweh and His creation.

Joe and Maria Rocha, of Portsmouth, Rhode Island are both alive today because of the information we shared with them over twenty years ago. They say so. Maria almost died from severe candidiasis until she used supplements we suggested. Before she accepted our advice, Jim sprang up in bed one night saying, "Maria is going to die if she doesn't do what the Lord reveals to us!" She introduced us before we spoke at Maria's House of Prayer healing service in Ocala, Florida as, "the people who saved my life." Yahweh did the healing and the saving, but He used us.

Her husband, Joe, came into Daniel Chapter One soon after my mother's passing, with the same kind of cancer, in the same location, as my mother's. I shared her story, as she wanted me to. He chose to use herbs and nutrients we suggested, not surgery, radiation, or chemo, and was healed. Thousands of people have been healed because of our products and the information we've shared. The United States Federal Trade Commission and Food and Drug Administration consider all those lives "irrelevant" anecdotes, the word they used in court, and seek penalties from us for not having "reasonable basis" for our information. They've censored our speech, so we can no longer share information with those who want it.

But we do have reasonable basis to support all we've ever shared. Ample! We have many testimonies (call it weak evidence, but evidence nonetheless), the long history of traditional medicine knowledge, God's

Word, and a growing body of scientific literature to back up what we have said and written. The people alive today after being sent home to die by their physicians are living proof of the validity of what we have been blessed to know.

"Only conventional cancer treatments (chemo and radiation) have been scientifically proven safe and effective in humans" is the government message they ordered us to carry, a false message from the prince of darkness and father of lies. We knew that we had to stand and fight.

CHAPTER 22

BROTHER'S KEEPER

first learned homeopathy to help Jim with his symptoms of multiple sclerosis. I had no idea what a great thing the Lord was about to do through our tribulation, I just believed that homeopathy could help my husband. My mother passed away in February, 1992. I began a condensed homeopathy program the following September. Every other month, The New England School of Homeopathy class was held in a hotel in Northampton, Massachusetts, Friday through Sunday. I drove with a customer who had become a friend, a local optometrist, and we stayed at bed-and-breakfasts so the cost was minimal. An inheritance of $5,000 from my mother, my grandchild share of my Babci's triple-decker, covered tuition and book fees.

David had meanwhile been sent out to the mission field with a word of the Lord. He first went to Hong Kong and worked with Bobby; from there went to the Philippines where he met and married Evelyn; and together they went to Bangladesh, where they ministered to Muslims for the next ten years.

The year after my mother's death, in September, 1993, 26-year-old Mary came to live and work with us. Her mother was a customer, and dropped Mary off one day at our store, asking us to help her. She suffered chronic ear infections, was underweight and generally sickly, and had been living in a women's shelter and from there, government housing. Mary received the Lord about a week after she met us, and moved in. (She's one of our spiritual children. In 2000 she asked me to fill in for her mother, who was in the hospital, in her wedding ceremony.)

In October of 1994, Mary was baptized in the Sakonnet River. Sally, whom we met in Holland and camped with in Israel, was visiting us from Oklahoma and joined in the baptism. Sean, a young man living with us, came to watch. He was not a born-again believer then, but is now (baptized in 2016). We had called other Christians to attend Mary's baptism, but it was "too late," and they were "too tired," reminiscent of the parable of the wedding feast in Matthew 22:3, in which the people first invited had excuses not to come, so the king had his servants go out into the streets and bring in those they found.

The air that night was balmy, the water unseasonably warm and smooth as glass, reflecting the moonlight. Sally and I walked into the river with Mary and baptized her, Jim and Sean watching from the shore. Back at the house, we enjoyed take-out pizza.

*   *   *

That year we also took over a small health food store in Warren, Rhode Island named The Lions' Den, started by a customer of ours in an old grain mill on the bike path. Unable to make ends meet, the owner asked us to buy him out. Three stores was one too many, so we eventually gave away the Fall River store to the son of a customer.

I graduated from homeopathy school in August, 1993, and started to practice. By then, the third Daniel Chapter One was operating, complete with an ice cream counter and a café we added in. One of the two athletes Jim hired to help in the store made an office for me by hanging sheets up in the back of the café. It was rustic, but nicer than my first office in the Portsmouth store, which was formerly a bathroom! (We had shut off the water, and stuffed old T shirts into the toilet bowl and covered it with wood for a makeshift desk.) In Warren, from an antique store I obtained a wooden secretarial desk (the middle of the surface was lower, to hold a typewriter) and there I sat taking cases, sometimes interrupted to flip a veggie burger or scoop ice cream for a patron in the store.

The Warren store became a mecca for serious athletes, most of them wanting to gain muscle. In those days, Jim's health was poor, and he tried to hide away while he worked on formulas for new products.

But word got out, and he was inundated with individuals who wanted to be measured, put on his computer program, and guided by him. It was a funny sight: Jim in the back of the store, sitting on a wooden crate surrounded by several muscle heads sitting on wooden crates, all hunched intently over a computer, oblivious to the cobwebs and grain dust forever falling from the ceiling.

Many of those men achieved record-breaking results, and one became the youngest person ever to win a Double Iron Man. That man was Paul Bedard, who years later starred in the Animal Planet series *Gator Boys*. He credits Jim with his athletic success. Jim also worked with world class and Olympic athletes, male and female, who found him through word of mouth.

At one point in those days of back-store counseling, he had a severe leg infection, but that didn't stop him. He continued to counsel people, his red and swollen leg weeping yellowish fluid. The infection, cellulitis, resulted from a wound he suffered in building the café, when he struck himself in the shin with a hammer while taking down a wall.

For fear of losing the leg, we went to the emergency room at Newport Hospital. The visit proved disastrous, and marked the last time we ever accepted drugs. Jim's face swelled as the IV antibiotics were administered, and by the time we got home his eyes were swollen shut. He threw the prescription in the trash, and sat with wet tea bags on his eyes.

Mary made Kloss's liniment from the *Back to Eden* book, a concoction of goldenseal root tea with cayenne, which Jim applied to his leg often. He also kept debriding his skin with a loofah and drank "detox" herbal teas to cleanse his blood. He eventually healed, though a round scar remains. He calls the scar his ebenezer, a memorial of the final turning point in our rejection of man-made drugs. *"Then Samuel took a stone . . . and called the name of it Ebenezer, saying, Till now has Yahweh helped us."* 1 Samuel 7:12

*   *   *

"Are we our brother's keeper?" Jim asked me one day in 2014, six years after the Federal government brought a civil lawsuit against us.

He didn't want my opinion, he wanted me to answer from the Word of God. He knew the challenge it was for me to continue helping people after the government ordered us not to. He was genuinely struggling with the question Cain posed to God when asked where his brother Abel was. *"Am I my brother's keeper?" Genesis 4:9*

The answer came to Jim in a dream. In his dream, he entered an old cellar made of stones, with a dirt floor. At the far end was a deep stone coffin, like a cave, where, by dim golden light, he could see sticks lined up against the walls. They turned out to be bones, which grew larger as they moved towards him, and he could see a person's name written on each one. When he woke up, he knew the answer was "yes," we are to care for our brothers.

We persevered as long as we could on radio, fielding an average of 100 calls per week as we had for many years. We fought the government order to stop answering health questions, were found in contempt of court, and came dangerously close to being remanded to a DC jail, avoiding incarceration but narrowly, by the grace of God.

Our home is open, as always. People come and go, and may stay a short or long time. We minister as need be. Presently a young woman is with us, recovering from addiction that nearly took her life. For a couple of weeks I put my life on hold to be with her, though I was itching to get back to work on this book. We plan our course; God directs our footsteps. What's more important, the human being He sends to us, or the other project we are working on? Yes, we are our brother's keeper. We are responsible for those the Lord sends to us, to give them the hope of eternal salvation through the gospel of Jesus Christ, Yahshua the Messiah, and to give those suffering in the body the hope of true healing. The kingdom of God is about the family of God.

"You're like my second mum" texted a British tennis pro to me yesterday, a young woman I've been helping with injuries. The government lawyers say we prey on people for profit, a false charge they cannot substantiate. Facts never seemed to matter in court.

"When you get in a tight place and everything goes against you, til it seems as though you could not hold on a minute longer, never give up then, for that is just the place and time that the tide will turn."

Harriet Beecher Stowe penned those words. I taped them onto the file cabinet in my office.

Weary at times with our court case, I've wondered if the people we risked fines and jail to help care as much about us. That's why Jim asked me, "Are we our brothers' keepers?" with utmost gravity.

I learned homeopathy to help my husband, who I am one with. With the same dedication we help others. *"Love your neighbor as yourself"* Jesus answered, when asked by a scribe which commandment is the most important of all.

" The first of all the commandments is, Hear, O Israel; the Lord Yahweh our God is one Lord Yahweh: And you shall love the Lord Yahweh your God with all your heart, and with all your soul, and with all your mind, and with all your strength: this is the first commandment. And the second is like, namely this, you shall love your neighbor as yourself. There is no other commandment greater than these." Mark 12:29

We fulfill the first commandment in obeying the second. He says whatever we do to others, we do to Him. An army of government lawyers, four FTC Commissioners, one administrative law judge, and four federal court judges ordered us to stop helping people. The panel of Supreme Court judges denied our appeal. Yet we have a divine duty to take care of our brothers.

CHAPTER 23

A RADIO PROGRAM AND A NETWORK

Two men in their late teens moved in with us shortly after Mary came to stay. Neither was a Christian believer, but both needed a place to stay after being kicked out of their parents' houses. Jim treated them, Sean and Tony, like sons. His son Eric was away at prep school, Suffield Academy in Connecticut, where he had been awarded a football scholarship.

The Lord stretched our tent pegs once again when Jim's parents moved in with us. In the hospital, the elder Feijo had begged Jim not to let him be put in a nursing home. Doctors told his wife and daughter that he had Alzheimer's disease, his brain was "eroded," and that he would never walk again.

"You can come live with me, Dad, but no drugs" Jim said firmly, and his father agreed.

Eric was home from school that week, and he and Jim carried Mr. Feijo in a chair, up the stairs to our apartment above the store. Jim's sister had a hospital bed brought in and placed in our bedroom. Jim and I slept on the floor beside his father, and Jim's mother slept on the living room couch.

Jim's sister and mother cared for Mr. Feijo by day, and Jim kept watch all night. No visiting nurses were called in, no hospice, the family cared for their own. Jim gave his dad our protein shake AM*PM, and Electro Carbs, and stopped all medication. The doctors had predicted that his father would lose all short-term memory. The drugs he was on apparently had been causing that, because his mind was restored when he discontinued the drugs and started taking nutritional supplements.

Thanksgiving came suddenly, and I was not prepared. All I had managed was to buy a turkey, with only half a mind to bother cooking it. Thanksgiving morning, Jim asked what I was going to do about dinner. No stores were open, so Mary and I drove to our Daniel Chapter One store in Warren where we found apples, potatoes, and carrots. We rushed back and got to work, together with Jim's mother. She was a great cook, and it was an honor to put together what would be the last Thanksgiving for Jim's father with her. Totally unplanned, we ended up with sweet potato pie, apple pie, mashed potatoes, and turkey with gravy and vegetables!

While we women were in the kitchen cooking, Jim's father became bored in the bedroom, climbed over the handrails of the hospital bed, and appeared, standing, before us. Jim's mother told him he looked like Mahatma Gandhi (the way he was dressed), and asked what he was doing there! He wasn't supposed to ever walk again, according to the doctors. That was another false prognosis.

For the months he lived with us, Jim's father had clarity of mind. He did not have Alzheimer's. Jim had him exercise, doing things like deep-knee bends, and Sean and Tony would visit him during the day to talk. He liked the boys, and they liked him. He had a rascally sense of humor, and would tease his wife and daughter. One night, in the middle of the night, he turned to Jim and told his son he had a gift. Jim thought, *Oh! Wow; the father-son talk we never had! This is it!* and leaned in to hear what his father was about to say. "You got the goddamned gift of aggravation!" Dad snarled. Well, that's the truth. Jim used to bounce his father on the bed to stimulate blood and lymph circulation, which was probably quite aggravating to the senior Jim when he wanted to rest.

When his father told him he did not want to eat any longer, though, Jim respectfully obliged and stopped trying to force him. Mr. Feijo had a heart attack and died soon after, on a day that we were away. His wife and daughter were with him. Jim's mother moved in with his sister. One and a half years later, she told her daughter she felt sleepy one afternoon, lay down for a nap, exclaimed, "It's so beautiful," fell asleep, and never woke up. She always said, the only thing she asked God for was to "go" in her sleep. He granted her simple prayer.

*   *   *

Between the time of Jim's father's passing and that of his mother, in 1994 we opened another Daniel Chapter One in Raynham, Massachusetts, and began the radio program *Daniel Chapter One Health Watch*. Neither was our idea.

An acupuncturist we met through Daniel Chapter One, Dr. Perry, told us about an integrative medical complex he was starting, and invited me in as the homeopath. Below the offices was an area of storefront, and he suggested we place our products there. We agreed.

"Why don't we put *Naturopathic Pharmacy* under the name Daniel Chapter One?" I asked in having a sign made, unaware that the law only allows the word pharmacy to be used by a business with licensed pharmacists. We did use it, but not for long.

After Tony (living and working with us), Joe (working with us), and I painted the store interior, Joe made shelves and we stocked the place. However, we noticed it leaking when it rained. For that reason we terminated the lease and moved down the street, into a bigger place, but not before a salesman from the radio station WPEP stopped in, his attention caught by that sign. John used to be a pharmacist.

Joe and Eric were there that day, and John tried to sell them radio ad time. "My father wouldn't be interested in ads, but he might do a radio show," suggested Eric.

Jim ended up contracting with WPEP for $75 an hour, one afternoon a week, for the two of us to do a live, call-in health program. We were so green, we scripted the first show the night before! John and the radio manager, George, patiently taught us the fundamentals, including production. John suggested the name *Health Talk*. After a couple shows of *Health Talk*, Jim came to me saying, "It should be *Health Watch. . . Daniel Chapter One Health Watch . . .* we are God's watchmen."

Thus, *Daniel Chapter One Health Watch* was born. To learn how to conduct the show, John told us to listen to a local chiropractor's popular health talk show. We found his show dry, so we only listened a couple of times. George told us to drop the name Daniel Chapter One, saying it would turn people off, and not to say "God bless you" for the same reason. We were limiting our audience, he warned.

"I don't care. I have to honor the Lord. He honors those who honor Him." Jim was resolute.

To the wonder of those working at WPEP, not only did our show grow in popularity, but the chiropractor began to say "God bless you" to his callers. *He* was copying *us*! Jim didn't like it, however, because it was insincere. Jim did not use the phrase as a gimmick, he meant it.

"May the Truth of Jesus set you free!" Jim shouted out one day to close the hour. Time up, off the air, he sat back grinning. "Let's see him copy that!"

*   *   *

We started with themes for the radio hour. After the show on fiber (we now call, the "everything you didn't want to know about fiber" show), we dropped the theme idea, and found that what people wanted was a free-flowing hour during which time they could call in with health questions. We began to let the callers dictate the content of the show.

Daniel Chapter One Health Watch became so popular on WPEP, we were eventually asked to do a national broadcast. For that, we had to drive up to Boston every Sunday evening. It, too, grew in popularity after a slow start. I had overcome my fear of the microphone, and we were having fun with the show. Jim made it fun. He came up with spontaneous phrases that stuck, which listeners repeated, like "Don't believe the lie, don't die!"

He used to tease me that I was boring, but listeners found my straight man persona (my true self) made the otherwise zany rants of Jim effective. We were yin and yang energy, opposite but interconnected forces, a balance that worked well. Listeners loved it, and we loved them! John said he never heard a talk show host greet callers with as much enthusiasm as Jim, "as if you're opening the door to people you invited to your party!"

Since the long ride up and back to Boston was increasingly burdensome, we decided to build a studio in our business building in Portsmouth.

To back up, after almost ten years of renting the building we started Daniel Chapter One in, we had the opportunity to move into the building next door after the chiropractor moved out. Palm readers had planned to take over his office, so we took a godly stand against palm reading. Nothing against the people, but God says have nothing to do with the practice. They probably thought we would be good company, a health food store beside their palm reading operation, but we felt responsible to let people know that in the Bible the Lord says palm reading is an abomination to Him. When they changed their minds about moving in, the landlord offered us the space with option to buy.

I didn't want to move. Because of his MS symptoms, Jim couldn't do any physical labor, and I dreaded packing house, store, and offices by myself. But we did move next door. Besides hanging curtains and wall papering the downstairs, we had to remodel the upstairs, which had been offices, into a livable home. We had a kitchenette put in, a section of floor tiled for a small dining area, and I painted the bedroom walls and hung curtains.

Then a man working with us, Kevin, told us about a property for rent down the street. *Oh, no!* I thought in protest. My husband said there was no way we could afford it. Jim was in a great deal of pain those days, pain that kept him up at night. He'd only fall asleep from exhaustion. One day he fell asleep in Kevin's car, and when he woke up, they were sitting in the parking lot of 1028 East Main Road. "This is the place I told you about!" Kevin explained.

"Nice. But I can't afford it."

Kevin nagged Jim to meet with the realtor, believing from the Lord that the place was to be ours. Jim didn't want to discourage the young man's faith, so told Kevin that if he called and set up a meeting, we'd go.

The property contained a three-story house, two-story business building, and numerous sheds. When the realtor asked for a bid, Jim threw out $176,000, a ridiculously low amount but one we still couldn't afford. While we were away on business, the realtor called to say the bid was accepted.

"Oh. Uh huh." I couldn't feign excitement.

"I don't think you heard me. They took the bid! You could have knocked me over with a feather!" he continued, trying to get me to understand the incredible deal it was. The owner further agreed to hold the note.

Ugh. I have to pack again, was my honest feeling. Mary no longer lived with us, nor did Sean or Tony. Packing up the entire store yet again, offices, and house was up to me. We did move again, in a single night, to be out by month's end as our landlord demanded. It was lightly snowing, as I and a couple of men Jim asked to help, moved boxes down the street to our new home and store.

That's how we ended up where we presently are, which proved to be a godsend. For the first time we had a house separate from the store, a store building with office space above it, and private, ample parking. In between Jim's spacious office and mine, was a room that would become our radio studio.

With John's help, we set up broadcast equipment and padded the walls of the room at the top of the stairs, above the store. We could then do radio any time, and did! Tom Starr of Talk America called often to ask us to sub for other shows whenever a host couldn't make it, or hadn't made payment. We would get up in the middle of the night - one, two, three o'clock a.m. – to conduct a live hour or two of *Daniel Chapter One Health Watch*. People anywhere, anytime, would immediately take to the show and call in, so it was a win-win for us and the network.

We had also made the risky decision to do a *daily* program, signing onto a $70,000 contract. That's the amount we agreed to pay, not to be paid. Jim and I both felt led to take the gamble, and it was a huge gamble. After that, we were on the air every morning, evening, and some nights!

Talk America Radio Network began using our program to build up a new, sister network, and for advertising revenue. We wouldn't have minded, except that during *Daniel Chapter One Health Watch*, ads for occult practices and sex products were being played. They allowed us no say in the matter. We decided to leave, and joined a new network owned by a radio talk show host, C. Wiley, and his friend.

* * *

We also kept busy with ministry off-air, the Lord continuing to send people to us daily. One special visit we had was from Theodore Stapp, whom we had last seen in the ministry house in Stockton, California. He surprised us by calling from a payphone down the street!

Ted was ex-military and could travel freely by military plane. Instead of going to the doctor one day for his scheduled heart check-up, he boarded one of those planes and then several more, flying a serpentine route across the country to get to us—to die. He was dying from heart drugs he had been on since contracting Dengue fever in mission work overseas.

He was in his late seventies, and fully prepared to die, but told the Lord he wanted to make one more trip: to visit Jim and Trish. He told us later he came to die with us. Instead, the Lord renewed his life and health. Within ten days off drugs and taking instead numerous supplements, he reported that the pounding in his head had subsided, and his rolling, erratic heartbeat had become regular. Jim and Gloria Portias called one day looking for him; evidently, he had been missing! He hadn't told anyone where he was going because he knew they would not agree with his decision to stop the heart drugs.

He lived with us for several months, then informed us that he felt strong enough to return to the mission field. He left us and rejoined Bobby to work with him in Vietnam, and later, on an Indian reservation in the States. Ted lived and served well into his eighties, with no health problems and without drugs or supplements. Products we gave him when he left, he gave away. He called and wrote infrequently. In putting together a witness list for the FTC trial in 2009, I tried calling but was unable to reach him. I finally reached a niece by phone, and she told me he had passed away a couple of years prior, in a car accident. He was a passenger; he never had a driver's license and never owned a car, since he had made a lifetime vow to only own what he could carry. He died instantly from the impact; instantly at home with the Lord.

*   *   *

Daniel Chapter One was growing. Jim's vision to streamline by doing away with labor-intensive foods and carry only supplements proved wise, and necessary to close the Warren location. The new Raynham store was large, and I had a satellite office there to which I travelled a few times a week. We purchased office furniture from the landlord, a great package deal, enough for both locations. My office desk in Portsmouth came with the deal, a beautiful mahogany desk with leather inlaid on top, previously owned by a lawyer. For the first time, we had professional, sturdy business chairs, glass display cabinets, metal file cabinets, and nice desks.

A fitness instructor, Emmy, and a pastor from a local church, Pastor Bill, worked with us for a time in Portsmouth. Joe helped out in Raynham, with John, ex-pharmacist and ex-salesman from WPEP. Jim's daughter, Jill, came to work with us, and later, her brother Eric also.

One day during our radio broadcast, the producer, Jonathan, told us over an ad break that the network was folding. "You didn't hear it from me, but this Friday is your last day."

It was wrong of the network to not let anyone know, and right of Jonathan to prepare us. By then we had people paying, some of them doctors, to help support our program. The Daniel Chapter One line of products had grown to almost 200 items, and was being carried in Biomolecular Nutrition Centers across the country. We felt responsible to our distributors.

Investigating options brought us to New York City. Saturday mornings we did one hour on WEVD, an expensive but busy hour. A New York doctor was interested in our product line and had invited us to visit his office. When we met him, his lack of interest in the efficacy of the products concerned us. He made it clear that he would promote anything that could make him more money. We did not want to be allied with such a doctor, so we cut the visit short, and used the rest of our time in New York to visit WEVD, where the manager had discussed with us the prospect of our doing a daily show, under a year contract. In the interim, a famous and egotistical doctor found out about our plans, and bought the time slot out from under us.

Standing on a busy street in New York City, Jim called Jonathan on his cell phone.

"What would it take to build our own network? Can we?"

"We could," answered Jonathan. "Normally, it would take (he quoted a figure I don't remember) and such and so amount of time. I could probably do it for (a lesser amount), and in less time."

"Let's do it then!" Jim saw owning our own network as a solution to the lack of control and lack of freedom we had on other networks, and a better way to utilize the money he had set aside for radio contracts. He gave it the name Accent Radio Network, ARN.

Jonathan had never built a network, but had the technical savvy and instructional books. With his father's help, he erected two pre-fab sheds in his backyard in northern Florida to house production. He set up satellite dishes among his pine trees. Twenty four hours of radio air time a day was then ours to use for the glory of God!

Daniel Chapter One Health Watch was the only program we had, however. That left too many vacant hours to interest advertisers, or listeners for that matter. We prayed for another foundational program. Jonathan called one evening, excited to have remembered Jerry Hughes and his conservative program *Straight Talk*. Jerry owned a Florida station, and had been a high-profile, professional talk show host on a major network. He left because of the tight control on what he could say and not say. Jonathan contacted him, and asked if he'd be interested in coming onto the new Accent Radio Network.

Jerry didn't answer right away, he had to pray about it. When he called back, he explained, "I told the Lord if He wants me to join ARN, to send a bald eagle to the station. I haven't seen a bald eagle here for years. Today I saw not one, but two bald eagles sitting on top of the station tower!"

CHAPTER 24

THE STOREHOUSE

"Is it a sin to commit suicide?" Jim used to ask not only me, but Pastor Bill, Emmy, son Eric . . . everyone working at Daniel Chapter One in the late 90s. Murder is a sin, but are killing and murder the same? We couldn't find in Scripture anywhere that suicide is a sin; not, at least, an unpardonable one.

He was desperate. The MS was debilitating, and he had suffered with it, and fought it, for years. He enrolled in a beginner karate class to keep moving, but as his symptoms worsened, he just wanted to end it. I gave him homeopathic remedies to the best of my ability, without much effect. We formulated products because of it, like Micro Cal Plus. But his difficulties getting around were not improving, and he felt he couldn't take it anymore.

As I drove us over a bridge in Massachusetts one night, he opened the door to jump. He looked down at the pavement but didn't jump out, fearing that the road might only leave him mangled, not dead, making it worse for me. At wit's end, days later he got down on his knees and repented of not wanting Daniel Chapter One, of not wanting to do business. He hated dealing with money. His breakthrough in healing came when he acknowledged that to the Lord and accepted that if God wanted him to oversee Daniel Chapter One, he would do it with all his might. He submitted by becoming willing to bring in the world's gold for the Kingdom.

Around that time, I gave him homeopathic Sulphur, and it caused a healing crisis. For days he pushed out huge gray stools that floated, old and putrid looking. With the MS, his intestines and bowels had become sluggish, a sign that not only were his cardiac and skeletal muscles affected but also the smooth muscles of his GI tract. Once his body was efficiently eliminating waste again, he began to improve.

*   *   *

Jim was almost fully cured by the time Accent Radio Network was formed. I began advanced homeopathy study that year through the New School (now the Renaissance Institute of Classical Homeopathy), around 2000. The dreaded Y2K never happened, but in 2001 the nation was traumatized by 9/11. I lost my closest childhood friend in the Pentagon that day. Everyone remembers where they were the moment they heard. I was in my office counseling a woman suffering from prednisone use, and the consult was interrupted by the news.

"*What does it profit a man if he gains the whole world, yet loses his soul,*" the Lord says. I had lost a dear friend and also a cousin to AIDS, and now lost a friend to terrorism; a dramatic reminder of the brevity of life and of the importance of calling upon the Lord, and toiling for the Kingdom, while there's still time.

I don't like to travel, never did. The Lord always had us traveling. Our trips changed in breadth; we were then making national business trips, mostly to visit our radio listeners. Always a hardship, but rewarding. Against the standard at the time in radio, Jim and I were conducting live broadcasts in public places. George at WPEP told us, "Radio is theater of the mind; never let people see you." That we disregarded, and started a new trend by doing so.

We were among the first radio personalities to meet and greet our audience, and made our cameo appearance in Las Vegas, at the Riviera Hotel and Casino, while in the city for the National Association of Broadcasters convention. Our names were on the marquee, scrolling in neon. Radio listeners from the Las Vegas station carrying *Daniel Chapter One Health Watch* sat with us, as we conducted and broadcast our program live. The producer that day was Pastor Wayne Harms of the Church of the Riviera. Like many in Las Vegas, he had several jobs; radio production was his third job.

Pastor Harms came to us after the program and asked about Gulf War Syndrome, which he contracted serving in the Gulf as a minister. He also developed skin cancer from the pesticide sprays, and therefore, said his doctor, he could not take antibiotics. Drugs would fuel his cancer. We suggested supplements to take, and he was fully healed by following our advice. He gave us his medical records, and an affidavit testimony to share with others. He only wanted to help others in the situation, not get us in trouble with the government! A perturbing fact is that he received vaccines before deploying, including the anthrax shot. Those records disappeared from his file. The government is a business that cares about the government, not the people.

We made many trips, "tours," one Jim named the "Save the Nation Tour." "Daniel Chapter One - Saving the Nation from Dr. Dum Dum and the Evil FDA" he had printed on the back of t-shirts we gave out, with "Save the Nation Tour" on the front. Hundreds of people turned out to be with us, in cities around the country, enjoying the simple, silly way we'd share the truth, unpretentious but profound.

Daniel Chapter One Health Watch visited Utah, Georgia, Florida, New Mexico, South Carolina, and Missouri, staying mostly in homes. The host stations treated us like celebrities everywhere we went, making sure we experienced unique local foods, and arranging day trips to sights. Listeners brought us gifts, and took us into their homes for meals and fellowship. We had love for one another. These were not business relationships, nor was it idolatry. We were brethren, equal, a community of the "living stones" Jesus refers to that form His spiritual church.

In South Carolina we saw J P Mouligne off, as he set sail for the *Around Alone*. His vessel was stocked with Daniel Chapter One sports supplements and health remedies for the arduous voyage alone around the world: Biomolecular powders, sports bars (we had some of the first, before the glutted market it is today) and First Aid remedies. He not only completed the race, he won it!

God's hands are on Daniel Chapter One, and those humble enough to receive what our biblically named company and a couple of nobodies have to offer. Not everyone can receive our unorthodox message, and many, even Christians, have greater trust in doctors than in the Lord.

Not that they see it that way. They f
that because they are experts and pro.

King Asa in the Bible became dis.
disease he sought not the Lord, but to the p.
and it proved fatal. A woman with a blee.
Jesus, "*had suffered many things of many physic.*
she had, and was not better, but rather grew worse.
encounter with Jesus, and her faith in Him, to he.
Asa, her trust in doctors did *not* heal her.

There have been those that listened for a time, th.
us. Some who have known us most intimately, later rai.
Not for any tangible harm done, but for the "danger" of
belief in the Living God, and/or because of their own sin.

When Elder Hennelly warned the Hixville Church ab.
misrepresenting us, we felt no need to rush out to defend ours.
God says not to argue about doctrine. When we later visited our go.
friends John and Eunice Buffam, then living in South Carolina, John
sat quietly at the table while Jim talked. He said, "I've been asking the
Lord if you are from Him, if what you say is from Him. He has assured
me that you are, and that what you say is true. Maybe if Hixville had
listened, they would have had the revival they were praying for. But as
for talking to them about you, I'm not going to touch that with a ten
foot pole."

The Buffams knew Rodney, knew his parents, and were happy that
he had been saved. Regarding the fact that his parents wouldn't accept
their son's salvation, Eunice said, "Some things from the Lord people
can't accept, when they happen *in a way* people don't expect."

As we were leaving, John took us aside in counsel: "The way you
are walking is very narrow. Don't expect others to follow. You just keep
walking as the Lord is leading you."

*   *   *

Those who have come against us, too many to describe in this story
(nor do I want to remember), have not had things go well for them.
Different men who worked with us tried to steal our formulas. The

know. One of the men dropped a set of weights on himself
ng bench presses, breaking bones in his face. Another man
nself, though he had come to know the Lord and repented
ars before. Another man who slandered us before repenting
a paralyzing stroke. The latter two had turned to mind-altering
anti-anxiety and bipolar medication, and I believe the drugs led
eir tragedies. Another had a heart attack after slandering us.

The Lord says, "*Whoever rewards evil for good, evil shall not depart
n his house." Proverbs 17:13.* We are not vindictive, the Lord says
ngeance is His. It's with fear and trembling that we consider the
ord's justice.

"*I will bless them that bless you, and curse him that curses
you . . ." Genesis 12:3* God does not turn a blind eye.

We pray for those coming against us now, and love them. It's hard
to love one's enemies, but Messiah tells us we must. He says, so what if
you love those that love you? "*I say love your enemies.*" We also fear for
them; wouldn't want to be them. And as Jim often says, "There but for
the grace of God, go I." We are the persecuted, but we are the blessed.

"*Blessed are those who are persecuted for righteousness' sake: for
theirs is the kingdom of heaven." Matthew 5:10*

*　　*　　*

We were greatly blessed in the years up to 2005. The early years
of ARN saw blooming prosperity, enough to buy a radio station in
Utah. Daniel Chapter One paid for it, but Jim had more than enough
to oversee, and wanted to reward faithful men and give them the
responsibility of ministry. That's a biblical principle, to teach and hand
down. I agreed, and the station was entrusted to Jonathan, and two
other brothers.

As always, people came and went in our life, and came in and
out of Daniel Chapter One. Our company was growing, and we hired
a full-time graphic artist who helped produce our *Bio Guide.* More
than a catalog, the *Bio Guide* was a testimony to the healing power of
Yahshua and His creation. We later produced *The Cancer Newsletter,* for

the same reason, and lastly, *The Most Simple Guide to the Most Difficult Diseases*.

The number of people we had helped climbed to the many thousands. We built websites to honor the Lord and His Ministry of healing through Daniel Chapter One, and posted true testimonials there.

"*Fear of the Lord is the beginning of wisdom*," Yahweh tells us in His Word. He taught us everything we know through divine revelation, through others, through traditional knowledge, and by personal experience.

In my homeopathy practice many were healed also of serious mental illness, like bipolar and schizophrenia, anxiety and depression, and of serious physical illnesses including cancer. The key is to support the body's immune system, and strengthen and balance one's life energy, the vital force. Drugs do the opposite. Drugs suppress the immune system, and weaken and disturb the vital force.

Of all those we've been used to help, one most precious was our spiritual daughter Mary, who became pregnant after marrying, but miscarried. After carrying another child beyond the said critical period, she bore a son prematurely. Jacob died in her arms hours later. She accepted it well at the time, her faith strong, but suffered a psychotic break later. With her paranoid and hearing things, her husband called me for help. We went to the house, where I gave her a homeopathic remedy that restored her mind immediately. She fell into a deep depression months after that, however, and "didn't want to bother" me. She later became suicidal. Driving to a bridge to jump to her death, her car ran out of gas.

Homeopathic Aurum lifted her depression, and a subsequent remedy restored her completely. Once again she has joy in the Lord. Despite being legally deaf, Mary has been able to produce wonderful music. Seven of her songs have been nominated for Grammys in the Gospel division. Of the time she was given antipsychotic drugs in the hospital, she said, "I didn't want to live that way. I just didn't want to live that way." The drugs made her a zombie, and had begun to worsen the limited hearing she has.

*　　*　　*

As people would pop back into our personal life, David and Evelyn returned from Bangladesh, a $100,000 bounty on their heads from radical Muslims. They lived with us for a while, then bought their own home. Others lived with us and worked with us, too many to enumerate. Boys Jim had coached kept in touch, now grown men, all doing well. Phone calls and emails from people whose lives we touched would sometimes pleasantly surprise us with the message that they had been born again!

In those our glory years, Jim lectured at colleges and universities, and conducted research at some. He was invited to present his science of Biomolecular Nutrition at Auburn University and Columbia University, and conducted research using his program on athletes at high schools and colleges including the University of Alabama, Boston College, SUNY Albany, Northeastern University, and the Naval Academy. An article about his computer program appeared in *The Journal of Sports Medicine* and in two different chiropractic magazines. North Kingstown High School in Rhode Island, Boston College and Gardner Webb University in North Carolina were a few of the schools that purchased Daniel Chapter One supplements for their athletes.

Jim's work with individual athletes continued, and he had many Number Ones in the world, like Chris Parrish, top slalom water skier, world record holder. Professional baseball player JD Drew, who was out with a torn patella tendon, contacted Jim and later credited him with saving his career. Bodybuilders and powerlifters continued to find Daniel Chapter One, most by word of mouth.

*   *   *

My husband told me one day that Daniel Chapter One had a couple million dollars saved in the bank. This was due to his righteous handling of the Lord's money. He kept expenses low, never owed anything so never incurred debt or finance charges, and basically kept living as we always had: simple food and clothing, heat kept low in winter, air conditioning conservatively run or unused altogether in the summer, maintenance of all properties minimal. We still don't have kitchen cabinets in the old Rhode Island farm house, and most of the furniture we have was acquired as used hand-me-downs.

We had given away millions of dollars over the years: houses, cars, and other help to people in need. Daniel Chapter One gave products freely to churches, stores, and individuals. We paid for the Israeli National Boys Softball Team and coaches to attend the Championship in Australia the year they qualified but couldn't afford to go. For our tiny ministry to have anything saved astounded me; but then, generosity is why the Lord so blessed us. He says if you're faithful with little, He will give you more.

"What should we do with this money?" Jim asked. "It belongs to the Lord, and I don't want to be guilty of burying the talent." He referred to the parable of the men given talents, the unrighteous man burying his so he'd have it to show the master upon his return. Better to use and multiply what the Lord gives!

I didn't know. I had no idea we had millions, and had no idea how we were to use it. We decided to pray about it, considering overseas missions, orphanages, the poor.

Daniel Chapter One rented a small, dingy space in Portsmouth, above the VFW Hall, for a warehouse. We had since closed the Raynham store, and consolidated everything including order center (4 phones) to the back of the Portsmouth store. Jonathan and his family had moved out of their dilapidated, moldy trailer after building a modest house to live in. His wife home schooled their children and a few other children in the old trailer.

We, together with the brothers working at ARN, arrived at the decision to buy land in Florida on which to build a warehouse, worship center, and school. Not for Jim and I, for others. A building for others to use, and a place for people in Florida to work. We bought 27 acres down the street from Jonathan. Jim hired an architect to draw up blueprints, and Jonathan got a quote for the building. But Jim thought the price too high, saying "We don't need the Taj Mahal!" He insisted on a basic, inexpensive structure, the way we had always done things.

CHAPTER 25

TIME TO REST

After working every day since 1986, except for business and missions trips which were as exhausting, by 2002 we were nearing burnout. Eric and Jill, out of college and working with us, urged us to let go and vacate.

"Dad, you and Trish need to go away and rest. You have an anniversary coming up; go somewhere! Leave, on vacation. Don't bring radio equipment, or any work, just go. Rest," urged Eric, practically pushing us out the door.

I had been feeling "brittle" lately, and Jim was clearly stressed. Eric was right. "Where would you like to go?" Jim asked.

"I don't know. Nowhere by plane. I wish we could have a quiet week at home, no packing, do nothing." But I knew that was impossible, we lived at Daniel Chapter One. The store, order center, and radio studio were in our backyard. People always came by asking for our help. We couldn't ignore them. "Ok, somewhere quiet . . . Vermont?"

Vermont it would be. Jim found lodging at The Cortina Inn, a Killington ski lodge in winter with off-season rates in summer. We'd be there in July, the quietest of times. After Jim overcame MS, a close friend bought him a set of golf clubs for his 50th birthday, to inspire him to exercise. He had put on a lot of weight and needed exercise. The Cortina offered golf packages for the week. Jim booked himself for a week of golf.

"But what will you do?" He wanted it to be a true vacation for me, as well.

"Don't worry 'bout me! I'll sleep in, hang around the pool . . . read. That's all I want to do: nothing!"

We set out for the first time since our honeymoon to enjoy a rest.

The Cortina was old but lovely, the lodge walls full of books and local artwork. We were practically the only people staying there. I perused the quiet halls, studied the paintings, read some of the books. I swam in the pool, which I had all to myself, and sat in the sauna. For two days.

Reinvigorated, I visited the front desk to investigate what else there was to do. I had had enough of doing nothing!

"There are tennis lessons here?" I asked, picking up the brochure.

"Yes. Anyone can sign up."

"Even a beginner? You have beginner's lessons?"

"Yes. All levels. There's a beginner's class this afternoon."

"Do you need special clothes? What can I wear?"

"Anything comfortable. But wear sneakers, you have to wear sneakers."

I signed up, and hurried back to the room where I cut an old pair of sweatpants off at the knee to wear with old running sneakers and a t-shirt.

The class was made up of a couple of little boys and a little girl. I learned the basics, with the kids. I heard the boys snickering at my pants. The girl was nice to me. The pro, I'm quite sure, was trying hard not to laugh. He did make some funny comments at my attempts. But I couldn't have cared less . . . I was in the fresh mountain air playing tennis!

"Guess what I did today!!" I greeted Jim that night.

He smiled. "Tell me."

I played the remainder of that week, both morning and afternoon sessions, my legs so sore I couldn't stand straight by week's end. But it was needed therapy, just what the Lord, our Doctor, ordered! Furthermore, He brought us there with a plan.

✳   ✳   ✳

The following year we revisited the Inn. I introduced Jim to the new tennis coach and they chatted, Jim working the Lord into their conversation. The coach exclaimed, "You remind me of a friend of mine! He sounds just like you. You have to meet him."

His friend, Scott Williams, was coach to professionals (Tommy Haas), author of *Serious Tennis*, and a zealous born-again believer in Christ. As zealous as Jim. They hit it off, and we had wonderful fellowship with him and his wife.

Two or three months later, we received an email from Scott, out of the blue: *The Daniel Chapter One Open has been approved by the USTA, to be held in November 2003.*

What?! A USTA-sanctioned tennis tournament in our name?

Scott told us he had applied for it, but was surprised that it was accepted. The USTA sanctions only a limited number of tournaments each year. The tournament was to be at the Deer Creek Tennis Resort in Deerfield Beach, Florida. He ran the tennis program at Deer Creek, besides running a tennis ministry, Match Point Ministry, teaching underprivileged kids tennis, centered on Jesus Christ and Christian values.

It cost us nothing and we didn't have to attend, but we did go. We wanted to see Scott and his wife again. We stayed with them in their small condo overlooking the tennis courts. The tournament attracted talent from all over the world. Women from Russia and China made it to the singles final, and a man from France, once ranked in the top 50 and who had beaten Andre Agassi, won the men's singles final. We were able to help him with a hip injury that weekend and beyond.

Before heading to Florida, I received notice of a homeopathic symposium taking place in Deerfield Beach the same weekend. I knew we'd be busy Saturday and Sunday, but asked Jim if I could attend the final day, Monday, which he approved.

The day of my seminar, Jim looked for something to do. Spontaneously, he stopped in at a realty office, and asked to see a house, a townhouse, and a condo. One of each, just to look. He called me during lunch break. "I'm going to pick you up. I want you to see some places with me."

I wanted to lay on the beach. It was hot that day, and cold back home. I had planned on getting some sun! Disappointed, I agreed to go with him. Uninterested, I rushed through the places, but liked the bungalow house. Though small, its layout would be perfect for ministry, and there was a room we could convert to a radio studio. I really didn't want to move to Florida, but felt the draw of the Holy Spirit. Scott was enthusiastic about our products, had seen their benefit personally and with others, and invited us to get involved with his ministry. Once again, the Lord had the sellers accept Jim's bid.

I dreaded shopping for furniture, didn't have the time. "Ask the realtor if any of the furniture can be left," I told him. It was old and cheap, but the house was ready to be lived in. They agreed to leave everything . . . *everything!* There was not a single thing we had to buy when we moved in, except for a couple of glass tables to set radio equipment on. This would be another ministry house we'd work out of, share with others, and use as a house church.

We flew back to Rhode Island, and in two weeks drove back down to Florida to live and work. Jim's children could run the Portsmouth headquarters, the responsibility would be good for them. It was time for us to step aside.

PART THREE

THE RAINS COME

"Whoever hears these sayings of mine, and does them, I will liken him unto a wise man, which built his house upon a rock: And the rain descended, and the floods came, and the winds blew, and beat upon the house; and it fell not: for it was founded upon a rock."

Matthew 7:24–25

CHAPTER 26

INTEGRITY TESTED

After Yahshua's death, resurrection, and ascension into heaven, His apostles continued to teach in His name as He had commanded, healing many. The rulers, elders, and teachers of the law met in Jerusalem, questioned Peter and John, and after ordering them to withdraw from their supreme council and tribunal (called the Sanhedrin), conferred together. *"To stop this thing from spreading any further among the people, we must order these men to speak no longer to anyone in this name."*

"Then Peter and the other apostles answered and said, we ought to obey God rather than men." Acts 5:29

"And daily in the temple, and in every house, they ceased not to teach and preach Yahshua the Messiah." Acts 5:42

Similarly, a commission of powerful people plotted against the Christ-centered teaching of Daniel Chapter One to stop its truth from spreading among the people. Driving that commission is a global commission manipulated by Satan with his promises of material wealth and power, the same temptation he used, unsuccessfully, with Yahshua in the desert.

Again, the devil took him up into an exceedingly high mountain, and showed him all the kingdoms of the world, and the glory of them; and said unto him, all these things will I give you, if you will fall down and worship me." Matthew 4:8–10

The Trilateral Commission is a non-governmental, non-partisan, private and secret "discussion group" made up of top political and business leaders around the world, with an emphasis on *international economics*. The group was founded in 1973 by David Rockefeller, with founding director and Marxist Zbigniew Brzezinski.

Brzezinski wrote in his book *Between Two Ages*,

> *"National sovereignty is no longer a viable concept . . . Marxism represents a further vital, and creative stage in the maturing of man's universal vision. Marxism is simultaneously a victory of the external, active man over the inner, passive man, and a victory of reason over belief."* . . . *"Such a society would be dominated by an elite whose claim to political power would rest on an allegedly superior scientific know-how. Unhindered by the restraints of traditional liberal values, this elite would not hesitate to achieve its political ends by the latest modern techniques for influencing public behavior and keeping society under close surveillance and control."*

The European community, North America (Canada and the United States), and Japan comprise the Trilateral Commission, its members interested solely in global commerce and elitist power. Founding Chairman David Rockefeller comes from the family who started the I. G. Farben cartel, a massive pharmaceutical cartel that provided the chemicals and poisons used in World War II. It was the leading industrial organization to fund Hitler's war chest, and to this day is behind the global pharmaceutical industry, including the Cancer Industry. The Rockefellers were the first to sell chemo and radiation to hospitals.

A working group of the Trilateral Commission is MUCH, the Mexico-US-Canada Health Fraud Group. Two agencies from each country comprising MUCH signed the Trilateral Cooperation Charter (TCC) in 2004, including the US FTC, the US FDA, and the Canadian Competition Bureau.

They did so in clear violation of the Administrative Procedures Act (APA) and the Federal Advisory Committees Act (FACA); they acted outside of the American Citizens and Congress. Said Attorney Scott

Tips in June, 2006, "Disguised as 'enhanced security,' the Charter is nothing more than an outright illegal usurpation of power by unelected bureaucrats in three countries who banded together to make their own rules. No constitutional process of law was followed in making this raw and unbridled power grab."

TCC claims "to provide a formal mechanism to work closely together to better protect, promote, and advance human health in North America. Its purpose is to increase communication, collaboration, and the exchange of information in the areas of drugs, biologics, medical devices, food safety and nutrition."

It is Satan appearing as an angel of light.

"The purpose (of TCC) is to make an end run around any domestic law that interferes with food and drug multinational corporate profits" says the founder of International Advocates for Health Freedom, John Hammell. In an article published by World Net Daily 04/04/2007, just three months before the TCC witch hunt that targeted Daniel Chapter One, Hammell explained:

"A key goal of the TCC is to limit the public's access to food supplements and vitamins . . . The TCC is determined to attack the Dietary Supplement Health and Education Act of 1994 by moving to merge our food and drug regulations with those of Canada and Mexico . . . Canada and Mexico define dietary supplements as 'drugs,' not food supplements."

To protect the interest of the behemoth global pharmaceutical industry, the TCC plotted to censor God given cures for cancer. The snare was being set for Daniel Chapter One.

In terms of spiritual warfare, *"we wrestle not against flesh and blood but against the powers and principalities of this dark world."* The prince of darkness opposes the light and seeks to destroy what Yahshua has created.

The Lord had placed a hedge around us for many years, and used us to His glory to help many people with herbs from His creation. He knew the persecution about to befall us; it is He who was about to remove that hedge.

*   *   *

As the plan was being laid to destroy our ministry, before we had an inkling of the perfect storm about to hit, Jim suffered another health crisis. More frightening than the MS, he began to have seizures. The first occurred while sitting with friends in a coffee shop. "It felt like my spirit left my body," he described to me when he came home, agitated. After that, his hand curled in painfully, his chest tightened, the muscles in his limbs contracted, and according to eyewitnesses, he let out a primordial scream. It took several men including an Olympic powerlifter to catch him and force the hand open at Jim's direction. The seizures continued, and grew in intensity and frequency.

On Thanksgiving 2006, he suffered violent seizures morning, noon, and night. That night we called an ambulance, and he was rushed through a rain storm to Newport Hospital. A doctor there dismissed him after midnight with a prescription for muscle relaxants. Our local GP and friend, Dr. David Johnson, referred him later to a neurologist, saying that his multiple sclerosis had returned.

Jim refused drugs, and the suggested CT scan. My homeopathy mentor, who used to be a neurologist, and my brother, William Haith, DO, agreed that an MRI was just as good, better, without the radiation exposure of a CT scan. The MRI confirmed no brain tumor, and my teacher pegged the problem as epileptic seizures.

Because Jim's children begged him to, he endured diagnostic testing. Eric was no longer working with us, but Jill saw her dad seize and was frightened. Heart breaking, she told her 2-year-old daughter that she couldn't walk alone with Grampy anymore. Everyone around us was fearful for Jim. Life had become a nightmare, and my servitude as a helpmate was tested.

When Jim wasn't seizing, he could do nothing but sit, motionless. He insisted on me being at his side at all times so I could stop a seizure by forcing his hand open. He slept in a recliner, I on a futon nearby. I had to wash and help dress him, and do everything domestic, including all the driving. Together, we were imprisoned by the strange phenomenon.

Evidently stress can cause seizures, as can strong emotion. A brief event of vexation precipitated Jim's epilepsy; in its wake, our mission was to cure it. A specific homeopathic remedy in the Homeopathic

Repertory, under the section "Convulsions, epileptic," covered all his symptoms. High anxiety was one strong, characteristic symptom Jim had developed, and from the first dose of the right remedy he felt at peace again. Just as his anxiety had been palpable, the peace that settled upon our house that night could be felt also.

"I think we're going to get through this" he said, tentatively hopeful. I thanked God, believing he was right.

It took three months, with doses of homeopathic Calcarea arsenica repeated every few days, before the final, brief whimper of a seizure. Chiropractor Dr. Ron Marsh adjusted Jim every day, sometimes twice a day. Jim waited three more months before beginning to drive again. He has not had another seizure since.

*   *   *

By Thanksgiving 2008, less than two years later, we found ourselves under another dark cloud—that of a lawsuit brought by the US FTC against Daniel Chapter One. Building plans in Florida were put on hold. My homeopathy practice closed. Ministry savings had to be dug into to pay hefty legal fees. Worst of all, our energies and focus were absorbed with court proceedings and legal briefs, pulled away from helping people and developing new products. Those bent on silencing us were using federal agencies to beat and bleed us. But we stood, and are standing still.

*   *   *

It all began with a letter we received in the mail from the Competition Bureau of Canada with complaints about our website. What does Canada have to do with us? Confused, we threw the papers away. We don't have customers in Canada, not that Canada has any legal jurisdiction, anyway, we thought.

We next received warning letters from the US Federal Trade Commission, with demands to see all our literature and certain product labels, and later from the US Food and Drug Administration. Those letters also complained about our website, about truthful information and testimonials posted there. We made no claims to have "a cancer cure," we simply shared the exact words of a handful of grateful people with a disclaimer, as we had on all our literature, in compliance with the law: "(This) is intended to provide information, record, and testimony about Yahshua and His creation. It is not intended to diagnose or treat disease." "These statements have not been evaluated by the FDA. This product is not intended to diagnose, treat, cure, or prevent disease."

The information we shared about separate herbs and nutrients we had gleaned from various books and research over the past 20 years, and said they can "*help fight* cancer." We explained how the herbs and nutrients work in the body, because it's no mystery. Some detoxify, some support the immune system, etc. According to the Dietary Supplement Health and Education Act of 1994, a company can make "structure/function claims." We were familiar with DSHEA, and believed it within our legal rights to say all that we said, and to share testimonials with a disclaimer. No customer in 20 years had complained. We felt we were being unjustly bullied.

"You have to get a good lawyer!" Dr. Karen Orr said, incensed. Her patients benefitted from our products, and one colleague she sent to us had a toddler healed of a skull tumor with Daniel Chapter One products. She told us that her teacher, a gifted chiropractor, had also been sued by the FTC for information he shared, and had won his case. "You should get *his* lawyer!" She managed to help put us in touch with the attorney, Jim Turner.

Attorney Turner was one of Ralph Nader's original "Nader's Raiders," activists in the 60s and 70s who investigated federal agencies. With a group of other law students, he had taken part in examining the FDA and exposing corruption within the agency. (Back then, for instance, the FDA allowed chemicals in foods to remain hidden, undisclosed on labels.) He's been a champion of health freedom for decades, and has won cases he argued against government censorship and prohibition. Besides the case of Koren Publishing, most notably he won the right for acupuncturists to use needles, and for the right to use the word "organic."

He took a long weekend to look at our case, then called to say he would represent us. Jim, who had been quiet for days, yelled when he got off the phone, "Yahhhh!!! He said our case could start a movement!!" The fight was on, we were not going to lie down. His head was no longer hanging. There *was* something we could do.

Before this, in prayer, the Lord had told Jim from the book of Isaiah that we were not to lie down and let them walk over our backs like a road. We were to stand for Yahshua, for His Truth. Now there was a prospect that He would use us to spearhead a movement that could lift the decades-long suppression of natural healing for cancer. We knew much of the history, and thought maybe, just maybe, Yahweh was about to remove that evil oppression from His people. When I prayed asking the Lord what to ask Him for regarding the lawsuit, not knowing His will, He answered me, *Pray for the peace of Jerusalem.* Jerusalem: God's people. Pray for the peace of His people, His holy city.

Then we received "The Order" from the Federal Trade Commission, half an inch thick. I read it first, standing at the front door where it arrived. It demanded a signature, saying we agreed to give up certain rights, to pay as yet undisclosed fines, to cease doing our ministry, and to send a letter to all our customers saying there is no science behind our products or ingredients in them, and only conventional cancer treatments have been proven safe and effective in humans. Below the signature line of the ordered letter, appeared the website and phone number of the National Cancer Institute.

"We can't sign this!" I ran with the papers to Jim. "We will *never* sign this letter!!"

Nothing could have made me angrier than being forced to advertise for the NCI. How could they? They couldn't make us sign something against our conviction - agree to their lie - and force us to advertise the NCI to people in our community! The US government cannot force a citizen to carry *their* message, or so I thought. Thomas Jefferson called it tyranny to do so.

Little did we know at the time, but we would later discover that it was part of the "enforcement and educational campaign" of the FTC, instigated by the Trilateral Cooperation Charter and its working group, MUCH. Coercion, censorship, and reeducation was part of the plan; how socialist dictatorships operate. The true goal of the "educational campaign" was to psychologically condition people not to try any other forms of therapy outside of the conventional cancer so-called "treatments," which in reality are toxic poisons more injurious than healing.

But we live in America, "land of the free!" We have a Constitution that protects our free speech, free assembly, free press, and religious freedom – don't we? We had broken no law. The US law says one has the right to free speech in commerce as long as it is not false and misleading. The FTC rules say that one must have "reasonable basis" for any health claims made. We had reasonable basis to say everything we said! Structure/ function claims for the ingredients came from books, the Traditional Herbal knowledge came from books, and our testimonies were all true.

The WHO, in their textbook on research methodology, refers to anecdotes as "weak evidence," not as "no evidence." Having a few anecdotes provides weak evidence, but, according to research methodology, when you compile many testimonies the evidence becomes stronger. In our case, add to the anecdotal evidence Traditional Herbal information and structure/function information, you have a three-pronged *basis* that is *reasonable*! Not "scientific proof," but "reasonable basis" to say that certain herbs may help fight cancer. We never claimed to have clinical studies on the products people used for their cancer, never promised or guaranteed a cure, never pretended to be anything other than what we are.

To call chemotherapy and radiation "scientific," "safe," and "effective" would be laughable if not so downright deceptive. I left experimental oncology (cancer research) when I realized what a dismal failure allopathic cancer treatment is, and that God has given us a better way. In light of the fact that our honest, strong opinion is that the Cancer Industry is fraudulent and harmful, the government was demanding that we bear false witness to our neighbor by sending their letter endorsing chemo and radiation. They ordered us to print it on Daniel Chapter One letterhead, put it in a Daniel Chapter One envelope, and send it with no accompanying letter. We could not lie for them.

Daniel Chapter One is innocent of the FTC charges of "false and misleading advertisement." We also happen to be the size of a nit in the relatively small world of dietary supplements. How did we come to be in the crosshairs of the world super power . . . for helping people? None of the agencies in Washington, DC, had ever heard of us, and no customer had complained.

As we would learn many months later, we were netted off an "internet surf" called Operation False Cures, conducted by the Competition Bureau of Canada, the US FTC and the FDA, in June 2007, instigated by the TCC. In September 2008, the FTC announced publicly that "enforcement efforts began with the FTC and its colleagues at the FDA and the Competition Bureau of Canada . . . surfing the internet."

Just five days after the September 18, 2008 press release about the FTC's attack on Daniel Chapter One and others, FTC Commissioner Rosch gave a speech in which he announced ". . . the results of Operation False Cures – a collaborative undertaking by the FTC, the FDA, and MUCH . . . to reduce consumer harm caused by online marketing of bogus cancer cures. . . There are a couple of points particularly important about this sweep. First, the FTC continues to work with its domestic and global counterparts in fighting deceptive and unfair acts and practices. This is an ongoing effort on the Commission's part – to coordinate and leverage our resources. Second, marketing bogus cancer cures is a particularly harmful practice. . ."

Before we were given due process, Commissioner Rosch, one of the commissioners who ruled against Daniel Chapter One, and who wrote the opinion, was patting the FTC on the back for helping consumers "avoid injury." The presumption was of our guilt, not our innocence. Our lawyers, Titus and Olson, looked into whether the commissioner's statement compromised his independence to vote and write an opinion in our case, since he had prejudged it. His words revealed explicit bias. By the time they discovered his speech, however, the FTC said it was too late to file any objection.

The September 18, 2008 press release was entitled *"FTC Sweep Stops Peddlers of Bogus Cancer Cures,"* and therein, the director of the FTC's Bureau of Consumer Protection was quoted as saying, "There is no credible scientific evidence that any of the products marketed by these companies can prevent, cure, or treat cancer of any kind. . . Many of these products are scams."

This was before any evidence had been collected!

It went on, "The companies will be required to notify consumers who purchased the products challenged . . . that there was little or no scientific evidence demonstrating the products' effectiveness . . . they also must urge these customers to consult with their doctors about the products."

From a note at the bottom of the press release:

"The Commission files a complaint when it has "reason to believe" that . . . the Commission is proceeding in the public interest. The complaint is not a finding or ruling that the defendant or respondent has actually violated the law."

So the FTC assumes the power to censor material and speech, levy fines, and basically tyrannize companies which may not have broken any law!

One hundred twelve letters had been sent by the FTC, resulting in 11 law enforcement actions challenging deceptive advertising. A later release would read. "All but two of the FTC's 11 cases have been resolved, with one headed for an administrative trial."

That "one" would be us, Daniel Chapter One, the only one to stand against the tyranny. Jim may have been willing to pay a fine, may have been willing to stop sharing information, but as he told the FTC at our deposition in New York, the letter they ordered us to sign and send was the line in the sand. Daniel Chapter One is a ministry of Yahshua, not a business, so money never factored into our decision. Our integrity did, and the honor and glory of Yahweh Elohim. Truth mattered to us.

CHAPTER 27

WITNESSES

The FTC Deposition of Daniel Chapter One, and of us, James and Patricia Feijo, was held in New York, which entailed a flight into Washington, DC, and from there, a train ride at daybreak to New York with attorneys Jim Turner and Betsy Lehrfeld. The morning of our deposition, a brother in Christ we didn't know emailed a comforting scripture verse. We received others like it; people all over the country were praying for us.

We were prepared and professional, though now I wonder why we bothered. The FTC lawyers were inept and unprofessional, their endless questions irrelevant to any truth in the matter. They snickered amongst themselves, and the lead attorney, Leonard Gordon, leaned back in his chair and played on his cell phone much of the time. They first locked me out of the room and spent the day questioning Jim, asking him over and over about the Cadillac he drives. (Since the MS and resulting weight gain, he needs a comfortable vehicle.) Betsy, stepping out to use the restroom, said to me, "They can't believe how small you are." She also explained why they kept questioning Jim about his car. They didn't have much else to complain about, and, she said, "They aren't used to people who can govern themselves."

I took a walk around the building while Jim was being deposed, and in one American history shop heard "Amazing Grace" being played over the radio. It reassured me that the Lord was with us.

Day two I was deposed by a female FTC lawyer whose questions were tedious and ignorant. I later complained to Jim and Betsy that the FTC lawyers were trying to fit a square peg in a round hole. When the two long days were finally over, on our way down in the elevator, Attorney Turner asked me what I thought about it.

"That was bullshit."

He smiled. "I didn't know Christians used that word."

"The Apostle Paul did; he said he considered everything in the world dung, bullshit."

Jim's daughter was also deposed, and had to leave her children at 5:00 am for a train from Rhode Island to New York. Two manufacturers of our products were also deposed. One was outside of the hundred-mile limit so was excused; the other sent a representative. Soon after her deposition, her lab told us they could no longer make products for us.

After our deposition, while we were still in New York, the FTC was willing to settle. Jim asked about the offensive letter we had been ordered to send, and was told that yes, we did have to send it, "because everyone else did." Gordon referred to all the companies sued as part of the internet sting. As previously mentioned, that letter was the line in the sand for us.

*   *   *

While in Albuquerque for a homeopathy seminar soon after, Jim and I met with an assistant to our lawyer, Mark Griffin. After spending time with us, Mark noted that we shouldn't be tied up with logistics of the lawsuit, that our time was best spent helping people. He suggested we form a team, with a PR person and a fund raiser, to conduct the work that was needed to see us through the case. Jim Turner agreed, and in short order we hired Pastor Paul as fundraiser, Jen Toone as public relations, Stephanie (Seve) Cordosi as videographer, and David Gornoski as writer.

Once the team was formed, Jim and I planned a trip to let customers and radio listeners know about the lawsuit. We made a PowerPoint presentation, and brought the team with us. Jonathan came to produce our radio program. We visited several places in Utah and Missouri, presented our case, and conducted live radio broadcasts. Seve filmed many people on location, on farms, in stores, in homes, and in an old historic building, sharing their testimonies and strong feelings about the government intrusion into our ministry. She hoped to make a documentary. Jen had to leave early, ironically, for her mother suffering from cancer treatment, and Paul turned out to be a Judas whose god is money, so we severed ties with him as soon as we got back to Rhode Island.

*   *   *

Our administrative trial was set for the following April, 2009. Until then, we were free to do "business as usual." But those months were consumed with answering legal briefs, putting together our defense, and constant harassment by the FTC as they put together their case against us. When Jim refused to hand over bank account and credit card records, they subpoenaed and received them directly.

Told by our lawyers to construct a witness list, we gathered a list of 80 people, each one I called personally. All were willing to come to Washington, most having been cured of various diseases, many cancer. The FTC protested, "We don't want to be in court for weeks!" and allowed us only ten, and gave us specific categories: three cured of cancer, three cured of other illness, some to testify that we are a ministry.

Daniel Chapter One paid for our fact witnesses to come to DC for that week, and for lodging and food. It cost us over $50,000, even though we all stayed in the oldest hotel in the city, the Hotel Harrington, and ate cheaply. The people that came, came at great hardship, leaving family and jobs to travel by plane, and train, and car to defend us.

Jim Turner assembled our expert witnesses, James Duke, PhD, renowned botanist, world's foremost authority on herbs, USDA (retired); Rustum Roy, PhD, professor emeritus at Penn State, world's leading materials scientist, teacher at the medical school of University of Arizona; Sally LaMont, naturopathic doctor; Jim Dews, world-renowned herbalist and pharmaceutical herbal manufacturer; and Jay Lehr, PhD, scientist, retired adjunct professor at Ohio State University.

The experts looked over our products and information and wrote opinion statements that we had reasonable basis for everything we said about the products named in the FTC complaint. Daniel Chapter One had to pay for the experts, in addition to the $10,000 every week being paid to the law firm of Swankin & Turner. We were grateful we had the provisions saved to do so; otherwise, we'd have been forced to settle, like some of the other herbal companies we talked to who had no choice because they didn't have the funds to fight.

*   *   *

It was as difficult as planning a wedding, but as exciting also, to be meeting and gathering with those eager to testify for us. The Lord brought us together from all over the country; a small, humble band of His, ready to fight for truth. We met the first night in DC with our lawyers, Jim and Betsy and Chris Turner. Sitting at an oblong office table, our witnesses introduced themselves to the lawyers, and each told their story. Ernie Jensen from Las Vegas, sent home to die by his oncologist when all treatments failed, healed of lymphoma. Still weak from past cancer treatments, he made the trip with his sister. Tracy Kulikowski, whose testimony shared on our website the FTC had most complained about, healed of leukemia and inoperable tumors on her brain, behind her heart, and on her liver over 10 years ago. She also turned to Daniel Chapter One after conventional medicine failed. Laura Rudin, whose dog lived long past the vet's prognosis, with superb quality, her glioblastoma (brain tumor) significantly reduced. Glenda Shaw, healed of a benign breast cyst, IBS, and high cholesterol.

Jonathan and his wife were there, and Kim, who worked in Florida at ARN came with her husband to support us and to film. Jonathan would testify in court as a fellow worker in our ministry, but that night his wife shared with our legal team how she was told she couldn't bear more children, and with our help got pregnant again, and again. We helped her daughter with kidney reflux. The doctors had said she may need surgery, or may have to live with it her whole life. She was cured with homeopathy and our products. We helped several of their children with health problems. Jonathan's wife cried telling her family's testimonies, everybody cried when they told their story. It was very emotional for us all.

Robert Hicks and his wife shared how their son Cole had drowned, not rescued until he had been underwater for 50 minutes. He was dead, but they had begged that he be airlifted to the hospital. There they agreed to donate his organs, when a nurse saw a flutter of life behind his eyelids. A true miracle, he was put on life support, where he again died once more, only to come back to life. After three months on life support, the doctors suggested his machine plugs be mercifully pulled. The Hicks family agreed, dressed him in a suit, and held a funeral for him that day. But after the life support was disconnected, his heart began beating on its own. He would live!

At that time, Kristi, a *Daniel Chapter One Health Watch* listener, had a dream in which she saw two boys drown. One's name was Cole, same as her son. She didn't know the Hicks family, but saw the story on the news in Alabama and felt led to contact them, after she contacted us. She had called in to the radio and asked, "What do you have for someone who drowned?"

By faith she bought First Kings at the Herbal Boutique in Florida, and went to Cole in the hospital. She entered his room, and in front of his surprised parents spoke to their comatose child, "Lazarus, get up!"

"I know you don't know me, but the Lord told me to give this to you," she said, putting the First Kings into Robert's hands. "Give this to your son!"

Robert cried telling the story, and again when telling how much we did for Cole at no charge. He shared that we always said, "Don't let money be an obstacle to getting what you need for Cole. Just let us know your needs." With homeopathy and our supplements, Cole was learning to walk and talk again when we met him in DC.

The people gathered at that meeting all told how unselfishly Jim and I availed ourselves to them, telling them to call morning, noon, or night, which they did. Jim Turner smiled at us and asked, "When do you sleep?!"

My brother flew in that night to support us at the trial. Dr. Mink, there to testify, arrived at court the next day with his wife. In the morning, those of us witnesses staying at the Hotel Harrington walked together to the FTC building down the street, where the trial was to begin at 10:00 am. We prayed together outside the building at 600 Pennsylvania Avenue.

Several black vans pulled up to the building, out from which came ICE police; Immigration and Customs Enforcement, "heightened security" for our trial.

CHAPTER 28

STAR CHAMBER

I t may have been an intimidation exercise, or maybe the government really felt threatened? The ICE agents would be our bodyguards for the time we were in the FTC building, to protect it and the government employees within. We were first screened with a hand wand inside the entrance to the granite and limestone building. We then had to walk through a metal detector, and were made to put our personal belongings through an X-ray machine. Our cameras, cell phones, and computers were taken and secured. A wand was passed over us again before entering the courtroom, which was on an upper floor.

The first day of the administrative trial was supposed to settle the issue of jurisdiction. We were ready to argue that Daniel Chapter One is a ministry, and therefore the FTC has no jurisdiction over it. Judge Chappell began by stating, without contest, that Daniel Chapter One *is* a ministry, but went on to say that the FTC still had jurisdiction over it since the ministry is involved in commerce.

In Jim Turner's opening argument, he laid out our mission, and how we always operated within the law. In conclusion, he stated: "Just to illustrate what a relatively small enterprise this is, even as an enterprise, they have about a thousand customers . . . This is not a serious business. This is a serious ministry."

Daniel Chapter One supporters, and fact witnesses and their families, were allowed in court for the proceedings. They filled the benches on the left side of the room. A handful of government workers sat on the right side, with three or four FTC lawyers in front. At the very start, Administrative Law Judge Chappell bristled at the sight of

Cole in his mother's arms, saying "the child . . . will need to leave the courtroom!"

Jonathan and I were removed also when Jim was about to testify. We would be testifying after him, so were not allowed to hear his testimony. I'm sorry I missed it, though witnesses later described it to me, and I have the transcript. It moved many to tears, including my brother, so I know the Spirit of God was speaking through Jim. During his testimony, Jonathan and I were made to sit in a room with ICE police guarding the door. If either of us went to the bathroom, or to get a drink of water, we'd be accompanied by one of the officers.

Meanwhile, Jim had not planned what to say. He trusted God: *"And when they bring you to the synagogues, and to magistrates, and powers, take you no thought how or what thing you shall answer, or what you shall say: For the Holy Ghost shall teach you in the same hour what you ought to say."* Luke 12:11–12

Without any forethought, his testimony was delivered with power, and with many more words than he should have been allowed. Tiffany Hicks, sitting in a sound proof room with her son, heard it over a monitor. She told us it made her jump to her feet and shout "Hallelujah!"

When asked if he believes that herbs mentioned in the Bible are "medicines," Jim answered, "Yes, for the health and well-being of an individual or individuals. . . The aspect of a drug—and what is happening today in this society is that they will call something a drug if it's a nutrient that shows benefits, and then they'll call a drug a nutrient or a substance that is equated to a nutrient. And that is the deception that is going on in the world, and that is the spiritual revelation, the fight that we have, and that's one of the reasons we're on the radio.

Drugs are chemicals that are created by pharmaceutical labs, they cannot create medicines. They cannot create herbs. They can't do anything to create what God has done. They mimic it, and every mimic, every mimic, every drug, has been a detriment to mankind.

The deception is that people need drugs, the spirit of Jezebel says you've got to have a drug and – the people are following a lie, which we believe is the lie . . . they say God didn't do it right so we need drugs.

We want people to know that God has provided everything in creation. . . . We see this as a war, a battle for people, for truth, and the differentiation of what is presented through so-called medicine as truth, is truth based on a bunch of people patting each other on the back with so-called science. . ."

At that, he was instructed to be sparing in his words. Short answers, mainly "yes" or "no," he had been told to give.

Attorney Gordon mocked the words of our corporation sole in examining Jim. "You declared that you have the full power to levy war?" Hand on his hip, leaning his weight onto the opposite leg, with glaring hubris he asked Jim if he was trying to be funny. Jim fixed his eyes on the arrogant young lawyer, and without blinking responded, "I take offense to that. There's nothing funny about anything that's going on here. It's about the Kingdom of God, about my Lord and Savior who died at Calvary. There's nothing funny about anything, whether the court's time, my time, and all the things that we've had to go through since you guys started this against us.

This is not funny, this is very serious, and I take my position with my oath to Jesus Christ seriously. I took my oath here when she asked me. My yes is yes, just like Jesus said, and my no is no. This is not funny.

What is war? Is it a definition that you have to use guns, or what is war, sir? Yes. You know what? I have to share with you that what you have done to us is attack and assault us and basically – if you'd look at the definition of terrorism, you would see what has happened to us, who is just a small ministry, the smallest ministry on the face of the earth, who have walked freely and brought the word of God to many people. If there's war, this is war.

The Lord God Almighty said we wrestle not, we don't wage war, with human beings; we wrestle not with what we see and hear but against rulers and principalities, authorities of darkness, and I know where we're standing. . .This is a war about truth, about evil and good, and so this is where we're standing. And there's a line that has been drawn, and we know which side you're on and which side I'm on."

"I'm on the side of evil?" taunted Mr. Gordon.

"Jesus said, if you're not for me you're against me, so obviously you're not for His Kingdom of God. This is not funny. The word *war* in there is intended because we are in a spiritual battle for souls. You're concerned about things that are perishing. I'm looking at you and everyone in here who needs the blood of Jesus Christ for the forgiveness of their sins and remission of their sins. It is a war. Daniel Chapter One is the sovereign existence to the Spirit of God here on Earth, the manifestation here on this earth. And we represent Elohim, Yahweh Elohim, the name above all names, and it is something that you might not understand, I know might be hard for you, but it's the way it is."

I testified later, along with Jonathan and Dr. Mink. Jill came to testify, but as the week dragged on, she was allowed to leave early to get back to her children. When it came time for our other witnesses to testify, Jim Turner came to us saying, "They'll only allow a few, not all. Who do we want to put on the stand?" But, they said we could have ten! *Not fair*, I thought. We chose Robert, Ernie, and Tracy.

When Robert began the impassioned account of his son, an FTC lawyer rose and interrupted with disgust, "Your Honor, I have kids too. This is irrelevant." The Judge nodded, and told Robert to return to his seat.

Ernie Jensen was sworn in next, beginning with his name. "Is it Ernest, or Ernie? You said Ernie, my paper says Ernest" teased the Judge. Solemn, Ernie replied, "It's Ernest. But I'm called Ernie."

As Ernie began his testimony, an FTC lawyer again jumped up, "Irrelevant, Your Honor!"

Judge Chappell agreed. "You may sit back down."

Ernie looked struck, like someone had slapped him in the face. He wanted to speak, he had come all the way from Nevada to speak on our behalf.

"Sit down!" Chappell ordered. Ernie may have been trying not to cry. "Look, it's not personal, nothing you did" said the Judge, as Ernie walked back to his seat.

Tracy was not allowed to speak either. All our witnesses were blocked as irrelevant.

But their testimony was heard that day, by the one the Lord appointed to hear. He was the security guard sitting outside the door of the courtroom. A big black man, with a young full face and kind eyes, whose job it was to keep watch on each person brought from the waiting room to testify. Each witness would be brought to those doors, to wait outside until ushered in.

"Hi," I smiled. He smiled back, and said hello. It was my turn, and I was waiting for the doors to be opened when it was time. I made small talk.

"What are y'all here for?" he asked. I told him we had a ministry of health and healing, and the government wanted to stop it. I explained that the people he had to guard were all there to testify for us that they had been healed.

"Yeah. That's what they tell me. Nice people, all of 'em. Really nice. Amazing stories. Drownin', and cancer. . ."

"Those stories are all true. They came to testify for us, but also for God, who healed them."

His eyes widened. "God healed them?"

"Sure He did. He does. Ever read the Bible?"

"Yeah I do."

"Well, God healed in the Old Testament. God through Jesus healed in the New Testament. God doesn't change, He says He doesn't. So why wouldn't God still heal?"

The man was intrigued, and smiled broadly. "Yeah, I guess He would. That's somethin'! All I was told is that this was about some people scamming people . . . but nobody's saying that. The people are telling me amazing stories. And they're thankful! Hmm, hmm" He shook his head. "I'm glad I got to talk to you."

"Me too" I replied.

The bailiff told us and our lawyers that the government spent a lot of money that week. "*A lot*" he added, with great emphasis on the word "lot."

We made friends with the ICE police, ate lunch with them in the cafeteria, and took photos with them outside the building. Some asked us for *Bio Guides*. After several days they were discharged, and then our witnesses left. We still had the day of closing arguments, our lawyers, Jim, and I.

GET INVOLVED ★ PRAY ★ JOIN US

VS

★ ★ Washington D.C. April 21, 2009 ★ ★

DANIEL CHAPTER ONE FREEDOM
MARCHES ON!

★ Hearing for Jurisdiction ★

When And Where:

April 21, 2009

10:00 a.m. in room 532

Federal Trade Commission Building

600 Pennsylvania Avenue, NW

Washington D.C. 20580

The FTC seeks to silence Daniel Chapter One ministry, to censor our information.

Daniel Chapter One argues that if successful, the FTC will violate our Constitutional Rights.

Daniel Chapter One maintains that our information is true, can be substantiated, and that it is within our rights to share according to First Amendment Rights of Free Speech, Freedom of the Press, and Freedom of Religion.

We say the Federal Trade Commission has NO JURISDICTION over a ministry!

If the Judge rules in our favor, our litigation is over. We will be free to continue to share truthful information about God's creation and testimonies of people healed by the Creator, Christ Jesus.

★ ★ ★ ★ ★ ★ ★ ★ ★ ★ ★ ★ ★ ★

A flyer made by Daniel Chapter One notifying its community of the first administrative hearing, FTC v. Daniel Chapter One, 2009.

Tricia visiting Jim on their 33rd wedding anniversary,
inside Devens federal prison, July 2, 2016

One afternoon I rode the elevator with the bailiff, from the cafeteria where I had gone to get bottled water. He said to me, "I know what you're going through."

"What?" I asked, trying to register the understanding and compassion in his voice.

"It's persecution. You're being persecuted as Christians. I'm a Christian too, and my pastor went through something like this. They questioned everything about him, to discredit him." We arrived at our stop, but he pushed the elevator button to go back up, to steal a few more minutes to say what he had wanted to say all week to us. He apologized, in a way, for working there. "I needed a job after I got out of the military. This is just a job."

The elevator doors opened again, and we parted ways, brother and sister in Christ.

*   *   *

The government had just one expert witness, Dr. Denis Miller, an oncologist who worked for Parexel International, a global company that tests drugs, including chemotherapy. Testifying for pay against the competition was nothing new to him; he had done so numerous times before. Twenty-seven times between 2004 and 2008, he provided deposition and trial testimony. He didn't work directly with cancer patients any longer. Included in his "qualifications," he was the recipient of research grants from the National Cancer Institute.

His company, Parexel, had been involved in various conduct controversies that called into question its ethics, and care for volunteers. In 2006, it implemented one particularly disastrous trial of a drug, TGN1412, where all the test patients landed in the ICU from adverse reactions. In MS drug trials, Parexel was guilty of "selective suppression," suppressing results that threaten the interest of any commercial trial sponsors, violating the integrity of the clinical research data. Parexel emphasized its "commitment to providing solutions that expedite time-to-market and peak market penetration." Evidently, speed and profit are its highest priority, typical of the pharmaceutical industry.

None of this came out in court, however. Dr. Miller was the government's prize piece in the game, paid well ($20,000) to testify against Daniel Chapter One and by whose testimony we were hung. The judge showed him respect he did not show Daniel Chapter One's expert witnesses.

The lawyers and judge discredited our expert witnesses for not being allopathic oncologists. Dr. Miller, though, had no knowledge of herbs. He didn't even have an answer when the judge asked him, "Is an herb a plant, or a plant an herb?" He answered that the question was outside of his expertise.

In the course of his testimony, he said he used to work for Cancer Treatment Centers of America, a place where people go who don't want to give up. He explained that many patients there have failing organs from past treatment (chemotherapy) and cannot tolerate any more, so they're treated with drugs like antidepressants. He stressed, "If I had cancer, I would trust my physician."

That's *his* belief, the belief the government wishes to enforce on all.

*   *   *

In his closing argument, Attorney Gordon kept repeating the phrase "double-blind placebo-controlled studies," insisting that such tests are mandatory for a dietary supplement to share *any* claim or testimony.

Judge Chappell asked, "If someone believes 7 Herb Formula will heal people, what are they allowed to say?"

Gordon was speechless. He groped for an answer he was not prepared to give. In pained, desperate silence he looked up to the ceiling, and from behind him I saw his ears turn red.

Fumbling, he questioned, "Will heal generally people?"

The Judge continued to ask, "What are they allowed to say?" To which Gordon finally said, "I think you would have to look in the testimonial guides to see exactly how far they can go as to their subjective belief," still not answering the question.

*   *   *

After the week-long trial, Jim and I remained in DC to visit with our lawyers, Dr. Sally La Mont, and Dr. James Duke at his home. We also visited Capitol Hill, where we hiked miles of marble corridors to meet with congressmen as could be scheduled. No congressperson met with us personally, but we got to meet with their young staffers. Some seemed genuinely concerned about our case. I wrote thank you letters to all. Nothing ever came of it.

Ron Paul knew about our case, referred to it in interviews and introduced a bill to the House influenced by it. But he wasn't there in the office when we visited, and his male staffer acted bored with our meeting, toying with a pencil most of the time and saying little.

*   *   *

Judge Chappell rendered his verdict, which was guilty as charged of "false and misleading advertisement," and he called for "fencing in relief" in the form of an extreme Cease and Desist Order on our information. He wrote in his opinion that the average consumer assumes that double-blind placebo-controlled studies have been done on our products. *What?! No they don't!* That is not a fact, nor has any attempt been made to prove it. It hasn't even been investigated by the FTC.

"Double-blind placebo-controlled studies" was the mantra of the FTC in the courtroom; the phrase by which they dismissed all our witnesses, Fact and Expert, as "irrelevant." Their demand for "reasonable basis" was turned into "double-blind placebo-controlled studies" by the magic of their own words, not by the letter of the law. They made up the rules of the game we were forced to play, and as they went along. About charging us with making statements we never made, they quipped, "You implied them." Our disclaimers: "not prominent enough," too small. Yet, there is no law about the size a disclaimer has to be! We were victims of a Star Chamber, with a beast of an agenda presiding.

Chappell also said in his final ruling that the average consumer cannot tell the difference between a placebo and a product that actually works. He wrote: "The 'placebo' effect of consumer expectations when taking a purported remedy makes it difficult for consumers to verify product effectiveness for themselves."

How insulting to the intelligence of America's citizens! You need the government to tell you a product doesn't work, after you experience that it does work, and you need the government to tell you that chemo and radiation work, after you've experienced it not to work?

In addition, he wrote: "A person who promotes a product that contemporary technology does not understand must establish that this 'magic' actually works."

The government lawyers were afraid to let our witnesses testify. Why not cross-examine them? They didn't dare. They couldn't risk the truth getting out, *because* people have reasoning minds. So they censor the truth, bury it, to force lies upon the people and limit choice. Given no counter message, people can be deceived. That's what having free speech is all about: the free flow of information gives people what is needed to form proper judgments, or at least, each his own judgment.

*   *   *

In December 2009, months after the administrative trial, we appealed before a panel of three FTC Commissioners and one Chairman, the required step before taking a case to Federal Court. Chairman Jon Leibowitz, and Commissioners Pamela Harbour, William Kovacic, and Thomas Rosch sat high above us. To see each other, we had to look up and they, naturally, looked down.

In his opening argument, Jim Turner made three major points: 1) The FTC has no jurisdiction over a ministry, and to extend jurisdiction would be unsound law and poor policy. 2) Daniel Chapter One did not violate the law. 3) If the law, as written or applied is such that Respondent's (Daniel Chapter One's) actions are held by the Commission to be a violation of the law, then the law is unconstitutional, either as written or applied.

He referred to our case as an integral part of a national debate, "a huge debate, and of the 130, 129 signed consent orders on this . . . the customers are the issue here. The customers are angry about having been interfered with in their own treatments . . . people are getting their money back from the FTC and signing the checks back over to the companies. You're stepping into a major social debate."

He presented the fact that in none of our material did we ever use the words "cure, treat, mitigate, or prevent," and tried to explain the difference of our language actually used, for example, "helps fight." "Their position is that these products help the body engage its natural ability to fight cancer, that's what they do."

He explained that we made structure/function claims, to which Chairman Leibowitz incorrectly said, "structure function claim, isn't that things like weight loss, fitness?"

Turner tried to explain what structure and function means, which is what we *legally* shared about our products, and also explained the paradigm difference between drugs and nutritional supplements, which DSHEA distinguishes. He said the law is *not* that double blind studies are required to make *any* health claim. The criteria that Dr. Miller and the FTC held Daniel Chapter One to is a requirement beyond the law.

He returned to the jurisdiction issue, and mentioned that on the internet, the FTC has filed a statement, a posted note, that it will not go after a 501(c) (3), even those nonreligious. The same protection should be afforded a 508 corporation sole. (Attorney Turner pointed out that Administrative Law Judge Chappell's final determination was that Daniel Chapter One is a nonprofit religious organization.)

Chairman Leibowitz challenged the FTC lawyer, "Don't you think the FTC ought to be very careful before it holds it to a higher standard . . . before it brings liability, because we are dealing with, you know, core First Amendment issues."

Gordon later complained, "The issue here is the way these (products) are sold. These are not sold in church basements." He said, "Daniel Chapter One and Jim Feijo are touting the products that they sell as alternative cures for cancer. And the stakes are extraordinarily high in that instance."

To which Chairman Leibowitz challenged, "But . . . certainly things like rosaries, and I'm sure other religions have similar materials, are also touted, in part or in whole, as having miraculous or extraordinary healing potential or powers. Why is this different?"

"Or, to put a sharper point on it, are there any higher stakes on whether or not you go to heaven?" added Commissioner Rosch.

The hearing turned out to be just for show. The FTC commissioners had their minds made up and supported the opinion and order of the ALJ, meaning the censorship Order prevailed and would have to be appealed in federal court. The first leg of a journey that may take us to the Supreme Court was complete. For Jim and me, it was time to shift gears and begin anew.

CHAPTER 29

COURTROOM VICTORY AND A RAID

We asked our co-counsel, Bill Olson and Herb Titus, to take over the case. They had written powerful briefs for Jim Turner for us, and had introduced the Religious Freedom Restoration Act to our case, of which they were well-versed. Moreover, they're brothers in Christ. We loved and respected Jim and his wife Betsy, but we *prayed* with Bill and Herb.

It was never our plan, but when it was suggested to us, it felt right. We asked the Lord what to do, our first law team had invested a lot in us – and we in them. They had worked hard for us and we'd been through much together. They cared about all the issues our case presented, but most about the Health Freedom aspect. We cared most about standing up for Yahshua. It is He who told my husband, through prayer, that we were to "take a new path."

Bill and Herb are Constitutional experts, another plus. Herb Titus helped found the first Christian Law School and was a one-time vice presidential candidate on the Constitution Party ticket. We met Herb through our journalist David, who had met him when he appeared as a guest on a radio program. Jim Turner graciously brought Bill and Herb on board to work with him on our case.

We agonized over the decision, and how to tell Attorney Turner. He was abroad, so we had to tell him over the phone, which we felt bad about. We then scrambled to secure our new counsel, to meet deadlines for filing an appeal in the US Court of Appeals for the D.C. Circuit.

We chose the District Court in Washington, DC to be accessible to Bill and Herb living in Virginia. Travel expenses would be less than if they had to travel to any of the other states where Daniel Chapter One had customers, the requisite for the district of our choosing.

Meanwhile, it was still "business as usual." Given the time of freedom, one we didn't know how long would last, we tried to make the best use of our days on radio helping people, and put our literature on a CD entitled "Health Information the Government Wants to Censor." We offered the CD to radio listeners across the country for a donation of one dollar to help cover production cost. *The Most Simple Guide* book, the *Bio Guide*, and the *Cancer Newsletter* we always gave away for free, upon request; we let people know that "now" was the time to get the publications, as they might not be available in the future. We had a legal right to proceed in this way, we were told.

With wrath ignited, the United States government filed a complaint in the US District Court for the District of Columbia, seeking injunctive relief enforcing the Order to cease and desist from certain activities and to force us to sign and send the "corrective notice . . . to past purchasers" of the four supplements people in our testimonials had used for cancer.

Jim and I didn't know what "injunction" meant, but traveled to Virginia to meet with our lawyers the night before the hearing. They were somber. Bill, Herb, their associate John, and a politician friend of theirs sat with us in their office and began, "This could be really bad for you," with the tone used to give one the bad news of a terminal illness.

"God's in control, we aren't worried!" Jim encouraged them.

"Usually we're comforting the clients," said Bill. "But with you, you're comforting us!"

We prayed and shared Scripture, and planned for the next day. John Miles would argue in court because he had the most courtroom experience. It was decided that Jim and I would not be present; we didn't have to be, and it would be too risky to give the judge opportunity to call Jim or me to the stand. We didn't understand, but accepted that. Then we took the train back to D.C., and from the station a cab back to the Hotel Harrington.

In the morning, Herb met us outside on the sidewalk. From there, he would go to court, and we planned to wait out the time at the

Lincoln Memorial. The Lord gave me a prophetic word for the day, and I shared it with Herb and Jim, above the noise of cars and cabs:

"Thus says the Lord, do not be afraid or discouraged by this vast army. The battle is not yours, but Mine. You will not have to fight this battle; stand firm and see the deliverance I, the Lord will give you. Do not be discouraged, I the Lord will be with you."

Herb said "amen!" pumping his fist in the air, and we departed. One other time, the Lord gave me such a word. Jim was being wrongly treated in Family Court in Massachusetts. We had to fire our lawyer when we could no longer afford him. The day we went to court by ourselves, I sat on the steps outside and prayed. The Lord said, "I will fight this battle for you." He did; for the first time, things shifted favorably towards Jim. For the first time, the judge did not mock or berate him, and judged righteously in his favor.

This day, the Lord told me that Jim and I were appointed to "go ahead of the army," and sing and praise Him, also from 2 Chronicles 20: *"Give thanks to the Lord, for His love endures forever."* So that's what we did, on the beautiful grounds of the Lincoln Memorial, with perfect peace.

*   *   *

In the afternoon we received the call that it was over, and were told where to meet our three lawyers. Sitting outside, enjoying lunch at a restaurant downtown, they shared how Judge Emmet Sullivan pushed back on the FTC, saying, "You want me to be your rubber stamp!" He rejected the Department of Justice's efforts to sanction Daniel Chapter One based on our argument that the District Court had no jurisdiction while the case was pending in the US Court of Appeals.

On the way out of the courtroom, a defeated and incensed FTC lawyer spoke to John through (figuratively) clenched teeth, "Call me when your client is ready to settle."

"I don't think that's going to happen" he calmly replied.

"Most people *obey* our orders!" she retorted.

We were jubilant. That day the Lord had the victory -- as He promised. During lunch, Jim called live into the radio show (we played a taped program that day), to share the good news with our listening audience. The lawyers squirmed, concerned over what he might say. But he was discreet, and simply thanked everyone for their prayers. We'd be home soon, and would be back on the air: *Daniel Chapter One Health Watch*, as usual!

*   *   *

Driving home from the airport, we got a call from Jonathan that his father died. It was unexpected; his father was young, close in age to me, and seemed healthy. He had been mowing grass for hay, on the Daniel Chapter One land down the street, as he often did, and suffered a fatal heart attack.

Jonathan had recently become adversarial with Jim, for reasons we didn't understand. We chalked a lot up to the stress of the case; everyone was on edge. But Jim was one of the first people Jonathan called to tell of his father's passing. Jim prayed with him on the phone, and later brought him a word from the Lord. Our momentary jubilation from DC was dampened, but we knew that a sovereign God was in control.

*   *   *

One week later, on September 22, 2010, I was brutally interrupted while playing with our middle, three year old granddaughter Hayden in my office. We had filled the center of a musical toy with Sesame Street finger puppets, and given it a quick spin to give them a ride. As they flew out, ejected upward into the air, we started to laugh. . .

"It's a raid! It's a raid!" Boots came thumping up the stairway. Alarmed, I turned to Jim standing in the doorway watching us play. He smiled, "That's Benny," but he was wrong.

"You should tell your friends not to joke around like that! That's not funny!" My heart was pounding.

Into the room burst armed men in black uniforms and bulletproof vests. One pointed a gun at Jim, another walked towards me on the floor. Hayden hid behind a small bookcase.

I was concerned, only, about her. "Don't you traumatize that child" I said in a low voice, rising up off the floor. An agent pulled open my closet door, behind which were books and homeopathic remedies.

"Glad we live in a free country," I couldn't keep from saying to him, and went to Hayden. It's said that fear is behind anger. I didn't feel fearful, I felt angry. I didn't know who these men were who stormed in so aggressively, or if they had a warrant. Ambushed as we were, I was unprepared to ask right questions. Hayden shook her head and pressed tighter into the wall when I reached for her. She wasn't going to budge. This happened within seconds.

Jim's cell phone was immediately confiscated and he was taken outside. I reached for my laptop on the desk a few feet away (a submission for my PhD exam had been left open on it, interrupted when Jim brought Hayden in to play), an eye on Hayden, but an agent said, "Don't touch that! You can take her outside." I reached for my purse. "Don't touch that! Don't touch anything" he ordered. I noticed his badge: FDA.

"I'm going to call my lawyer. Can I call my lawyer?" I moved towards the phone.

"Yah, you can call your lawyer."

Herb answered the phone. "Herb, there are men in here, in my office . . . we're being raided! . . . I don't know our rights. What should I do?"

"Did you see a warrant?" he asked.

"No."

"Tricia, you've got to see the warrant."

"Do you have a warrant?" I asked, hanging up the phone, reaching again for Hayden.

"It's somewhere, downstairs, I think. Take the child outside" the agent commanded.

I pried Hayden away from the wall and the bookcase, took her in my arms, and we left, down the stairs. Uniformed men filled the room downstairs, and our computers lay in pieces on the floor. One agent was slowly, meticulously filming the walls of the room with a camera.

An agent locked the door behind us after we exited.

Jill, her infant Mya, and an office worker who was six months pregnant, were standing at the back of our house. Jim was talking to a State trooper on duty, a man we knew as a customer. A local police cruiser blocked our driveway. The parking lot held several black government vehicles. I called Herb back, and he asked that the warrant be faxed to him.

I knocked on the back door of the store, asking for the warrant for our lawyer and access to the fax machine. The agent disappeared, then came back with a couple pieces of paper which he let me fax from the office. Once again locked outside, I heard back from Herb: "This is only Part A. I need Part B! Fax the entire warrant."

Once again I knocked on the door, and requested the remaining pages of the warrant.

"I have to call my lawyer, and see if I can give that to you," the agent responded, locking me out again. He reappeared, additional pages in hand, and let me back into the office, locking the door behind me when I left the building.

Jim was not upset, but I was. Minutes before our radio program was due to begin, however, I suggested, "Hey! I still have my cell phone. Maybe we should do the show from my phone?"

We called in to ARN, told them the situation, and the producer narrated news of the raid during *Daniel Chapter One Health Watch*, as we broadcast our two hour program live from the parking lot using my phone.

Listeners were calling in, shocked and enraged, some crying. The more we talked to them, the calmer I felt. We didn't know what was happening, didn't know if it would be our last time on the air. Through my office windows we could see agents rifling through my personal things. We kept reporting live, as we watched the men wheel boxes of our personal property, files and computers, out of the building on hand trucks and into the backs of their SUVs.

Four surreal hours later, they left. The office women had already left for home with their children as soon as they were allowed to. We walked into the back building, into a mess. My office was trashed. I opened file cabinets, and found them empty. My client files had been taken. A knot of indignation gripped my stomach.

Harvard Coach Bryan Fetzer was living with us at the time. When he came home that evening, we recounted the day's events to him. I had to take homeopathic Ignatia that night for my stomach, a grief and shock remedy, only after which the pain subsided enough that I could sleep.

Attorney Herb Titus told us we needed to obtain additional counsel, criminal defense attorneys. The next day I still felt sick, but we drove to Providence to meet with a criminal defense attorney, Herb DeSimone. While waiting for him, reading the Bible open on my lap, the Lord gave me this promise from Isaiah 43:2: "*when you walk through the fire, you shall not be burned . . .*"

Attorney DeSimone agreed to take Jim's case, but said I'd need my own lawyer. At the elevator, I told Jim I didn't like that. "I feel like they're trying to separate us." But it's the law; or, at least, the judge would demand it. Mr. DeSimone suggested a colleague down the hall from him that could represent me. Another visit to Providence, and I was handed an agreement by Attorney K. B., requiring a $75,000 retainer, $25,000 of which was non-refundable. Under duress, pressured and exhausted, I signed it.

The Providence lawyers called us to their office days later. After another half hour drive into the city, we met with them only to be told, "Well, you're going to be indicted." They could have emailed or phoned. "That's it?!" I said to Jim outside. Resignation? We're sitting ducks? What's the point of having a *Defense* attorney? *Fight for us*, for crying out loud.

The next day, Bryan offhandedly mentioned that he knew of someone who worked for a firm in California that had won cases against the FDA and the FTC. My ears perked up. I asked for the name of the firm. He didn't know, and she wasn't there anymore, but . . . he managed to later obtain the name, Sanger & Swysen.

We had already signed agreements with the two lawyers in Providence. But I wasn't comfortable with them; literally lost sleep over it. I asked Jim for permission to call Sanger & Swysen. He consented, then I prayed. I told the Lord that if we were to switch council, to have either Sanger or Swysen answer the phone. Lawyers almost never answer their office line, a secretary does. I had googled the firm; they were prominent Santa Barbara, California attorneys (Bob Sanger represented Michael Jackson for 17 years).

A woman with a lovely French accent answered the phone. Her name was Catherine Swysen. She spoke with me for at least half an hour, listening intently and asking questions. She arranged for her partner and husband, Bob, to call us, and the next day Jim and I talked to Bob together for close to an hour. He told us we should have asked for business cards of the agents who raided us so we could investigate *them*, and shared other proactive steps that could be taken. Jim asked if he would take our case. Bob didn't want us to rush into it, and suggested we talk it over and get back to him.

"If you're willing, I don't need more time," Jim said. Bob agreed then to take our criminal case. He said he couldn't promise that we would not be indicted, and indictment can mean the death of a small business, but he promised "We'll at least try to slow this train down."

We recouped some of the retainer money from the Providence lawyers, not all of it, and Attorney B. withheld the $25,000 "non-refundable" portion.

We have since called the office of Sanger & Swysen many times. Never again has either one answered the phone.

CHAPTER 30

TO OBEY GOD OR MAN

The year before the raid, after the FTC administrative hearings were over, Jim had knee replacement surgery.

From old football injuries and past surgeries his knee was destroyed, beyond repair with homeopathy and nutrients. We tried. Walking had become painful, stairs excruciating. Eric, involved with a company that serves orthopedic surgeons, gave his father the name of a reputable surgeon.

Surgery went well, though it was complicated by the artificial ligament screwed into the bone, and a bone cyst. (The GORE-TEX ligament was, by then, shredded.) Jim informed the surgeon that he wouldn't take any drugs, and he had no need of any before, or after surgery. He accepted general anesthesia in the Operating Room, but refused antibiotics, anti-inflammatory drugs, relaxant drugs, painkillers, and blood thinners. Without exaggeration, he had *no* pain! Prior to surgery I gave him homeopathic Phosphorus, to ease any grogginess after surgery, and Arnica before and after, for pain and swelling and bleeding. He used our GDU and other supplements, and had no pain, minimal swelling and discomfort, and healed quickly. The surgeon was so impressed, the following week he called another surgeon into the room and suggested they do a study on our protocol. He asked us to write down exactly what Jim took, which we did. They may have wanted it for personal information, since their hands would be tied to share it with any patients. Doctors must adhere to "standard protocol" to protect their licensure.

Months later Dr. Lehr also had knee replacement surgery, and couldn't take painkilling drugs. I sent him the remedies that Jim took, and he likewise had no pain and healed quickly. Other people we've talked to who have had knee replacement surgery say they had great pain despite the drugs.

*   *   *

After we secured Bob Sanger's council for the criminal investigation, we appealed the Order of the FTC with Attorneys Titus and Olson in the US Court of Appeals, in an attempt to reverse the unconstitutional "cease and desist" order against us. It was decided that Herb Titus would speak in court. Jim told him that most of all, he wanted proclaimed that the Lord Yahshua is The One we stood for.

We met with Herb in D.C. the day before. He explained that he would only have 10 minutes for his argument, which he could use all at once, or 8 minutes before the FTC lawyer, and 2 minutes after the FTC argument. Jim said, "Just make it about Yahshua."

We stayed in the same hotel. The morning of the court hearing, I encountered Attorney Titus stepping out of the elevator, looking dapper in his suit and tie, but distracted and anxious.

"I've lost my glasses," he said. "I need my glasses!"

"They must be in the room?" That was the last place, he said, he had them. "Let's go look again, I'll help." He had trouble finding the right elevator button, and I realized he truly couldn't see.

After turning the room over, in despair he got down on his knees and passionately implored the Lord, "Jesus! Please help me find my glasses!" When he straightened up, he took a couple steps to the nightstand and picked up his glasses. They had been hidden under something, right under our noses.

"I think the Lord just showed me not to trust in my own sight" he said, as we rode the elevator down to the lobby to meet Jim.

*   *   *

I don't remember exactly what Herb said before the panel of three Federal Judges, but his argument centered on the "reasonable basis" issue. The FTC lawyer, I remember, said, "All they (Daniel Chapter One) had to do was say that the products and information were based on the Bible."

The Judge caught him in that lie and said, "Oh, really? That's all they had to do?"

"Well," the lawyer shrugged, "It'd be a start."

It was a disappointing, anticlimactic day in court. After much preparation and money spent to appeal in Federal Court, it was over in minutes. All three federal judges ruled in favor of the federal government agency. The onerous FTC Order was upheld.

Time to gear up for our appeal to the US Supreme Court.

*   *   *

An Australian videographer, Ben, and a woman from Missouri, Krystle, contacted us to propose they make a documentary about the Daniel Chapter One story. We had to let our videographer Seve go when we could no longer afford her services, so we told Ben and Krystle we were sure we couldn't afford such a project. They offered to do it for free. They both had other freelance work that would support them, and they cared deeply about our case. "It's a humanitarian case, really," said Ben. "It's about basic human rights."

They arrived in Rhode Island, coincidentally, the week our brief was submitted to the Supreme Court. Attorney Bob Sanger felt we had a strong case. The brief he wrote with his associate Stephen Dunkle was substantial and compelling. In addition, two amicus briefs were submitted on our behalf, by two different law firms, each with two citizen groups behind them. Amicus briefs are written pro bono - at no charge – and present to the Supreme Court that the case is of national importance. Two Health Freedom Groups and two Religious Freedom Groups supported the fact that the case of *Daniel Chapter One v. Federal Trade Commission* was of national importance. Jim Turner wrote one amicus brief, Herb Titus and Bill Olson wrote the other.

We waited to hear if the Supreme Court would accept our case, while Ben and Krystle filmed.

The day they arrived happened to also be the first day of Grand Jury hearings in Providence regarding Jim, and me, and Daniel Chapter One. Jonathan from Florida and others were subpoenaed with records. Anyone who worked with us or had worked with us in the recent past were targeted by the Feds and had to stand trial before the Grand Jury. Neither we nor our lawyers were allowed to be present.

Ben and Krystle picked Jonathan up and brought him to our house. There, they interviewed him on camera for the documentary, which he consented to despite being distraught. Off camera, he broke down crying, saying he missed his father. Jim and I ministered to him, praying with him and trying to comfort him.

On camera he talked about the various times we assisted with his children's health needs. When Ben asked about our relationship, he didn't say we were "like family," which we would have said. From the witness stand in the FTC administrative hearings, he had testified that we were like family. I thought it odd now that he minimized our closeness, but it had been a stressful day for him. Traveling outside FL, in itself, was discomforting for a homebody from the farmlands and cow pastures of northern Florida.

Also interviewed and filmed were Mary, Coach Fetzer, and Tony Petrarca, a sister and brothers in Christ, and some local Daniel Chapter One customers. Dr. Ron Marsh granted an interview, and spoke eloquently on the issue of freedom of choice in health care. Another local chiropractor (who we had helped with health problems, and who used our products) declined to be interviewed, choosing to shirk the light of attention regarding our case rather than stand up for right. (For all the people willing to come to Washington to defend us, there were those – cured of cancer even – who admitted to fearing the government too much to testify.)

Carol and Al Mello gave a video testimony in their home in Massachusetts. He had been subjected to Agent Orange in Vietnam and developed asthma, diabetes, and a rare cancer as a consequence. He was on hospice care after conventional cancer treatments failed, when his neighbor told him about Daniel Chapter One. After taking our products for a time, he was well enough to dismiss hospice. When they called one day and he answered, the hospice worker exclaimed, "You aren't supposed to be here!" It had been at least four years since then, this day when Ben and Krystle interviewed him. He brought us out to his garage to show us his classic car collection, cars he exhibited at car shows. Not only was he still alive, he had quality of life.

Al looked into the camera and asked: "If they stop these people, what's going to happen to me? And to other people like me? It's your choice! This is still America."

His testimony was typical of the testimonies the FTC lawyers mocked. He was the kind of person they made fun of. I can laugh at myself in almost any situation, but fail to see any humor in another person's suffering, or in their salvation and gratitude. Al's question demands a serious answer. Why would anyone want to prevent him from getting the information, and products, that gave him hope and saved his life? How, in America, could he not be allowed choice?

Jim and I went with Ben and Krystle to film our old location, the place where Daniel Chapter One started, and then to the trailer park where we used to live. After filming, sitting in the car at the trailer park, we received a call from Herb and Bill: the Supreme Court denied our case.

"What do we do now?" I asked.

"Nothing you can do. You're at the end of the road."

We had filed all the documents, three sizeable briefs, just that morning. "How could they have read everything so fast?"

"They probably didn't."

I realized there was no chance, really, that they would have taken the case. They turned us down with no explanation.

Bill went on to say that maybe we'd do better with other lawyers. We could appeal to the Supreme Court "en banc," which is to the entire bench. Slight chance it would do any good, but we could. He said sometimes certain lawyers have more favor with the Supreme Court. "Basically, we are disparaging ourselves to you."

The mood had turned glum. Ben filmed the entire conversation from the back seat of the car, and resumed filming us back in the office. Jim and I didn't know what to do, if we should spend the money for one, last, desperate appeal or not. And, what about what Bill had humbly, honestly shared? Should we seek new council?

We decided to call Bob. The criminal investigation was underway, and now we had the FTC Order to deal with, maybe a last ditch effort at the Supreme Court. Herb and Bill had worked hard, and were clearly discouraged. Maybe they didn't want the case anymore. We were spending money on two law firms, it made sense to consolidate.

Attorney Sanger was not eager to take the case. Jim told him he felt led to put all legal matters under one roof, under one head. We didn't exactly beg, but close to it. Bob finally agreed. He would take over the FTC case. He wasted no time in reading mountains of court transcripts to come up to speed on it. He did appeal "en banc," and we were again turned down. It was no longer "business as usual" at Daniel Chapter One. We had to comply with the FTC Order, or risk monumental fines and/or imprisonment.

*   *   *

We tried to resume *Daniel Chapter One Health Watch*, but without answering health questions. People called in for help, and we'd say, "Sorry, we can't answer that." We had the answers, but couldn't share them. Jim was frustrated, and said to me, "We are disobeying the Lord! Do we fear men, and not Him?" I guess I did, because when he decided to help people asking for help anyway, we started to disagree for the first time. He suggested I remove myself from the radio ministry, and so I stopped co-hosting the program with him. He kept at it alone, mostly discussing spiritual matters, but when a health question came up, he answered it best he could with restraint.

I was unhappy being apart in ministry, and after several weeks rejoined him. We decided to change the name of the program to *Daniel Chapter One Censored*. People often called in because they had been given the number by somebody, and had no clue they were endangering us by asking health questions. The name suggested the new situation.

Regular listeners knew the difficulty we were in, and their hearts went out to us as well as to the callers seeking help. That's when, with no prompting by us, people started calling in to help others on the line. We had four phone lines, and listeners would call in, with the questioner still on the line, "I know what they can do!" "I can tell them what I did!" We let them speak. We no longer had free speech, but citizens out there did!

It was wonderful, God's people helping each other. It took Jim and me out of the equation, and we never wanted it to be about us. Truth is truth. No man should be looked up to as 'the one.' We were ecstatic; the Lord said He would make streams in the desert!

Many called in to encourage us, also. One man, Tim Weisner, called to say if we sent him the letter the FTC wrote, he would film himself burning it and place the video on You Tube. To the 70s song "Smiling Faces" by the Undisputed Truth playing in the background, Tim lit the FTC letter and filmed it going up in flames, declaring "Jesus is my healer!" He then took a few moments to share the gospel, and said, "What's happening to Daniel Chapter One is a miracle. It has God's fingerprints all over it. We were looking too much to Jim and Trish . . . we need to link to each other!" He ended with his arms raised, praising God.

That marvelous season was short-lived.

*   *   *

Accent Radio Network in Florida was raided, as we had been. Jonathan was clearly rattled, especially over their demand for his computer files. When I talked to him that afternoon, after the agents left his premises, I had never heard him so shaken.

"Jonathan, you have nothing to worry about. They're after Jim and me. You're the straightest arrow I know . . . your files aren't going to incriminate you. You aren't responsible for us answering health questions, or for any of our material." I was sure the government had just tried to shake him.

He didn't want ARN in his backyard anymore, and suggested we move it to the land down the street. The network studio could be set up in the double-wide trailer, on the property we had purchased for a warehouse. We let families live there off and on, but presently it was empty. Jim agreed, and we paid Jonathan and his friend the following weekend to move all the equipment and the satellite dishes down to the field.

Soon after, we heard from FTC Compliance with complaints that we were violating the Order by letting other people answer health questions on our radio program, by not sending their deceptive letter, and by not turning over our customer list.

If we were going to be shut down and/or go to prison anyway . . . why keep *trying* to comply at all? And, we naively thought, maybe we could rouse public support through civil disobedience, enough to push back the injustice. The documentary was being made, and people all over the country were writing to their politicians demanding access to health information and justice for us. We were collecting thousands of names and comments on an online petition, and signatures on paper petitions. And, bottom line, Jim felt he had let Yahshua down by turning people away who came to us. Like the disciples of old, he believed he had to be willing to be imprisoned for the sake of the Lord and His Truth.

If we were going down, we'd go down unflinching. *Daniel Chapter One Censored* was renamed *Daniel Chapter One Alive*! We resumed the old format, prefacing our statements with "The government doesn't want us to tell you this, but . . ." The ax was about to fall, so we chose to stand and proclaim the truth with the time we had.

CHAPTER 31

NETWORK STRUGGLES

Jonathan emailed Daniel Chapter One distributors and radio stations early one morning to say that we were finished, Daniel Chapter One would no longer be broadcasting a radio program. The office phones began ringing as soon as the work day began, abuzz with confusion and distress. When we saw the email he sent, we couldn't believe it. Why would he do such a thing? "It's inevitable" was his explanation. "And I didn't want the network to go down like C. Wiley's, not telling anyone right up to the end."

But we aren't C. Wiley, nor are we like him! And we had not thrown in the towel, not yet! The end wasn't "inevitable" in our eyes, we were still hoping and trusting. It was strange that Jonathan would do such a thing without talking to Jim. We called around to let everyone know that it was not true, the email was sent without our knowledge, and that we were still doing everything we could to stay alive.

Jerry Hughes had warned us about a possible unholy alliance between Jonathan and the previous owner of the station we acquired, Duane. Jonathan was working with us and had started Accent Radio Network with us, at the time we purchased the station from Duane. Duane did a political talk show we aired, and at one point had started a network that failed. We hired Duane to help with affiliate relations for ARN, and paid for him and Jonathan to attend a National Association of Broadcasters convention in Las Vegas to promote Accent Radio Network. We later found out they were there on our dime, not to promote ARN but rather, their own prospective network.

"I hate to say anything, but Jim, I think you should know . . . I think Jonathan and Duane are planning to start their own network. Or to steal yours." Jerry was reluctant to say it, but felt he had to alert Jim. That had been several months earlier. Jim continued to somewhat trust the men, but fully trusted Jerry.

We called Jerry later in the day, to tell him the email wasn't from us. He had already gone on air and told his audience it would be his last week of *Straight Talk*, and that he was quitting radio altogether. His health was poor, he was taking chemotherapy for cancer, and he felt too fatigued many days to do his three hour program. As was his style, he would bow out with grace. His listeners were in tears.

As a homeopath, I know what "ailments from bad news" means. "Jerry's health will probably worsen now," I said to Jim. Radio was his life-blood. He was the best in his field, and it was keeping him alive. Jim assured Jerry we would keep ARN as long as possible, and would continue with or without Jonathan. It was settled, and Jerry resumed his show.

Then Jonathan quit. He sent an email to Jim to say he was resigning as Manager of ARN. He was done. He wouldn't talk to us anymore. His brotherly love had been swallowed up by fear and cares of the world.

Our producer in Florida took over and ran the network by himself for a long time. When he called it quits, we still were not ready to pull the plug. Everyday people not only called in with health problems, but to pray, and to sing praise to the Lord. It was an anointed time. We'd shut it down if and when Yahshua told us to.

The day before our producer's last day, the owner of a radio station in Missouri called and asked if we'd like to move Accent Radio Network to their location. The producer there could continue to produce *Daniel Chapter One Health Watch* (we reclaimed the original name), as well as run the entire network in-house. It was a tremendous offer, and we had no other option.

David drove down to Florida from Rhode Island, packed up the network, and drove the equipment up to Missouri. There the producer had to grapple with a tangled mess of wires, managed to sort them, and got the equipment up and running. Sound quality wasn't great, but we and our listeners bore with it.

When someone slashed the tires of a person's car at the station, the station owner grew nervous about having ARN under her roof. She appreciated that our products had healed several people she knew, including her mother, but knew that the government considered us outlaws. We could move to the garage outside, she said, and the producer's nephew could run our network from there.

He made a valiant effort, but neither the sound nor the technical quality was professional from the garage. It was time to call it quits for the network. *Daniel Chapter One Health Watch*, however, would prevail on other networks. Daniel Chapter One still had a national voice.

CHAPTER 32

ACCOMMODATION OF LOVE

When we were sued by the FTC, I didn't tell my father right away. I didn't want to cause him to worry. He had always led a quiet life, was a model citizen and respectful of authority. When I did tell him, with some hesitation, that we had been sued by the government but were fighting it, he surprised me by saying, "Good for you, Tricia! Fight those bullies. You and Jim, stand together. Stay together on this, and stand up to them."

Dad was wise, his words always measured. Thinking back, and I have many times, his response reflected righteous anger. Not only was he angry over his daughter being bullied, but also about the growing size and power of the US government and changes in the nation.

"It's not the America I grew up in" he'd say. He hoped that with a new president – 2008 was an election year – we'd see tyrannical, out of control agencies like the FTC reined in and realigned with the Constitution. "It trickles down from the top" he commented.

When Jim and I grew disgusted with mounting legal bills and still no justice, and considered proceeding without legal representation, my father counseled, "Lawyers, and I have no use for any of them, help you navigate the shoals," suggesting that we'd shipwreck without them.

Dad prayed for us every day. My sister lived with him, and said she often heard him crying out to the Lord at night on our behalf, from where he kneeled by his bed. I hoped the stress wouldn't make him sick. I shared everything good with him, and despite the years of litigation, there was plenty that was good. We spent quality time with brothers and sisters, nieces and nephews, children and grandchildren, and with my father and his best friend Natalie. I kept him abreast of our travels around the country. I shared homeopathy papers written for my PhD with him.

*   *   *

In 2011 I was finishing a PhD program in homeopathy and working on a thesis. My hard drive crashed. My work was lost in the crash, and I had to start over. During that time we had opportunity to buy an inexpensive auction car in Florida, a 2004 Jaguar, and decided to drive it up to Rhode Island to replace my 1995 Jag (which we had bartered product for!) We visited Dad and Natalie in Massachusetts. He wasn't doing well; he had a persistent cough, had lost a significant amount of weight, and was generally weak. The man who hiked Mount Washington at age 78, was at 84 slowing down at an alarming rate. We gave him our nutritional ENDO24 to drink, and he reported feeling better.

His doctor dismissed the cough. Jim and I decided to drive the '95 car down to Florida before the winter. It was on its last leg, so we'd retire it to fairer weather rather than get rid of it. It was worth next to nothing and in need of repairs; we'd get little for it if we tried to sell it.

The four people remaining at Daniel Chapter One-- David, and three office workers-- couldn't believe we were driving it all the way to Florida. No one thought we'd make it. We left on Thanksgiving, knowing the roads would be pretty clear. We did make it, but the car stopped running as soon as we got there.

Days later, I received a distress call from my sister, and then my father. I had called him from the road on the way down, again when we arrived safely, but now he was asking me urgently to come home. His condition was critical, he knew. Dad never asked for anything. Jim immediately bought a plane ticket for me to return to Rhode Island. He would follow later for cheaper fare.

I had a thesis deadline, and didn't know how long I'd be at my father's, so I packed a suitcase full of research books, and lugged it and a computer bag through the airport, to fly for the first time alone, to my father.

*   *   *

Dad wanted his family to be with him, together, and for there to be "no squabbling" amongst us. Not that there ever was, but his anticipation was, "when the patriarch is gone, dynamics change." He referred to other adult children he had seen fight over money and important decisions to be made after the death of parents. He made my brother his health proxy to head any medical decisions regarding his care. Knowing Larry and I were from two different health camps which held opposing principles to the other, he feared arguments would arise. He wanted no trouble, certainly not because of him or over him. And he never wanted to be a burden to his family.

I was vacuuming the house before leaving Florida, attempting to bring order to a situation I could. Jim told me to put the vacuum down. Mundane cares of the world, he said, "stop." I obeyed, though frustrated. "Let's pray" he said, and brought me a word of the Lord in which the Lord said He was sending me to my family to bring His word. Jim finished the chore after dropping me off at the airport.

*   *   *

We three kids convened in the hospital, and stayed at our dad's house together. Dad was petrified of cancer, which he might have, and to enter the hospital, because of my mother's treatments and the fact that once in, she never walked out. He'd recently confided in me that he "did *not* want to go down the road she did." He referred to the chemo and radiation, which he supported at the time but came to see was useless torture. He cried when he told me that, acknowledging that Jim and I never supported the conventional treatments, though we did support their decisions. He regretted their decisions, and said plainly, he did not want that kind of treatment.

He was diagnosed with lung lymphoma. It remains for God to know how and why such a disease developed, but he did have skin cancers (basal cell carcinoma) from the sun (he was fair, blue-eyed) that doctors burned and cut away, which according to Traditional Chinese Medicine and homeopathic principles is suppressive treatment that drives the illness deeper. Skin illness suppressed manifests in the lungs. Besides that, he had been prescribed a heart drug (after a mild heart attack, after shoveling heavy snow) that according to the PDR can cause lung cancer.

At any rate, my father was not one to take a lot of anything, supplements included, and although I had helped him with a bone spur, digestive issues, and allergies over the years, he wasn't willing to take our products at the amounts I suggested. He couldn't, his vitality was too low. He also feared suffering a protracted illness, and didn't want to burden his children in any way. He would rather die than that, or to enter a nursing home. He made it clear to me what he did not want done, but the decisions rested with my brother.

In the hospital he was put on about 20 different drugs. He would never walk again. In and out of sleep, groggy when awake, his main suffering was anxiety; the panic felt by a drowning man. He was drowning, in swollen lymph nodes and fluid and phlegm in his lungs. We took turns staying with him through the night, taking shifts so one of us was always with him. One morning my sister and I woke about 4:00 in the morning, neither able to sleep and both feeling it urgent to get to the hospital. It had been my brother's turn at the hospital that night.

We three siblings sat in a visitor's room together. My brother cried, knowing Dad was dying as he had been trying to tell everyone he was. He was scheduled for an open lung biopsy later that day.

"He won't be able to survive that!" I spoke up, though I tried hard not to. "Look at how weak he is! A biopsy? What for? He doesn't want their treatments anyway . . . what's the point?!" I promised my dad I'd go along with the doctors and my brother, but my heart was ripping. I had to speak what was true.

Anguished, my sister said "But maybe they can do something . . . ?"

My brother agreed there was no point, that a lung biopsy done in my father's condition would do more harm than good. After some discussion, we decided to take Dad home. My sister would return later, and my brother went to the house to sleep. He explained the hospital system to me, saying the oncologist would be making his rounds around 7:00 am. He instructed me to use the acronym for Care Measures Only. "Just tell them CMO."

I stepped out of the room for a few minutes to use my phone. That's when I saw them: an army of white coats, coming down the corridor like Roman soldiers, coming to take my father. I blocked the door. The head doctor attempted to move by me and enter the room; I asked if he was there for Mr. Haith.

"Who are you?" the doctor asked, with authority and an edge of contempt.

"I'm his daughter and my brother, Dr. Haith, is his medical proxy, and he said to tell you there will be no biopsy, CMO. He's CMO."

"What? No biopsy?" He had not been informed of this. Mr. Haith was scheduled for surgery; the surgeon had a job to do.

I looked frantically over at the nurses' station, got one's attention, and she confirmed, "Yes, it's true, Dr. Haith changed his father's status to CMO." The oncologist had no choice but to turn on his heels and walk away, medical students in his train.

While we waited to take Dad home, my brother had a brief encounter with one of the nurses at the Nurses' Station, an older, Polish woman named Urszula. "You are doing the right thing!" she told him with certainty. "They'll test you 'til your dying breath! Better to get him home. You're a smart family, you're doing the right thing." Deeply grateful, he embraced her. He had started to second-guess himself, and she confirmed his was the right decision.

We did the best thing we could do. We brought Dad home and cared for him together. Hospice came in daily to help. His favorite nurse prayed with us, and other people including his parish priest came often to pray. My brother put in writing that after he returned to work in Maine, I was to be allowed to continue to give homeopathic remedies instead of prescription drugs. He threw out most of the drugs.

As Jim had done for his father, I slept on the floor beside my father's bed. One night, he leaned back against the pillow, hands behind his head, elbows out, posturing as he would when star gazing or telling us camping stories when we were kids. Then he proceeded to narrate the New Testament story of the life of Jesus, enlivening it with comments such as, "Imagine Joseph, not yet wed, his wife-to-be pregnant . . . the social shame," his voice low, and intense.

When he got to the book of Acts in the story, he quoted Peter and John's reply to the Sanhedrin when ordered not to teach any longer in the name of Jesus. "They said, judge for yourselves whether it's right in God's sight to obey you rather than God . . . We cannot help speaking about what we've seen and heard."

He finished by mentioning that Paul wrote letters from prison, epistles, which became important books of the Bible. Too tired to talk any more, he concluded with a chuckle, "Well, I've talked your ears off."

I was so grateful to God! I heard my heavenly Father speak through my earthly father that night. Instead of "Jesus," Dad said "Messiah," straining for breath and pronouncing it through his teeth so that it sounded like the Hebrew word for Messiah, "Mashiach" (ma-SHEE-ach). I'd never heard him use that name before, and I doubt he consciously did that night.

*   *   *

As Dad wished and the Lord appointed, he died with his children around him and getting along. All his grandchildren got to see and speak to him, as did other family members and neighbors, and Jim arrived in time to pray with him. We broke bread together and praised the Lord. Dad had clarity of mind, having planned his entire funeral and written his obituary. He did it his way, with final dignity.

The only time doubt and fear gripped my brother again during that difficult time, I laid hands on him and, in obedience to the word I received through Jim, brought him a word from the Lord. Right away his faith and resolve returned. A Catholic allopathic physician, and a born-again Christian homeopath, the love that united us was greater than any differences that might have divided us. There was room for us both.

As Health Care Proxy, he wrote a statement for hospice regarding our father's care, ending with: "Comfort only. He is protected by allopathy, homeopathy, osteopathy, sibling cooperation, family love, humility, hospice, and ultimately all derived from the Lord, Yahweh."

*   *   *

My father died in December 2011.

Soon after, people working at ARN quit and we moved the network to Missouri.

The following May, 2012, we had to appear again in court in DC, this time on contempt charges. That, we knew, could mean jail.

CHAPTER 33

THE HOLE IN THE NET

After being sued, we started a legal defense fund at others' suggestions. Not much came from it, and the Lord told us that He wouldn't let help come from those outside of Him. We stopped asking for financial help, believing we were to trust Yahweh. Some people have made donations to the ministry of their own volition and continue to do so.

Before David came back to work with us, he was working fixing generators. He'd often stop by for products, and one day approached Jim with an envelope, saying "This is from the Lord." It held $1,000. As you may recall, Jim met David at the boat dock, when Jim handed him $100 dollars saying, "I believe the Lord wants you to have this." From strangers to brothers, a gift given in obedience had come full circle.

David later got sick on the job, and was unable to keep working around petroleum. Jim offered him a position at Daniel Chapter One, so he came to work in the warehouse. His road to recovery was long and difficult, but he used only supplements and homeopathy and the Lord honored that. He was and is Jim's right hand man, a trustworthy brother. When Jim faced prison for the civil charges, David offered to go in his stead, saying that is sometimes allowed in a civil case. He was willing to go to prison for his brother.

*   *   *

In May 2012 we had to appear again in Emmet Sullivan's courtroom, this time for contempt charges brought by the FTC. We felt that if one person was helped in the time we defied The Order, any punishment was worth it. The Lord says, *"What you do to the least of these, you do unto me."*

We didn't fight the contempt charges. Instead Attorney Sanger defended us on grounds that our "noncompliance" was due to our deep religious convictions. Judge Sullivan didn't care, and listened while the FTC lawyers listed their grievances. We pleaded the Fifth, so as not to incriminate ourselves if indicted on criminal charges, but Jim asked our lawyer if he could say something about where and why he stood. No, that was not allowed, but Bob assured him, "Oh, they know how you feel."

The FTC played recordings of our radio show in the courtroom. We heard people ask questions, and heard our caring answers. Jim and I were not ashamed nor embarrassed by the recordings, had no reason to be. I found myself looking at the government spy who recorded the shows, wanting to say, *you have a problem with this?* It was obviously not about money, not about advertising/marketing. It was also evident that we were trying to comply with the government order, but had an overriding compulsion to help people in need.

"We have a voice," I wrote to Jim on a piece of paper.

People would often call in to *Daniel Chapter One Health Watch* to give "praise reports," but when they did so after The Order, as the tapes proved, Jim and I would stop them and say, "The government won't let you share that on this show."

Nothing appeased the FTC. Although the letter had not been sent, we had turned over the customer list. The government argued that our customers had no expectation of privacy, we argued they did. We lost.

Rather than expunge testimonies on the website, Jim had blacked out disease and product names. The FTC wanted it all *gone*. And the big issue remained the letter.

What were we going to do about the letter? The government objected to our attorney's idea that they, the FTC, send the letter, saying "It has to be believable," and "We're a small agency with limited funds." The judge agreed that we couldn't pick and choose what parts of The Order we would comply with, our compliance had to be total.

With no time to pray, Jim set a fleece before the Lord. He took coins out of his pocket, and told the Lord that if he was to sign and send the letter, it would be heads; tails, he was not to. He pulled a coin from his pocket and blindly slammed it down on the table. Tails won; Jim could not sign the letter. He told Bob he could not.

"I'll have you remanded to a DC jail this afternoon!" snapped Judge Sullivan.

He called in two marshals with yellow handcuffs in their back pockets. Jim stood up in defiance, the judge ready to arrest him. Jim took the hotel room key from his pocket, and his cell phone, and placed them on the table near me.

Although he was the named Respondent and I shouldn't have been made responsible, the FTC and DOJ lawyers then flipped it on me. "She has to send the letter!"

The judge fumed out of the courtroom when Bob asked for a few minutes with us. Before he left, he said he wanted an answer about what I was going to do when he returned.

I began to tell Bob that I could not sign that letter either. "They killed my mother with those treatments. I will never sign that letter!"

"I get it" Bob said stopping me, color rising in his face, beads of sweat on his forehead. He couldn't waste any time. "You don't have to sign it; you're only court-ordered to send it." He pulled the order out from a file, and showed me where, in fact, we were court ordered to *send* the FTC letter.

"But there's a signature line at the bottom!"

"That's only suggestive. All you have to do is send the letter, can you send the letter? With your own letter to follow it?"

I looked at Jim. What should I do?

Jim once again took coins from his pocket, five coins this time, and told the Lord that more heads, or tails, I should send it, or not. I knew whatever came up he would accept. "Send the letter" won. "Ok Trish, send the letter."

"If she sends it, you get out of jail, so why not you send it in the first place?" Bob said to Jim. "Can *you* send the letter?"

Jim thought for a moment. Yes. He agreed to send the letter.

The Lord promised us He'd make a hole in the net. That was the hole. Never in the six years we had been fighting the FTC, did a lawyer point out that we did not have to actually *sign* the letter. That technicality ended up making all the difference. Had we not sent the letter, we would have been *imprisoned indefinitely* until we agreed to send it, without a trial or jury.

The judge ordered us to reappear in a week.

* * *

Back in Rhode Island we had thousands of letters to send. We hired a local printer to print the FTC letter on Daniel Chapter One letterhead, personalized as we had been ordered to, along with personalized envelopes. We were racing the clock, since the letter had to be received by the government spy in our database by the next court date. The printer at the print shop broke, and production was slowed. Then the Post Office ran out of stamps. I told everyone it was a matter of our freedom, that if we didn't get this done we were going to jail! They probably thought I was making that up.

Two women who worked in our call center labored with us late into the night for several nights, to get the monstrous job done. We had to hire someone to help with the database, which was not organized to do such a specific job: letters had to go out to customers of the "challenged products," going back five years to the present. My fingertips were sore from affixing thousands of stamps. We had to check each letter to make sure the name coincided with the name on the envelope. Any mistake, and the government spy might not get his or her letter exactly as court ordered. We barely made the deadline.

The judge called it our "day of reckoning" the following week in court, and asked irritably if the websites could be taken down completely since the DOJ and FTC lawyers were still complaining about content. Yes, answered Bob, and the judge asked how soon. Could they be down by after lunch? Yes, Bob replied.

He called his internet technician during the lunch recess and had him take down our sites completely and lock them up. (Through that process, we lost a lot of material.) When we resumed, despite a pathetic attempt on the part of the FTC to still complain about the sites (a universal page had been put in their place) there was nothing left for them to complain about but the radio program.

The judge ordered us, "Do whatever to make them happy." We were to write a declaration that said we would stop answering health questions, even in part, and Judge Sullivan wanted it to satisfy the FTC lawyers by noon the next day. We were flying out in the morning. He also ordered us back to court the following week; we still had contempt charges on our heads. The declaration was emailed between lawyers, to and back again, through many revisions to get it just right. Finally, late at night, Jim signed it.

As we boarded the plane in Baltimore the following morning, our lawyers called to say the government lawyers still weren't happy; they wanted the word "forever" put into the declaration. Jim explained that we were about to board and had no access to a printer, and said it would have to remain as it was.

When we landed in Providence, we received another call: the judge pushed back on the FTC, and had already lifted the contempt charge! No need to go back next week. Our lawyer said he probably saw that the FTC lawyers were being petty and mean spirited, and he judged the declaration good enough. We were free, and would not need to return his court.

*   *   *

Eric had a 65th birthday party planned for his dad when we returned home. Over grilled burgers and chicken, we celebrated with friends, members of Daniel Chapter One, and family in our yard. Children, grandchildren, brother and sisters, nieces and nephews were there, happy to think it was all over and we could get on with our life.

The radio show had become problematic because of production inadequacies, and the fact that we could no longer answer health questions in any way or in part. We decided to call it quits, after 18 years. It was time. The government had succeeded in pulling the plug on *Daniel Chapter One Health Watch*.

Jim worked to keep products in stock. We moved from one manufacturer to another, through no fault of our own. One closed soon after we started with them. Each time, new labels had to be made; it was like starting a product line from scratch. Not one to get discouraged, Jim pushed ahead to keep the products available that people had come to depend on.

After receiving the government letter, many customers wrote back to us, offended by the FTC. They knew we had been forced to send it. The letter made them furious, even though its contents had been abridged somewhat by the government: the contact for the NCI had been omitted, and it stated clearly that "the FTC found," rather than its message appearing to have come from us. We had *not* signed it.

We never followed it with our own letter. The government letter had cost thousands of dollars to send, a cost we couldn't afford to repeat. Instead of letters, we sent out postcards with a line-wide offer, "Buy One Get One Free," which was well received. We determined to move forward. Once we sent the letter, our line in the sand, we submitted to full compliance with the other elements of the order, namely the government censorship.

I had imagined that discontinuing the radio show would leave a gaping emptiness in our day and in our hearts. But soon enough we settled into a new routine, and had more time to do other things. The ones hurt were the listeners, who we missed greatly, and the general public, anyone who might ever want the chance to call in to a people-to-people, spiritual program with solid answers to health questions. The government stopped the free flow of information, and if they did it to us, they've done it to others, and will continue.

Nothing was ever found false in any of our information. The legal "Finding" was that we were guilty of "false and misleading advertisement" based on the "no reasonable basis theory," "*not* based on the falsity theory." The FTC didn't have a single consumer complaint that we hurt anybody or as much as misled anybody. The FTC said we *might* harm someone someday, which is "prior restraint." Prior restraint is an injunction on something before it occurs. In the United States, prior restraint by the government is forbidden by the Constitution. There can be no prior restraint argument, according to the law. Otherwise, anyone can become a target with no evidence of harm or wrongdoing. In our case, the government had *no evidence of harm* from our products or information.

Daniel Chapter One products are God-created nutrients and herbs that are considered GRAS, "Generally Recognized as Safe," by the government. We can still sell our products and do as of early 2015, but we cannot tell you how to best use them. We cannot share any of the thousands of true testimonies of people who have been helped by specific products for specific conditions.

The "double-blind placebo controlled studies" the FTC and FDA demand, the gold standard for drugs, are out of our reach financially (one hundred million dollars for one product) and would be unethical even if we could afford it. (You have cancer, I know herbs that can help your body fight it, you may be in the group getting those herbs, or you may be in the group getting nothing but a placebo.)

Double-blind placebo controlled drug studies can be manipulated, the statistics can be manipulated, data may be covered up altogether (as was done with the arthritis drug Vioxx), or the knowledge about a drug is still incomplete because the drugs have been fast-tracked onto the market place. Drug combinations are never studied, yet most people are prescribed more than one drug at a time. All drugs have negative side-effects that are more likely to manifest in your body the longer you are on them. No drug cures.

The choice between plant-based, natural medicines or chemical drugs should be yours to make. You need information to make that choice.

CHAPTER 34

THE PROCESS

Spring and summer saw us working feverishly to keep afloat while keeping aligned with the government order. None of our materials could be shared anymore. We hired a marketer to rewrite the *Most Simple Guide*, without saying anything specific, and to write nonspecific material for websites which we had to rebuild from scratch. She also presented to chiropractors at seminars we were invited to. No longer having to support ARN and the radio program saved us thousands of dollars each month, but not having a voice cost us more. We had never advertised, did not know how, and the idea of marketing was distasteful to Jim and I. He was frustrated and angry, and our lawyers past and present thought the order unnecessarily onerous. But it was what it was.

Ben, making the documentary, had placed many of the testimonies he had collected on You Tube; the government made us take them down. With Stalinist zeal, government lawyers sought to expunge any traces of people we had helped, all Daniel Chapter One testimonies that glorified Yahshua. They made every effort to eradicate any record of the good effects of our products and of our ministry. In the raid on us, people's affidavit testimonies, some with medical records and pictures, were taken by the agents, along with thousands of people's signatures on paper petitions. By capitulating to the government's coercion, we thought we had at least shaken the FTC off our backs. But, had we?

In September 2012, we received a certified letter from the FTC, a legal brief demanding fines for the time past that we did not send their letter, did not turn over our customer list, and kept trying to help people. They demanded $11,000 per violation, per day. We had to go back to court.

It wasn't the first time, but it was one of the few times that I cried. After reading the brief, I dissolved into tears and cried out loud, "Lord, I don't want to deal with these people anymore! I just don't want to deal with these evil people anymore!" He held me together, and I regrouped.

*   *   *

The land in northern Florida lay fallow after we moved ARN to Missouri. Before that, Jonathan and his family had used a portion to grow a vegetable garden. A pastor we knew well asked Jim if he could now use some of the land to plant blueberry bushes. We knew him from when his son David worked with us on the Health Freedom Fight. His other son, Chris, had started a website on which he placed Daniel Chapter One material. The FTC complained about it, but Judge Sullivan said he had "valid free speech" as long as we were not behind it. Both men were called to testify before the Grand Jury in Rhode Island, and gave testimony to the Lord Jesus Christ.

Farming blueberries was Pastor Steve's livelihood; he took no money from his congregation. Jim offered him as much land as he could use, saying it belonged to the Lord and should be used for His Kingdom.

We, meanwhile, were not sitting around waiting for the next ax to fall. We had ministry work to do! We visited Lakeland, Florida where we had several distributors, met with them and with past radio listeners, stayed in homes, and taught how to worship freely. Free church and free worship is that which is Holy Spirit led, not contrived and organized by men. We broke bread as the Lord taught at the Last Supper, prayed, and sang, worshipping the Lord in Spirit and in Truth.

There is equality among the priesthood of believers. The Lord says *"When you come together, every one of you has a psalm, has a doctrine, has a tongue, has a revelation, has an interpretation. Let all things be done unto edifying." 1 Corinthians 14:26* This is not the practice within most church buildings, but it is the form of worship we have been involved in all over the world, and we teach it to others so that they might have greater freedom to worship by His Spirit.

*   *   *

The following May, 2013, Jim and Daniel Chapter One were deposed in Washington, DC by the US Department of Justice (DOJ), regarding ability to pay civil fines. The purpose of the deposition was for the government to collect data, a financial fact finding mission. One whole day was set for the deposition of the ministry, and the next whole day for that of Jim Feijo.

I was sick and tired of such formal, pedantic proceedings. Tempted to not dress up and wear instead jeans or sweatpants, and t-shirts, out of respect for our lawyers, Jim wore a suit coat, dress shirt and trousers, and I wore a white shirt with dress pants. Missing my dad and his solid support, I slipped on his Citizen's watch that morning. Gold in color only, it cost about $30 when new. I wore it caring for him when he was dying, in order to time his pulse, and after he passed my sister told me to keep it. It would be something of him with me that day, since I couldn't call as I usually did and he wouldn't be praying for us as he usually did.

Jim and I sat on a bench facing a giant, smiling face of President Obama, and beside it, a giant, smiling face of Eric Holder, while waiting to be brought to the specified meeting room in the Department of Justice building. After that wait, we were told to put our personal belongings through an x-ray machine, then were made to stand in a clear Plexiglas cubicle, one at a time, until a man on the other side granted us entrance and escorted us upstairs.

We recognized the young man as one of the government spies who testified against us. He seemed nice, I wanted to talk to him as a person but didn't know quite what to say. We were mutually cordial.

I could have been prohibited from sitting in the room when the deposition was held, but was allowed to accompany Jim both days. Bob sat between us. The DOJ lawyer did not tell me to leave, as had the FTC lawyers in the past. That was an answer to prayer. Jim and I prayed beforehand to be allowed to stay together and not be separated.

The day was long, the questions tedious and all about money. I kept silent, unacknowledged at the end of the table. I had not been sworn in, and was expected to keep quiet and invisible. The DOJ was salivating to discover how much Daniel Chapter One and Jim Feijo were worth.

It's redundant to depose the two, Daniel Chapter One and Jim Feijo, so the second day was much of the same as the first. We sat again at the large office table that filled most of the room, and Jim answered many questions over again. A new, male trainee sat beside the DOJ lawyer Jessica Gunder, sitting across from us, there to observe and learn.

I read my Bible. I prayed. I listened. I grew frustrated at the line of questioning, which was then directed at Jim's personal worth. He is not the greedy con man they think he is, or were falsely trying to depict. We live simply and own nothing, everything is in the name of the ministry. Others use the cars, use the houses, and if we die tomorrow everything stays in the ministry. We've never had insurance, personal savings, a retirement fund or any such accounts. We do not have the lavish lifestyle of mega preachers that the government kept trying to portray.

Jim gave brief answers, too brief I thought. Ms. Gunder was asking leading questions and begging the question. I held my tongue, until she made comments about me. Leading up to it, she asked Jim about his "collections."

"I don't have any" he stated.

"Coins? Gold? Silver? China? Antiques?"

Jim shook his head and answered no after each.

"Watches?"

"No, I don't even own one."

Eyes straight ahead on Jim, without as much as a glance at me, she said, "Ohhh, come on, I see your wife . . . she has a *beautiful* watch . . . and a *gorgeous* bracelet."

Jim was stunned. What was she was talking about? What beautiful, gorgeous, *expensive jewelry* (from the tone of the assertion) was she referring to? Where did she get those things?!

The stenographer typed away, word for word.

I sprung to my feet, and across Bob said to Jim, "That just went on the record, and that needs to be corrected!"

Then I directed my words to the government lawyer, pulling off the watch and setting it down with force in front of her, from across the table.

"My father passed away last year and this was his watch! It has nothing but sentimental value! Look at it! It's cheap metal!" I was livid. Attacking my husband was enough to endure, but her smug comment about the watch was more than I could bear. I wanted to grab her by her tweed business suit jacket, and scream that she didn't know what she was talking about! None of the lawyers who've come against us have known what they were talking about.

"And this bracelet? You think these are diamonds? It's glass!!" I was fuming, thinking: *you foolish girl, you foolish, envious girl.* The "gorgeous" bracelet she referred to was a thin braid of leather with glass beads interspersed, that I paid $15 for in a clothing store.

She sat speechless. Bob told me to sit down. Jim said, "Be quiet, Honey."

A recess was suggested. We left the building. Outside on the sidewalk, Bob came up to me and said quietly, "Good for you Tricia! That needed to be said. Just don't do it again."

Jim shook his head, smiled, and said, "*Myyy* wife."

After lunch, we reconvened. The trainee didn't come back. Attorney Gunder took only another 15 minutes or so, and called it quits for the day. We shouldn't have had to go back, but then, we did recess abruptly. The FTC did not contact us again until after we were indicted on criminal charges, the following year.

*   *   *

The CID, the IRS, and the FDA were involved in the raid on us. In his book, *World Without Cancer* (1974), on p. 49 author G. Edward Griffin describes exactly what the government does to those who help people with cancer naturally; exactly what the government did to Daniel Chapter One, "*Once an individual has incurred the wrath of the FDA, he can expect to find himself the target of harassment from other agencies of the federal government as well. Probably first at his door will be the man from the IRS to scrutinize his tax records with a determination to find something wrong. If the defendant sells a product, the Federal Trade Commission will take a highly personal interest in his operations."*

On p. 417, regarding the difficulty and futility of fighting their might, he wrote,

> *"Regardless of one's financial resources . . . he cannot hope to match the unlimited resources of the federal government. Private citizens must hire attorneys. The government has buildings full of attorneys on the tax payroll just waiting to justify their salaries. It matters not to the FDA how long the litigation drags on . . . part of its strategy (is) to bankrupt the defendant with astronomical legal expenses."*

> *"On top of this financial handicap, the defendant must face the fact that there are very few judges or juries who will have the courage to decide a case against the FDA . . ."* (p. 418)

The FDA had visited us several times before, seeing that we're a very small operation with children and babies in the workplace. Yet they raided us with full force: armed, loud, and threatening. One must ask, why?

As an aside, back when Daniel Chapter One was in its infancy, an armed agent came in undercover and proceeded to take honey off the shelves. He also embargoed some name brand sports supplements. We called the company, whose lawyer contacted the FDA, who in that case wrote a letter of apology to us. Shades of things to come: the situation has only worsened under a government now larger and more tyrannical, proof that their thuggery will only grow if not reined in. Is there a tipping point in the future, I wonder, or, a point of no return?

After the raid on us, the Grand Jury proceedings began and continued into the following year. We heard nothing for a couple years after that. When a journalist for the conservative magazine *The New American* wrote an article about our case, our lawyers asked us to intercept it from being published so as not to "stir the hornet's nest." Every step along the way, with every legal team and new development, and especially once the criminal investigation was underway, Jim and I were asked to remain quiet and not grant reporters interviews. But by silence, tyranny continues unnoticed!

Yet we obliged, suppressing our strong desire to speak out. We know the media twists things. Herb Titus put it this way to us, quoting Scripture: "*Be wise as serpents, and gentle as doves.*" Unless the Lord told us otherwise, we agreed to show restraint.

We were indicted in May 2014. That brought a flurry of media attention and attorney activity, and Jim and I were subject to the all the unpleasantness of being accused criminals. When we lost our civil case against the FTC in 2010, the *Providence Journal* was alerted before our lawyers knew. Herb and Bill found that surprising, but it shows how the government uses the media to promote their side of a story. Mainstream media sources play right along. We were on the front page of, no less, the Sunday edition, with one perverted "doctor" (an unlicensed psychiatrist) who has made it his life's mission to deride natural healing, quoted as saying, "The administrative law judge simply tore their arguments to shreds." He doesn't know us, and he wasn't there. The only way he got to weigh in on our case, was that the FTC used him as one of their puppets.

After the criminal indictment, we had to appear at the Providence federal courthouse for arraignment. Newspapers and television stations had a field day. Reporters came to our storefront and house, and camped out on our front lawn. We refused interviews. Because we happened to be visiting Jill and the grandchildren once when the media showed up, they accused us of fleeing or hiding to prevent scrutiny. The media purposely made us look guilty. We tried to ignore them.

Jim was arraigned first, on several felony and misdemeanor charges. At his arraignment, he had to be fingerprinted and photographed. The scanning machine broke after his left finger prints were successfully scanned, so the officer said he'd take the right prints later.

The following week I was arraigned, and Jim again. While a reporter waited out front with his camera, I was photographed and talked to a probation officer as Jim had before me. Then we went to have fingerprints taken. My lawyer objected since I only faced misdemeanor charges, and I was dismissed from the procedure. Jim went to have his hands scanned again. That's when the scanning machine broke a second time, again when it came to Jim's right hand.

"You aren't going to get this guy's prints!" said the officer. The machine failed only those two times for Jim, and worked otherwise for others. The Lord is sovereign.

On their way out, the door lock broke. After passing cells surrounded by agents, an officer punched in his key code on a keypad high on the wall, then attempted to use a key to unlock the door. That proved oddly unsuccessful, and he had to call and wait for someone to come let them out.

"*That's* the power of God" said my lawyer, Tom Briody, as we walked down the hall.

Because Bob and Stephen are licensed only in California, we had to hire criminal defense attorneys in Rhode Island as well. We hired Tom to represent me, and Chuck Tamuleviz to represent Jim. They are working together with Bob and Stephen, and are responsible for filings in Rhode Island.

Our case was continuing to be exceedingly expensive, with no end in sight. The ministry account had dwindled significantly, after we had spent millions of dollars on legal expenses to this point. The remaining funds were depleted between the four criminal defense attorneys.

With bank accounts exhausted and closed, and revenue way down, we were barely making ends meet. Jim always said it would have to be "a Gideon experience." Gideon was a judge who went to war for Israel. According to the biblical account in Judges, chapter 7, the Lord reduced the size of Gideon's army substantially so it would be clear that God's power, not human power, won the battle.

CHAPTER 35

TRIALS AND BLESSINGS

In the fallout from our legal battles, most people working with us left. We were down to one man in the warehouse and two women in the office; down from once having a full house including three graphic artists. We also cut back on personal bills as much as possible. We terminated all phone land lines we didn't absolutely need, including my office line. I no longer practice formally, although I continue to work with special cases as the Lord leads.

Not all fruit born from the government assault on us was bad. Good came out of it too. We met people we otherwise would not have, and have had opportunity to help many with their health problems, lawyers included.

We may be avoided and whispered about in our hometown, by those who don't know us personally, but true friends and believers have been there for us, with encouragement, and prayers. The bond of love between us has grown sweeter and tighter. It's been an ideal time to witness about the love and faithfulness of Yahshua, and to talk to others about what really matters in life.

One of the greatest blessings the Lord has wrought through the evil of others has been the fulfillment of Jim's vision for the land in Florida. Besides the planned warehouse, he saw a school, a farm, and a community ministry there. After ARN was moved off the land, it lay unused for many months, a desolate reminder of what once was.

Now Pastor Steve and his family live there, overseeing their ministry, Sowing Seeds Farm. Children's voices carry in the winds that sweep over vegetable and herb gardens, and the grounds teem with animals. Disciples live and work on the land in harmony.

We met Steve's family when his son David, 19 years old at the time and still living at home, worked with us as part of our early support team for what we called the Health Freedom Fight. When we traveled to Lakeland, Florida to do a presentation, Steve and his wife invited us to stay in their home and to use their car. We were blessed by their fellowship.

When Jim told the pastor that the land was his to use for blueberry farming, Steve went to inspect the property. He found several varieties of berry bushes growing wild in the wooded area behind the front roadside field. He would cultivate the wild berries instead, and eventually moved into a trailer on the property with his wife.

Steve's son, Chris, moved with his family onto the land as well. He, his wife, and their four, home schooled children farm the land with Steve and Deborah. A baby boy has just been born to him and his wife, their fifth child, the first baby to be born to them while on the farm. They named him Judah, the Hebrew of which is Yahudah, meaning High Praise.

Besides the trailer, the property came with a barn, an aviary, and animal pens, now being utilized. Worship services have been held in the barn; one on the Sabbath, which is Saturday, and one on Sunday. The aviary houses ducks and chickens, and the stalls house sheep, goats, and a donkey. Livestock guardian dogs protect the chickens, and Zebu cows graze in the field. Zebus are a special breed that only grow to three feet in height; useful for milk, but manageable for children.

As part of the Sowing Seeds Farm ministry, men and women have been welcomed from Steve's church in Live Oak, and Jacksonville, Gainesville and Lakeland, to learn how to plant and grow their own food. People from the congregation take home the freshly grown vegetables. It's the perfect solution to provide for people's needs: give them a way and a means to provide for themselves.

Sowing Seeds Farm also obtained several horses, which the land can both accommodate and feed, two Paso Fino mares and a stallion. The horses are named for their gait, literally meaning "fine gait." They seemingly glide, rather than move in a horse's commonly jarring fashion under the rider. Underprivileged and abused children have been brought to the farm and taught to ride the horses as therapy. Several homeless people have been brought to live on the farm, and Chris has a vision for a house to be built on the property which could accommodate people recently released from prison.

As it is for Daniel Chapter One, the mission of Sowing Seeds Farm is to do as Jesus did: meet individual's physical needs to reach them spiritually. In His earthly ministry the Lord Yahshua healed and fed people, and while doing so taught them spiritual truths. The early church was a spiritual church made up of believers who met in their homes, lived together, and had everything in common.

Life on the farm has not been easy. The families have been tried and tested through health problems primarily, acknowledging spiritual warfare and that the Lord's grace is sufficient to see them through. Two of the cows died last winter, one right after giving birth. A neighbor invited them to give the calf to a cow she had, which may or may not succeed. The calf took to nursing from the neighbor's cow without problem. Chris saw it as hope for the future, of the redemption and renewal of Yahshua.

Out of death, comes life; out of tribulation, victory.

CHAPTER 36

BANNED

After writing the previous chapter, on the evening of March 31, 2015 we received an unexpected, expanded order from the DOJ completely shutting down Daniel Chapter One.

"Banned from selling dietary supplements. . ." it read, the sentence set in boldface type.

Nearly falling off the couch, I read the words out loud to Jim. The lawyers, Bob and Stephen, couldn't talk to us for a few days but wrote that we would discuss it later. "*The Voice* is almost on" I said, looking at the clock. We did what we did most Tuesday nights: watched the singing competition, then went to bed.

When I awoke, unfamiliar sadness met me in the morning, as if someone close to me had died. When my sleepy brain came to, I remembered the new federal court order. It hadn't been a dream. Daniel Chapter One, after 29 years of ministry, had just been handed a death sentence.

Days before, I heard the Lord say to wait upon Him, with emphasis on the word *Wait*. At the time, I didn't know why. The Lord told us again clearly, "Wait," when Jim and I prayed about the shutdown.

That Friday, which happened to be Good Friday, we talked to the lawyers. Bob said, "I don't know what got into that judge." Judge Sullivan further ordered that Jim and Daniel Chapter one must pay $1,345,832.43 as equitable monetary relief, due in one week with interest accruing afterwards, and $3,528,000 as a civil penalty. The shutdown was immediate, no wind-down time. "Give them what you can," our lawyers instructed, and said they'd get to work on an appeal.

Jim offered the lawyers more money for the work they now had to do that was not part of our financial agreement, but they refused to take payment, saying, "We just want to try to make a bad thing better."

Jim wire-transferred $60,000 from the critically depleted Daniel Chapter One bank account to the FTC. That was all we had left.

A friend of Jim's had come to visit, and needed a ride to the airport early Sunday. Jim drove him and I stayed behind, settling into a plastic lounge chair behind the house. It was Easter morning. The sky overhead cloaking palm trees and adobe, tan, and pink colored houses was serene, as was the man-made pond mirroring it.

"DOOOOOO!   DOO-DOO-DOO! DOOTOODOOTOOOOOO!!!" A loud, short, and then long, magnificent blast of a shofar sounded from miles away.

The ram's horn! Stirred, I sat up. It sounded again, piercing the stillness with the strength of its blast.

Nothing had changed, but everything changed for me.

I ran inside and googled the significance of the shofar. It's used, for one, as an instrument of spiritual warfare, "*And if you go to war in your land against the enemy that oppresses you, then you shall blow an alarm with the trumpets; and you shall be remembered before Yahweh your God, and you shall be saved from your enemies.*" *Numbers 10:9*

The blast of the shofar represents the shout of God's victory over sin and death to the believer in Yahshua. The Lord, He is King; victorious, and will come again at the sound of the trumpet! The battle is His. Hallelujah!!! I was dancing inside when Jim came home, no longer downcast, certain that our wonderful Lord and Savior had blown that horn for *my* ears. There was nothing to fear or worry about.

In the coming days I spoke with many people, customers, distributors, who wept over the vindictive, mean-spirited destruction of the Daniel Chapter One ministry. I comforted them with the revelation of God in the shofar. Yahweh is in control. It will be all right! He is preparing for battle, and is coming again soon.

While speaking to one of our distributors in Florida, a woman came on the phone and told me about the breast cancer she had and how the Lord healed her with Daniel Chapter One products. I continue to hear many such testimonies, every day for months now since the shut-down, from people calling in the hopes they can still obtain the products.

The federal government said it sought to "broaden coverage" of the FTC order "to enhance the compliance monitoring . . . necessary to protect the public." Without a consumer complaint of any harm or deception in the three decades of Daniel Chapter One, they had to protect whom? The SS wing of the Nazi party stood for "Schultzstaffel," which means "protection squad." The protection was not of the people. Concentration camps were first used to imprison "unfit members of society" including "members of minority religions."

Judge Sullivan's newest order read: "The FTC order did not achieve its purpose of protecting the public and demonstrate that they likely will repeat their fraudulent activities and victimize consumers unless practices are more significantly curtailed." The injunction against Daniel Chapter One and Jim Feijo is based upon "the degree of consumer harm." But the government had no evidence of *any* harm.

"I'm really sorry we can't get our hands on those great herbal products . . . but, God's still going to get the glory! Boy, we miss you so much! A lot of us studied under you . . . we're all your students. Now, even though you can't sell the products, you need to come back on the radio and give all that commitment you gave us all those years, showing how much you love humanity. . . keep in mind, can't nobody suppress knowledge and truth!" Al from Georgia left his message on the answering machine. I continue to receive many like it. The problem is that we've been bled out financially, and doing a radio show was expensive. Money to support the radio ministry came from the sale of supplements.

*   *   *

We began to dismantle Daniel Chapter One as soon as we returned to Rhode Island from Florida. With income cut off, we had to terminate all contracts we could, shut down phone lines, and let go the few people left working with us. The sign in front of the back business building, Biomolecular Nutrition Center, was painted over white, and now stands blank, weeds climbing up its long legs.

The radio room has become a dusty receptacle of books and papers, the sound-absorbing foam hanging off the walls in parts. The store below is dead quiet, dark, and full of boxes of products we brought up from the warehouse. Kid's toys litter the floor from happier times when the office girls brought their children to work, including Jill and our grand-daughters. I didn't feel like straightening up.

Customers initially came to the door begging to be let in to get what they needed. We had to turn them away. One man from Florida, a retired truck driver, came by just to say hello. Jim pulled out his phone camera with Frank's permission and recorded him sharing a testimony of his mother and how she was healed of metastasized breast cancer with Daniel Chapter One products. Such testimonies never cease.

The other day a man called for GDU, saying that his wife had arthritis and was told she'd need surgery, but after using the product "She doesn't have arthritis anymore!" He went on to say that his sister-in-law was bedridden after given prednisone, for three months, but after starting on the ENDO24 was up walking around again.

One has to ask, what hate is this against us, against all these people?

I continue to field messages left on the main office line we kept active. Many days I'm encouraged and blessed in talking to the person I call back, whether by their testimony, gratitude expressed, or prayer we pray together. I've taken on that job to protect Jim, the named Respondent in both the civil (FTC) and the criminal case (IRS and FDA), but realize that it must be God's design for me, the weaker vessel, to be filled in this way. Talking to past Daniel Chapter One customers renews the spirit within me. I have no regrets, and am grateful for the work and the ministry the Lord had us do.

Back in the days we defied the FTC order, it was mostly Jim's idea and his lead to help people anyway. It would be easy for me to blame him now, to get angry with him, but when I talk to the people who call, I'm reminded that we did it for them. Out of love for neighbor, brothers and sisters, we kept helping people when an unrighteous government order told us to stop. I have no regrets. But I need to be taken back to the compulsion we felt then, and the compassion I feel when talking to people we've helped is how the Lord brings that to me.

Before we left Florida, our friends had a surprise Going Away Party that turned into a "Happy Retirement" party for us. Jim read to the small group gathered that evening in the Coldren's kitchen from *1 Peter, 4:12, 13: "Beloved, think it not strange concerning the fiery trial which is to try you, as though some strange thing has happened to you: But rejoice, inasmuch as you are partakers of the Messiah's sufferings; that, when His glory shall be revealed, you may be glad also with exceeding joy."*

Rejoice, we did! The group clapped at the end, not sure what else to do, and because God's Word is mighty and worthy of applause. Then we enjoyed the party. Why worry about tomorrow, today has enough problems of its own, the Lord says.

However, joy just washes over our undeniable sadness. We feel more hurt for others than for ourselves: our hearts ache for the elderly woman who called asking for ENDO24 for her sick husband, for the people who call because they don't want to be experimented upon with chemo, for the young parents who don't want to drug their children.

As of April 1, 2015, we can no longer sell Daniel Chapter One products, and have been further court-ordered not to give them away or distribute them in any manner, nor transfer formulas, other information, or data bases to anyone else. Thirty years of hard work and success the tyrants want buried. The court order commands us to destroy our customer base within 15 days of government notice.

Separate from the civil case, on April 15, 2015 we appeared in Rhode Island Federal Court on a motion to dismiss the criminal charges brought by the FDA and the IRS. Judge McConnell at one point said, "Sounds like a First Amendment Rights case . . . religious freedom. You can argue that to a jury, not that I'm telling you to. But I'm not going to dismiss it today."

Outside, our lawyers told us it went "very well" despite what we heard. "The prosecutor doesn't like this case. He wasn't really against you, usually a prosecutor is. . . ". Small comfort, we had just been shot down again. Again, a judge sided with the government, and there was nothing we could do. We'd have to go to trial.

Meanwhile, I began to prepare to restart my homeopathy practice, and to possibly begin teaching.

Some people have sent in checks of support and encouragement. I've written to each personally, though there aren't words adequate to express our gratitude. We maintain hope and have the Lord's peace, get up every day, and go about our non-business.

We next received a call from our legal team, the two lawyers in California together with our two criminal defense attorneys in Rhode Island, saying it was urgent that we conference.

CHAPTER 37

THE DEAL

The government had made an offer, a step towards resolution. If Jim pleaded guilty to one felony and one misdemeanor, the AUSA promised no jail or prison time, and all charges against me would be dropped. Our lawyers felt this was a great deal. I asked what it meant for Jim, what ramifications there are for being a convicted felon.

"Your travel may be restricted, you can't own a gun, you may not be able to vote, and probably can't get a teaching job." Nothing we cared much about, except the freedom to travel.

When I asked what it meant for me, my lawyer Tom said, "You win!" Not how I would put it, but the Lord did promise me the morning after the raid that the flames would not touch me. He also said to me, "And morning never came," back when I was planning to write this book from prison.

Prior to the plea deal offer, while negotiations between our lawyers and the government were ongoing, the Lord gave me *Matthew 5:25–26*, "*Agree with your adversary quickly, while you are in the way with him . . .*" In light of that, Jim and I believed that a deal was something we were supposed to agree to, so without any more discussion we said yes, we would take the deal.

Brightening, Jim said "One hurdle out of the way!"

But the next morning we received another call, this time from the lawyers telling us that the prosecutor, Donnelly, called back to say he could no longer offer no prison time because his boss in Washington wouldn't let him. Our lawyers said he was apologetic, embarrassed even. Bob, and Tom later, explained that Donnelly's "boss" in the IRS

Department had said, "We have to get a felony out of this" when Bob tried to talk them down to a misdemeanor.

The felony could mean five years in prison, the misdemeanor, another full year. It would be far riskier to go to trial, according to our legal counsel. A jury is unpredictable, a courtroom is often not a place of justice, and, they told us, the judge would look more favorably upon Jim for accepting a deal and entering a plea. On the other hand, if he pushed to go to trial, he'd likely suffer "trial penalty" that would result in maximum time, much more than six years, and possibly prison time for me as well.

We didn't want to base a decision on human reasoning. We strained to hear from the Lord, because all that mattered to us was to do what He wanted us to.

The wording of the charges in the plea was not definite yet, Bob suggested. The felony involved employee withholding tax, the misdemeanor "putting unapproved drugs on the marketplace." We had a problem with both: the tax issue because, we sincerely thought, according to our 508 filing with the IRS we were not responsible for independent contractors who paid their own taxes. The "drug" issue we found most offensive. Daniel Chapter One products are not drugs, the FDA knows they are not drugs. It's a perversion to call God-created herbs and nutrients drugs. Bob suggested that it was reasonable to request the wording be changed.

While in Maine visiting my brother and his family, we received an email with the final deal to sign. It was not what we had been told. Besides the nearly quarter million dollars they wanted us to agree we owed the IRS for "employee" withholding tax from 2007–2008, the charges included others that were not supposed to be part of the deal. The misdemeanor still included the word "drug."

"Can't sign it," we told them, feeling betrayed. Bob agreed it was different than what had been discussed. Chuck took it back to the prosecutor, and it was rewritten. The government refused to omit the word "drug" from the FDA charge however. It was the final and best offer we'd get. Jim finally signed an email copy of the deal on his cell phone and sent it. "They need a hard copy signature, can you get it to Chuck today?" urged Stephen in an email.

Jim's computer had crashed during our last Skype conference, so there was no way for him to print out the deal and sign it. The office computers, the internet in the back building, had all been shut down.

During that conference with Stephen, Chuck, and Tom, Jim became distracted by the sudden computer crash (distressed that he may have lost everything on his computer), and mumbled something to which Tom (who earlier had charged with frustration, "Do you want all our work to go out the window?!") said, "Jim you sound tired. Look, you made some bad business decisions is all" to which Jim took umbrage and firmly said, "I did everything I was supposed to do!" As far as he was concerned he had always done things according to the law. The government chose to ignore our documents, and made their case against us unfairly. They disregarded the Constitution, the Bible, and our religious corporation sole, as it suited them too.

Back to the push to get a hard copy signature to Chuck in Providence: We had been shut down with the typed name of Judge Sullivan, not even a signature. Yet they required a hard copy signature from Jim? "Because it's a very serious matter," said Tom. It was not a serious matter when the government shut us down completely? As an aside, the same judge who 'signed off' on the injunction against us – rubber-stamped it, basically – also was presiding over Hillary Clinton's email scandal and the Lois Lerner IRS scandal. Perhaps ours is *not* such a serious matter to him.

There are no coincidences. God is sovereign and purposeful, so we put the brakes on. We would not sign the deal. If they accepted the electronic signature we would have honored our word, but they did not. We had no way to print a hard copy. We prayed, the decision before us again heavy.

"What about Esther?" I asked Jim one morning. She took her chances, saying "*If I die, I die*" and went before the king for the sake of the Jewish people.

"Right. It's not about us," replied Jim, "We should go to trial for the truth."

That night he sent all our lawyers an email stating our position: we would go to trial.

Bob called us at home that evening, "What happened?" He re-numerated the reasons we had agreed to the plea deal, primarily that it was the best way for us both to avoid prison. Although Donnelly reneged on his promise of no prison for Jim, he did promise to remain neutral, and that everything against me would be dropped. "Not to be paternal . . .," said Bob, tugging at us to reconsider.

We once again acquiesced, but asked to see the itemized list of "employees" we were said to be responsible for withholding tax from, since the monetary figure seemed excessive. The next day Jim's computer started back up, as surprising as when it crashed. We received the list of names, and I went ballistic. Many were people we had given money gifts to, to help them. Large sums of money. And others were independent contractors hired to do a job like help with the radio tower in Utah, much as we had hired our lawyers to work on our legal case; not "employees" of Daniel Chapter One!

When we spoke to the lawyers about it, they said it would "open a can of worms" to contest the list. While the government would, most likely, leave people alone if Jim accepted responsibility, they would go after them if he did not. What could he do? He did not want the people on that list harassed. He would not sacrifice others to save money or his own flesh. Since the Lord hadn't given us a clear word on what to do, Jim based his decision on the principle "consider others more important than yourself."

Down to the wire with the time we had from the government, he signed the hard copy. We gave up our right to a jury trial. Coerced? Of course we had been. The whole case against us has been coercion from the start. Due to Jim's computer crash, we at least had the additional opportunity to take a stand, and did with the email saying we would go to trial. We did not fear. We just wanted to go to trial, or not, for right reasons.

* * *

Summer passed quickly, and Jim entered his plea before the judge. We were asked to babysit Mya that week, our youngest granddaughter, so I stayed behind with her the morning of Jim's appearance before

Judge McConnell. Jim later told me that as the prosecutor laid out the charge of putting unapproved drugs on the marketplace, specifically referring to 7 Herb Formula, he took his lawyer aside and said, "These products have never harmed anyone, and FDA approved drugs kill thousands of people every day!"

Chuck said he'd see what he could do. When asked by the judge if he had any objections to the language of the counts, Chuck said, "With respect to Count XIX, Mr. Feijo admits . . . that there was not an application made to the FDA about 7 Herb Formula, and he admits that the FDA did not approve or render any approval of that product . . . He also, and I don't want to quibble over things that don't really matter, He did ask me to add to the proffer, if you will, that in the years 7 Herb Formula was marketed, he is not aware of anybody. . .suffering any harm from their consumption of the product."

To that, Prosecutor Donnelly addressed the judge, ". . . Mr. Feijo wanted it added to the statement of facts . . . (that) nobody was ever harmed by 7 Herb Formula, *and the Government has no evidence to submit otherwise.*"

His statement went on the record. Chuck felt the morning went well. Jim's sentencing date was set for January 12, 2016.

Next, Jim had to go for a presentencing interview, several weeks later, for the purpose of a written report for the judge prior to sentencing. Molly, a new probation officer there, would not allow me in the room for the interview. So I typed out a timeline for Jim: dates of graduations and jobs, marriages and births, all on one sheet of paper. He would have struggled without that; as it was, the interview was 2 ½ hours long.

"She asked questions I've never heard asked before" said Chuck afterwards.

She asked Jim about how he got saved, about how and why we traveled to China and Israel and Poland, and about his faith. She also asked, "How do you feel about what the government's done to you?"

"Sad" replied Jim, honestly. "Sad that I can't help people anymore like I used to."

*   *   *

I tore the ivy off the stone wall in front of the house with great fervor. It felt liberating to rip the thin branches out from the crevices they had crept into, from where the ivy clutched stone; to tear away and then gather yards and yards of the vine rope adorned with giant green leaves and throw it in a heap of yard trimmings. Until then, I hadn't noticed that the wall had become completely obscured.

"A lazy man lets vines grow on his walls," the Lord showed me in Proverbs later that day. I don't know that it was laziness, but something kept me from paying attention to it. Despair? Depression? Apathy? Now that the criminal case looked like it was coming to an end, whatever the reason, my inertia was dissolving. Jim said he thought I wanted the wall that way, so purposely left it alone. I removed the ivy because I thought it might be destructive to the wall. At any rate, it felt good that day to yank it out.

We were able to plant a small garden in the summer, with time we hadn't had for years. Reminiscent of when we first started Daniel Chapter One, we planted lettuce, tomatoes, kale, cucumbers, Swiss chard, beets, and Asian pears; home-grown food to defray grocery bills.

In the fall, tomato vines hung brown from the sticks they were tethered to with pieces of nylon, a few final green balls bowing their withered stalks. All else has been uprooted, and the bare earth was waiting to become frozen and covered with snow until spring's thaw, with the expectation of next year's planting.

But no man knows what tomorrow may bring.

The evening of Jim's presentencing interview we heard from Herman and Yvonne Matthews, whom we met and stayed with in Newfoundland on our honeymoon, and visited with Jill a few years later. We caught up in brief over email and Facebook. Tragically, their daughter Kimberly passed away at age 19, two weeks after giving birth to a daughter whom they've raised. Their granddaughter, now 21, is getting married in November. I explained why we cannot accept their invitation to visit Canada at this time. Our tribulations pale in comparison, but I shared that the good Lord has been our strength, as they said He's been theirs.

Other voices from the past came back to bless us, and to be blessed by us. Rodney called soon after Daniel Chapter One was shuttered.

"Hang in there, God's got something better!" He had a stroke 10 years ago and his legs and guitar-playing hand have been paralyzed since, confining him to bed and a wheelchair. When he first left Daniel Chapter One he slandered our church, but later repented and came to visit, servicing our bicycles and washing our cars as a gift. Then we lost touch again, until after his stroke. When we were sued by the FTC, unbeknownst to him, he called asking for help to get a door for his wheelchair van, and Jim, without hesitation, bought him a door.

*　　*　　*

Meanwhile, the third Republican Presidential Debate aired last night. During the debate, it was said that the Obama Department of Justice is political, that they shame and destroy those they don't like and exonerate those they do. Lois Lerner will face no repercussions for her illegal bias against Tea Party groups and obstruction of justice (she destroyed her emails and the IRS completely destroyed the computer hard drives), while the same Department of "Justice" punished General Petraeus for sharing classified information with his mistress. Speaking of classified information, Hillary Clinton is an exposed liar, yet it is said her "performance" during the Benghazi hearings was so good, the week was the best of her presidential campaign.

Two of the candidates on the debate stage know about Daniel Chapter One, Rand Paul and Mike Huckabee. Both men are sympathetic to our plight. Ben Carson was asked a question about his involvement with a dietary supplement company described as settling a deceptive advertising suit. We've spoken with the founder and owner of that company; he claims that he, too, was wrongfully sued and had little choice but to settle. We tried to get him and others to band with us, but the supplement industry is too divided and competitive to join forces. Every company owner is fighting for his own life, uninterested and afraid to serve the bigger picture.

As a further aside, the FTC administrative law judge who issued the first Order against Daniel Chapter One, Judge Chappell, has presided over major national trade cases, like the suit against Whole Foods. He ordered the grocery store chain to split up and sell stores "to

FTC-approved buyers." There again, the government harasses who it wants to.

We're small, but we've been playing with big players. Washington attorneys watching our case with interest "don't know how such a small ministry has been able to fight the government" as we have. I used to find it amusing, but realize now that Jim's wise stewardship and the grace of God, which has allowed us to do the impossible, has not helped our cause. The beast is not impressed. It rages at us in vehement hatred. We are Daniel before the king, David against Goliath.

> *"And when the Philistine looked about, and saw David, he disdained him: for he was but a youth . . . And (he) said to David, "Am I a dog, that you come to me with sticks?" And (he) cursed David by his gods." 1 Samuel 17:42*

They either think we're bigger than we are, that we have cleverly hidden our net worth from them, or they despise our insignificant size. Before the judge, during our Motion to Dismiss, prosecutor Donnelly described Daniel Chapter One as "a very sophisticated operation," legal phraseology used against a criminal enterprise. The more "sophisticated" the "fraudulent activity," the greater the punishment. They have to pretend that we're big and bad to justify their harsh treatment of us. Chuck argued against the insinuation. For one, he presented the fact that nothing was ever hidden, there were no offshore accounts or things of that nature.

Most people we talk to understand the political nature of our case and Big Pharma's involvement. Many express that the real criminals are those operating within our corrupt government, including administrative agencies like the FTC, FDA, and the IRS, which wield unlawful power. The Constitution begins with "All legislative Powers herein granted shall be vested in Congress." The word "All" makes it an exclusive vesting of the legislative powers in an *elected* legislature.

The Supreme Court rendered a decision in 1984 (*Chevron v. Natural Resources Defense Council*) which requires judges to defer to "any reasonable interpretation" of an ambiguous statute by a federal agency. That ruling basically requires judges to abandon due process and independent judgment. The decks are stacked on the side of the federal agency in court cases, perverting the entire "judicial" process.

Tyrannical administrative agencies do not fool all the people, and never fool the Lord. Their successes are fleeting. He will ultimately judge and will vindicate us one day. He told me our house will stand:

> "*As the whirlwind passes, so is the wicked no more: but the righteous has an everlasting foundation.*" Prov. 10:25

> "*The wicked are overthrown, and are not: but the house of the righteous shall stand.*" Prov. 12:7

For eight long years, throughout the frustrating battle with the FTC, FDA, and the IRS, the Lord has kept His promises and preserved us. He tells us to be content with food and clothing. Even if the government takes our properties and possessions, we're to be joyful and are prepared to remain so. They cannot take our greatest treasure.

CHAPTER 38

JUDGMENT

Jim's sentencing was postponed one week, to January 19, 2016. Dark clouds descended over our old farm house the night before, and the storm came. Rain pelted the windows and roof, and strong, violent winds shook the building into the night, felt most in the upstairs bedroom. We were quiet, not fearful, though we did not expect to see justice in the morning.

"I'm sorry." Jim didn't say for what, and I didn't ask. It was understood. He knew the hardship his decisions had been on me, and would be, and for that he apologized. He was not apologetic, however, for doing what he thought was right in the eyes of the Lord. We said very little to each other that night. Jim fell asleep despite the noise of the storm and the shaking of the house, but I couldn't sleep. So I got up, wrote the following poem, and stuck it in a card for him to find in the morning:

1986

Oh blessed year! We had begun /selling health food, souls to be won! / No eye or ear knew what He had planned/come 2015 and all was banned.

Standing firm, we trust in His grace/His Truth, His Life, they cannot erase! / They stole peoples' stories, censored our speech/ The Constitution they did breech.

But the Lord, He is sovereign/ He reigns on high!/ He's coming again , that day draws neigh./ He'll scatter our foe, burn them like chaff/ our tears He will dry, and He'll make us laugh.

"Patience," He tells us to trust in His plan/ "My peace I give you, not that of a man."/ He sees what they're doing, knows what they've done/ while we are to look to The One, to The Son.

He's done it before and He'll do it again: / causes the drought, and then brings the rain. / He gives and He takes for His holy desire/ and lovingly works to bring us higher.

Inside the card I wrote, "Whether free or in prison, I'm with you."

*　　*　　*

I sat in the courtroom the next morning on a bench behind my lawyer. Jim sat with his lawyers, Bob and Chuck, below and to the right of the judge (to my left.) Several government agents involved in the raid on Daniel Chapter One sat on benches across the aisle, to my right.

"I'm going to Spain!" I heard one say.

"You're going to Spain?!" laughed another.

The room was buzzing with many animated conversations, like a house party. All of a sudden, it became quiet and tense at the order to stand for the judge.

Judge McConnell began by thanking family and friends who had submitted letters of character reference, saying it was hard not to be moved by them. None of the people he spoke to were there however, just Jim and I.

Prosecutor Donnelly spoke at length. "Obviously there's a lot of positives that can be pointed to . . . there are many factors here that might say the court should spare Mr. Feijo a prison sentence. . . however, the government comes before you and asks that the Defendant be sentenced. . . some just incarceration time to send a message . . . "

He talked about other businesses "that take the time and expense to do proper testing that the Food, Drug, and Cosmetic Act that Congress requires everybody to do, in order *to protect the public*. . . don't be marketing new drugs that need the FDA's approval before you can do so."

Bob explained, "What they had here were herbal supplements . . . We're finding out in the treatment of cancer that there's all sorts of intangibles that people didn't understand previously, including faith and including taking herbal supplements that really aren't explained by science yet . . . the big picture of who is a criminal, who really needs to be punished so that they get the message, I don't think that's the case here."

He talked about Daniel Chapter One being lawfully structured as a Corporation Sole, explaining, "The Catholic church has used the Corporate Sole configuration." He told the judge that for many years Daniel Chapter One paid all taxes, despite being a church, until learning that it qualified to be tax exempt. Later, in closing, Jim explained how and why he established Daniel Chapter One as a Corporation Sole and lawfully obtained an EIN number and filed as a church able to do business. The judge said he never heard of a Corporate Sole.

Bob pointed out the alleged "employee" list as not being accurate. Besides the people listed who Jim gave money to in charity, Jim considered people who worked in the ministry as independent contractors. Chuck explained that Jim had no malicious intent, "This wasn't some type of very sophisticated undertaking that involved concealment of things. . ."

After both sides argued, the judge closed by saying, "There is an element of needing to adequately deter the public . . . and then there's the catchall of promoting respect for the law. Mr. Donnelly's right. We just can't have this continue."

His scathing pronouncement was similar to that spoken by the Sanhedrin (the Jewish judicial and administrative body) when they conferred among themselves regarding the activity of the disciples: *"But that it spread no further among the people, let us straightly threaten them. . ." Acts 4:17*

As modern-day disciples living a life dedicated to Christ, we met with the same intolerance as the early disciples did from the Sanhedrin, who demanded social conformity over conformity to the Word of God.

McConnell asked Donnelly for his recommendation. Donnelly replied, "One year and a day in prison."

The US government bent the letter of the law and used contemporary agency rules to hang us. Denying the actual words of the law and denying the spirit of the law, the original intent of which was to protect people from fraud and harm, they twisted the law and added to it, in order to meet their agenda: to destroy the Daniel Chapter One ministry of Yahshua and to silence His prophets.

Chuck and Tom were confident that Jim would get no prison time. They're familiar with Judge McConnell, who, they said, "never gives prison time for these types of charges." In pleading guilty, Jim avoided "trial penalty," the penalty incurred when one insists on a jury trial. Ninety-seven percent of federal cases are settled out of court, a kind of horse trading among lawyers, and the three percent that go to trial risk having the proverbial book thrown at them. Jim technically could have been sentenced to many years, and most likely would have been.

The judge pronounced a sentence of six months of incarceration followed by six months of home confinement while on supervised release, with a monitoring device, restitution of $218,408.04 for the said uncollected withholding tax, and a three-year probation. When Jim made his way over to me, the first thing I said was, "There's somebody you've got to meet in prison." He nodded with a tight smile.

We five walked back to Chuck's office and sat down around a conference table. Jim was resigned. Chuck and Tom expressed astonishment, and looked somewhat deflated.

"We've gotten nothing but beat up for years . . . we didn't expect anything different," Jim offered wearily. The lawyers commented on how well Jim was taking the sentence. Bob said with sincerity, "Jim, you're a good man."

Jim had to wait for "assignment" and was to self-surrender February 9th, to begin the six months in prison. His attorneys thought he might be sent to New York, but he could be assigned anywhere a bed was available.

CHAPTER 39

TRIUMPH

Jim was assigned to the Federal Medical Center Devens, in Ayer, Massachusetts. Eric flew in from Nashville to spend time with his dad and me in Florida, but an impending snowstorm cut Jim's time with us short.

"Honey, get up. I have to go." Jim shook me softly, early in the morning the day before he was supposed to leave. With bad weather threatening the Northeast, he couldn't risk not getting out in time, and managed to get the very last seat on a flight into Providence. He had to be at the airport in an hour. The time to say goodbye had come abruptly.

*   *   *

The morning after we dropped Jim off at the airport, I dropped Eric off. He had to leave in the pitch dark before dawn. I pulled away from the terminal and drove slowly, carefully back into the blackness. My night vision is poor, and the artificial lights above seemed to dance in blurry stars. I squinted hard, straining to adjust my eyes to the road, and gripped the steering wheel harder.

A long week passed, and still I hadn't heard from my husband. I tried calling the Federal Medical Center, but got no answer. A friend in Rhode Island dropped him off February 9, about 1:00 pm, watched as he entered the facility, and no one had heard from him since. It was like the prison hospital devoured him.

Prior to his surrender, Jim asked if he could bring some of our supplements with him: GDU for pain, and Electro Carbs for leg cramps. He was told no, a doctor would see him inside who would give him any drugs he needed. In my imagination, he may have been refusing drugs, or vaccines, so maybe was held hostage and being punished. Or, maybe under the stress he had a seizure, or. . .

It was President's Day weekend. No one answered the phone at the prison and no lawyer returned my email. All I wanted to ask was, when can a new inmate place their first phone call? I scoured the website, and even kept asking Siri on my phone, but found no answer. I did read, however, that if a convict has a present health problem or health history he may be assigned to that federal prison. A blessing in disguise. Jim's past health problems recorded in the presentencing report to the judge may have kept him out of New York, and placed him a little more than an hour away from his daughter, and more or less near to other family members and friends.

By the seventh night, my worry had grown overwhelming and I couldn't shake it off. I cried out to the Lord, begging for His mercy. I sang, I prayed, I shouted, I cried. I did not, could not, trust the government. We are in a spiritual battle, and Jim was in the belly of the beast. The next afternoon I returned home from the fruit stand after purchasing a couple of giant avocados, 2 for $1, of no significance except that I remember it as the time, the moment, when I first heard from Jim. I opened the email on my phone and saw the invitation to CorrLinks, a restricted, monitored email service for federal correctional facilities. I rushed to the computer and frantically went through the process of accepting the invitation and of getting connected. Jim's prisoner number popped up. Oh, Hallelujah! He was there. He had a number, a wonderful number!!! He was 09729070, and I could now access him. I emailed him I Love You!!!!!!!!!!!!!!!! Later that day, he called.

He had spent the past eight days in a tiny cell called "the SHU," the Solitary Housing Unit, dressed in an orange jumpsuit. A guard gave him a Bible in kindness, and a blunt pencil and some paper. He read, and wrote letters (which he later mailed to me), broke bread by himself with the Lord, and prayed for mercy to be let out so that he could contact me and his children, for our sakes. He had endured a thorough physical including a total body X-ray scan, a test for TB, and "crazies" screaming every night. He wrote that he didn't mind the screams so much, what he hated was the darkness after nightfall. "I like light." Food would come by cart at meal time and be pushed through a slot in the door. He said he was beginning to respond to the sound of the cart like Pavlov's dogs. All he could see out a small window was barbed wire and snow.

His first email to me read:

2-17-16

Great day yesterday. Went to a Bible study with all inmates at the camp. There is a reason I'm here. Met several believers and Mauricio has lent me one of his Bibles. Real interesting stories of the saints in here. The Lord blessed me with shoes, free old but boy they're great. Also shower shoes more like boats free also. And a radio I bought but thank the Lord. And a sweatshirt awesome.

The Lord moves everything and He said if we asked for bread He wouldn't give us a stone. Really you are able to know where I am and how I am. Reality is I'm supposed to be in the hole 14–18 more days. His grace and mercies extended not just to me but to you and Eric and Jill. HalleluYah! I surrendered to Him he is sovereign and His will be done Amen.

Last night topped a great day watching and receiving the Lord working his will displaying his omnipotent sovereign power over All things. I mean All Things.

Pray that the Lord allows me to serve the saints here they are a remarkable group, trophies of Yahshua.

This time in prison is truly from our Lord! Yah determined that I get sentenced and there was nothing the lawyers could do. There was nothing the USAG Donnelly could do but give his recommendation and that the judge could do. He felt he was making the sentence but Yahshua had already planned and was just using them to execute His will. Let others know and if you ever write Bob please let him know how grateful I am we are It is as it is to be because Messiah ordained it to be. HalleluYah!!

His emails were quick and poorly punctuated; streams of consciousness. He never wanted to take much time, as others were lined up and waiting to use the computer. He also had to pay for time on the computer, as he did phone calls, so he kept communications very brief.

It would be three months before I'd see him again. I surprised him the first day I visited, and we both cried for joy. I tried not to hug or kiss him because the guards watch and I didn't want to get kicked out. I visited every weekend after that, for 6 hours every Saturday and every Sunday. We'd sit at a wooden picnic table, or on plastic chairs indoors, nothing to do but talk, or not. It was heavenly just being together.

The week Jim was in the SHU, the Lord had me helping others despite intense back pain, which didn't quit until I heard from him. Besides being called upon for homeopathy, one young man in prison needed a legal brief formatted, which I had never done before but managed to do. I also had to type and fax a digital copy of a compliance report to the FTC; part of the court order requirement. I suddenly had to learn to do a lot of things I had always relied on my husband to do.

Meanwhile, out of solitary and in general population, Jim brought light and life to the prison camp. Many of the inmates told me he had a positive effect on all the men. He won most over with his humor, and by the warmth of his genuine love for the Lord and for them. Before long he was asked by the elders of the ministry to take a leadership position, through the laying on of hands, and to take charge of the worship music. Jim is not musically gifted, but he's leading singing, teaching the men songs he knows mostly from our days at the Hixville church, scripture verses set to music. We laugh at what the Lord has done, and is doing, with us both.

Yes, we laugh. We joke. We adopted a couple of names from a *Three Stooges* episode we once saw, and use them fondly for each other in jest, King Rootin' Tootin' and Queen Hotsie Totsie. Our love is strong, and being strengthened, for each other and for the Lord.

Jim has been blessed with a loving relationship with his son and daughter, as I have been, and Jill visits her dad every weekend with her three daughters. The Lord has healed many relationships in our life that the enemy sought to destroy. Before passing away, Ray called to repent of spiritual offenses from the time in Poland, and his son, Jesse came to live with us one summer. Jesse's grandfather, Bolek, called to thank us. Jim's best man and his wife, from the former First Christian Church of Hixville, came by to visit and to acknowledge wrongs done by the church. We have a good, caring relationship with Jim's ex-wife, the mother of his children. We praise Yahweh Ropheka; He is the Lord Who Heals.

Not the enemy, Satan, nor the government has crushed our spirits. We have Yahshua's friendship, His joy, His peace, His hope, His salvation. We have His victory. Already won, but the story isn't over.

California Attorney Stephen Dunkle has worked hard on our civil case appeal, pro bono, arguing both the total shutdown of Daniel Chapter One and the enormous fines as unprecedented and unjust. He entered the oral argument in court in DC on March 7, 2016. We are still waiting for the judges' opinion.

No matter what happens, this story will have a happy ending. The Lord is the author of it, and He has already promised to make our end better than our beginning. For Jesus, being nailed to a cross was not a defeat but rather, His greatest victory. Our faith is not contingent upon situation or circumstance. Faith is believing in things unseen, hoping for what is not yet realized. We will never give up.

When we were first sued by the FTC, along with 130 or so other companies, we reached out to some of them seeking mutual support but none responded. At the urging of others, we also attempted to start a legal defense fund but nothing ever came of it. We talked to author G. Edward Griffin about our case, and asked him to possibly speak at a rally we tried to organize in Washington. He was willing, but the rally never materialized. David, our journalist, talked to the actor Chuck Norris about our case. He was sympathetic, as many people have been, but nothing came of the contact.

The Lord told us over the eight year battle that we would get no help from the outside. World Net Daily and Natural News, online publications, covered our story in several articles, God bless them, and a few other newspapers and several radio programs have given us fair coverage. A handful of believers, brothers and sisters in Christ, have sent money donations and continue to. Other than that, we've stood alone.

In the garden of Gethsemane, Yahshua said, "*you shall be scattered, every man to his own, and shall leave Me alone: and yet I am not alone, because the Father is with Me.*" *John 16:32*

He told his disciples: "*Blessed are you, when men shall hate you, and when they shall separate you from their company, and shall reproach you, and cast your name out as evil, for the Son of man's sake.*" *Luke 6:22*. His obedience to Yahweh earned Him condemnation and crucifixion from the world, but He knew that a divine, master plan was unfolding, so He endured the pain with abounding grace and love.

The government's ruthless treatment of us and Daniel Chapter One is a sign of the end times: "*This know also, that in the last days perilous times will come. For men shall be lovers of their own selves. . .false accusers . . . fierce, despisers of those that are good.*" *2 Timothy 3:1–3*

We are constantly being encouraged, for "*We know . . . all things work together for good to them that love God, to them who are called according to His purpose.*" *Romans 8:28* Joseph was thrown into a well by his envious brothers and sold into slavery, an evil that Yahweh intended for good. Joseph later said to his brothers "*But as for you, you thought evil against me; but God meant it unto good, to bring to pass, as it is this day, to save many people alive.*" *Genesis 50:20*

So we run and faint not; we fight the good fight; we know our future is secure. We are a couple of nobodies, saved by grace. But before the Lord, we can say we stood, and, like Job, did not throw away our integrity when tested. We stood, as Daniel did, doing what we believed Yahweh expected of us, not fearing the fire or the lions' den.

> "*And in nothing be terrified by your adversaries: which is to them an evident token of perdition, but to you of salvation, and that of God. For to you it is given in the behalf of the Messiah, not only to believe on Him, but to suffer for His sake*" Philippians 1:28, 29

From the inception of Daniel Chapter One to now, we have stood for Him unwavering, as we've been called to do as His watchmen. And through the apostle Paul, He assures us of justice and reward one day: "*Henceforth there is laid up for me a crown of righteousness, which the*

Lord, the righteous judge, shall give me at that day: and not to me only, but to all them also that love his appearing." 2 Timothy 4:8

And that is how this story is sure to end. The ultimate ending will be a glorious new beginning of a story without end, infinite.

EPILOGUE

Daniel Chapter One and James Feijo fully lost the civil case on appeal, May, 2016.

Three Circuit Judges in the US Court of Appeals affirmed the district court ruling that shut down the ministry, Daniel Chapter One, disregarding its compliance of nearly three years (from the time our contempt was purged, May 24, 2012 until the ban, March 31, 2015.) As to the egregious fines we cannot possibly pay, the judges wrote: "courts considering a defendant's ability to pay a civil penalty look beyond the funds and assets currently in the defendant's possession."

Perhaps it is not yet over. We still hope, and pray, for justice on Earth, as we pray for our nation. America may yet see righteousness reestablished, based upon the Constitution and natural law, its citizens allowed to be free as Almighty God created us to be: free to pursue life, liberty, and happiness – even when it comes to our health. Government is supposed to secure those rights, not destroy them.

Ron Paul introduced three bills to the House that would have saved us had they passed: The Health Freedom Restoration Act, to force the FDA to comply with the commands of Congress, the First Amendment, numerous federal courts, and the American people by codifying the First Amendment prohibition on prior restraint; the Freedom of Health Speech Act, requiring the government to actually prove that speech is false before the FTC acts against the speaker; and the Testimonial Free Speech Act, legislation that would prohibit the federal government from censoring an individual's account of his experience with foods and dietary supplements. (As explained in *Government Bullies*, by Senator Rand Paul, in the foreword by Congressman Ron Paul.)

Maybe another righteous congressman will resurrect those bills. Maybe they'll pass in the future. A morally justified, concerned public can sometimes achieve the impossible! Votes matter. Voices matter. If Americans for health freedom stand together and fight for right, perhaps the out-of-control, tyrannical FTC and FDA will yet be reined in by Congress and realigned with the Constitution. If not, the public health will continue to be seriously jeopardized by the abusive campaigns of those agencies against alternative medicine.

Rather than wholesale targeting a type of medicine, the FTC and FDA should make case-by-case judgments that are reasonable and true, based on fact of injury. They should not be allowed to terrorize businesses, or ministries, just because they don't agree with their message, or because their lobbyists don't condone them. "If a church were to seize such power, imposing its 'religious' view of health and healing, the courts would scream 'separation of church and state', and rule in favor of individual choice," wrote attorneys William Olson and Herb Titus. "But when a government agency invokes the name of "reasonable basis," the courts bow before the altar of so called "science" – actually scientism – and permit the agency to run roughshod over the health care practices and programs outside the "mainstream." *(Federal Trade Commission v. Daniel Chapter One, A Story of Government Suppression of Alternative Medicine,* www.lawandfreedom.com*)*

According to Congressman Paul, the president can use his authority and order the FDA and FTC not to pursue these types of product cases unless they have clear evidence that the provider's claims are not true. No new law is required; the agencies could simply be made to follow the law as it is written, and not be allowed to rule beyond the law.

In his first message as President, Thomas Jefferson said that the liberties of a nation cannot be thought secure when we have removed their only firm basis, a conviction in the minds of the people that their liberties are the gift of God. Perhaps if the people of America who believe their liberties are a gift of God become more prayerful, and more active, and stand up to the government when it acts with tyranny, the present oppressive situation will change.

For three decades, we exercised our Christian faith and the liberties granted us by Almighty God; liberties that our forefathers acknowledged and wrote the United States Constitution to protect. In the time we walked in freedom, without government intrusion, we were creative, innovative, prosperous, and generous. We contributed to the welfare of many individuals, to our community, and to society. We harmed no one, and helped many. We never asked for anything, and we took nothing from anyone including the government.

Today, Jim is banned from selling, marketing, or advertising any dietary supplement for the next 20 years. He is barred from "any health service," so he cannot return to counseling athletes. The federal court order forbids him from selling or giving away Daniel Chapter One, its products, its customer list. They've forbidden us our livelihood, and at the same time, have ordered us to pay millions of dollars in fines and penalties though we have nothing left.

Thirty years of hard work and nearly 200 excellent products the US Government has destroyed. As a result of the vindictive, mean-spirited motion of the FTC and DOJ banning the entire line of Daniel Chapter One products, and of the federal judges who granted and upheld it, countless people will suffer and lives will be lost that could have benefitted from our safe, natural, and effective products.

The last of our ministry funds were taken by the FTC and distributed to Daniel Chapter One customers. Many sent the checks they received back to us; some multiplying the amount, with cards and letters sharing testimonies, expressing outrage and a desire to obtain the products again.

The silver lining to the ban on Daniel Chapter One may be that now Jim and I can speak, teach, and write about natural healing according to our Creator's design. Someday, I hope to write a book about the insights and approach we were given to healing cancer and other illness, and publish it—*uncensored*. Unfortunately, though, the fact remains that you cannot obtain the unique products we developed, to accompany the information. Unless, the Lord works a miracle.

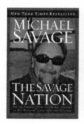    

CPSIA information can be obtained
at www.ICGtesting.com
Printed in the USA
FFOW03n1418101017
40928FF

The Last Old-Time Ranger

John H. Riffey

Vishnu Temple Press
P O Box 30821
Flagstaff AZ 86003-0821
(928) 556 0742
www.vishnutemplepress.com

The Last Old-Time Ranger
John H. Riffey

by
Jean Luttrell

Table Of Contents

Photographs

Photographs are courtesy of National Park Service unless otherwise acknowledged.

Foreword

Most people picture a Park Ranger as a kind, helpful, rugged, outdoors person, who wears a Smoky Bear hat, and lives and works in the forest. For some reason rangers are always in the forest.

Yet, if you had asked me when I was a kid, I would have given you a much different answer. I would have told you that while indeed rangers are kind, helpful, outdoors men; their hat is a straw sweat-stained cowboy hat, their uniform is a plaid shirt and twill trousers and they live and work near the Grand Canyon, not in a forest.

Of course, my idea was formed by contact with a real person and not based on a stereotype. This real person was John H. Riffey, Park Ranger at Grand Canyon National Monument.

The Monument was a lonesome, remote outpost along the north rim of the Grand Canyon. My grandfather had a ranch 22 miles away, which by Arizona Strip standards, is considered nearby, and he and Riffey were close friends. Consequently, during my summer stays on the ranch I saw Riffey often. All of my ideas as to what a ranger was, what a ranger did, how a ranger acted, looked and talked, came from Riffey.

In my eyes Riffey seemed to be more like a local rancher than a government official. His life mirrored my grandfather's, only he had a better house on his "ranch." He did the kind of things that my grandfather did. He mended fences, maintained the roads, fixed machinery and did whatever was necessary to keep up his "ranch."

While he was the law on the Monument, if he had a lawman's revolver, I never saw it. In fact, the only outward clues to his official status were the Grand Canyon Monument sign at the cattle-guard entrance to the park and the faded and chewing tobacco spittle-covered words on the door of his old Dodge pickup: "U.S. Government, For Official Use Only."

Riffey started out as a fairly typical ranger in a young National Park Service. There were few rangers and they were sprinkled far and wide in remote places. They were expected to do everything that needed to be done to keep up their assigned area and serve the visitors. However, after World War II things began to change. Visitation to the parks grew rapidly. Suddenly simple things were not so simple anymore.

Rangering had to evolve to keep pace with the sweeping changes overtaking the Service. The do-it-all ranger gave way to the highly trained specialized ranger. The broad work of the old timers was subdivided into law enforcement rangers, interpretation rangers, resource managers, maintenance men, etc.

Rangers who once spent most of their day in the field were now being forced to spend more and more of their time in the office going to meetings, filing reports and drafting plans. Though not relished, these things needed to be done if the Park Service was to properly fulfill its mission to preserve and protect the parks. The bigger the park, the more it was visited and the greater the pressure to change. Park Service survival demanded change.

But the Grand Canyon National Monument was a small, out-of-the-way place. It attracted little attention from visitors or park administrators. For Riffey the upheaval elsewhere in the Park Service did not, and need not, apply to his world. He did not need a uniform to identify his authority, and he had to be a generalist because there was no one else to do the dozens of jobs that needed to be done. And unlike his counterparts in busy areas, he had time to sit and chat with his visitors.

Nevertheless, pressure to change, even at Toroweap was inevitable. In the 1950s Riffey began to feel the pressure to conform to the new ways. In time it grew to the point that he felt he would either have to comply with the new directives or be forced to quit. Still he resisted or, more accurately, quietly ignored directives that he saw as impractical or nonessential.

In the end Riffey was not forced to quit, because his outstanding work (even when it wasn't accomplished exactly as the bureaucrats prescribed) could not be denied. The land and the visitors to the Monument were well cared for and Riffey, the custodian, was universally held in the highest esteem.

The Service began to realize this old-time ranger was not a relic of bygone days but a treasure. He was a living tie to a simpler time—a credit to the character and values of all rangers and the embodiment of the true spirit of rangering.

When John Riffey's days ended, the National Park Service memorialized this spirit in an extraordinary gesture of recognition. They asked his widow if she would permit his body to be buried at his ranger station. So in death, as in life, John H. Riffey's spirit still resides at the Grand Canyon National Monument.

Here then is Riffey's story.

Chuck Luttrell, former National Park Service Ranger,
Lake Mead National Recreation Area

Acknowledgments

Without my son Chuck Luttrell's insistence that I undertake this project, there would have been no book.

Liz Roberts, who with her husband Clair Roberts, hosted the April 21, 2001 Tall Tales Rendezvous and produced a booklet containing the stories told that day. The booklet gave me a starting point for my research.

Art Gallenson for providing stories, suggestions and inspiration.

Jim Riffey for entrusting me with family photos and memorabilia.

Dove Menkes who has a great deal of information at his finger tips and, if he doesn't have it, knows where to find it.

Hazel Clark & Tom Martin, editors and publishers.

Ben Luttrell who supports my endeavors.

And thank you to these people who provided essential information: Anthony Williams, Sharon Carter, Phil Shoemaker, Gale Burak, Howard and Pearl Ferris, Judy Elsley, Alta Hansen, Myron Best, Robin Hunter, Mary Allen, Trynje Seymour, Ray Schmutz, Martin Litton, Rose Houk, Gene and Marvyl Wendt, Edie Eilender, Dave Mortenson, Michael F. Anderson, George Billingsley, Michael Ebersole and Joe Rumburg.

I would also like to thank the many librarians and archivists who helped by finding books, photos and records: Susan Eubank, Mary Alice Watrous, Lee Gregory and Michael Quinn.

Chapter 1
The Wake

John H. Riffey's wake—the time before and after his funeral when people gathered to tell stories about him, to laugh at his original one-liners and remember his wisdom—started on July 12, 1980, in my mother's tiny living room in St. George, Utah and has continued with annual reunions to the present time. So who was this man? What made him special?

I met Riffey when I was ten years old. He and Laura, his first wife, took a special interest in me and during my growing-up years they invited me to their home, took me interesting places and gave me excellent advice. But because Riffey was someone I had known most of my life, because he was so very much like my dad, I never thought of him as anything other than ordinary. And that, of course, was part of his charisma—he never made you feel that he was anyone special.

On July 12, 1980, when I entered my mother's home a few hours before the funeral and found the room crowded to over-flowing with people from Portland, Oregon; Tucson, Arizona; Cortez, Colorado and many points in between, I was amazed. I knew why I was there. Riffey was my special friend. But, how had this ordinary man commanded the attention of so many people from such far away places?

My wonder increased when I found an even larger crowd at the Spillsbury Funeral Home. Here were ranchers, business-persons, educators, students, people on welfare and all levels of education from grade school dropouts to PhDs—all there to pay their respect to a man they greatly admired.

My memory of the viewing at the funeral home is dimmed by time, except for one clearly remembered detail. It was the only time I ever saw John Riffey in full ranger uniform. I have since been told that there was some discussion about whether or not Riffey should be buried in his uniform, because he never wore it while on the job. According to one source, Ron Smith, Riffey's good friend and founder of Grand Canyon Expeditions, said something to this effect, "He's the kind of person that makes the Park Service proud. He belongs in uniform."

Indeed, Riffey was the kind of person that made the Park Service proud. After forty years of outstanding performance, after being recognized by the Department of the Interior with the Meritorious Service Award, it would have been inappropriate for him not to have been in uniform.

The funeral service was held in a Mormon place of worship, the St. George Stake Center, but the mourners represented all denominations—Mormon, Catholic, Protestant and even a large group of Mormon Fundamentalist (Polygamists) from Colorado City, Arizona.

Riffey was not a religious man, but his wife Meribeth was a devout Catholic and had arranged for the scripture lesson to be read by Rev. Edmund V. Campers of El Cristo Rey Catholic Church.

Three eulogies were given. Riffey's nephew from Cortez, Colorado spoke first, referring to the deceased as Hauert, his middle name used by his family. Jim told of his uncle's family background.

The next speaker was Ray Schmutz—a rancher, a good friend of Riffey's and a Mormon Bishop. Ray started his remarks by saying, "Mr. Superintendent, be very careful whom you choose to fill Riffey's shoes. They are very big boots." Then Ray said, "Riffey was not a religious man. He was more like Abou Ben Adhem." He quoted the poem in which Abou Ben Adhem awakes in the middle of the night, sees an angel and learns that his name is not

16

included in a list of those who "love the Lord." Abou Ben Adhem asks the Angel to write his name in the book "as one who loves his fellow men." The next night the angel returns and shows Ben Adhem a list of those "whom love of God had blessed." And Ben Adhem's name led all the rest. "And that, my friends," said Ray Schmutz, "was John Riffey."

The third eulogy, delivered by Grand Canyon National Park Superintendent Richard W. Marks, outlined Riffey's outstanding employment record and mentioned the Department of Interior Meritorious Service Award, which he received in 1970. However, this prestigious award was eclipsed by an even more esteemed honor. In a highly unusual move the Park Service allowed Riffey to be buried in Tuweep Valley near the ranger station where he had lived and worked. This was the highest honor the Park Service could have awarded him, and if there was bureaucratic red tape involved, it was cut with amazing speed.

The distance between the funeral service in St. George and the gravesite in Tuweep Valley is roughly one hundred miles. This meant transportation had to be arranged. Immediately Riffey's good friends and owners of Lake Mead Air, Earl Leseburg and Art Gallenson, solved that problem by donating the use of their airplanes.

Art Gallenson had almost total recall of these events. He told me that Lake Mead Air donated five airplanes, but another airplane was needed. According to Gallenson, Earl Leseburg approached the director of operations at Sky West Airline in St. George and said, "We need to get another airplane down to Tuweep for this funeral. I think with all the help Riffey's given you guys over the years, bringing you water and taking care of your people especially when you got hung up, you should give them an airplane for this funeral." The officials at Sky West, well acquainted with Riffey and appreciative of his help with river rafters who had been helicoptered out of the Grand Canyon, quickly agreed and donated a pilot and a nine-passenger airplane.

After the funeral service, Gallenson remembers there was a problem when it came time to load the casket into the airplane. It wouldn't go through the cargo door without being tipped to one side. Leseburg assigned Gallenson the duty of distracting Meribeth, Riffey's widow, while the casket was loaded. Gallenson says, "Now Riffey would have understood, but Meribeth might not have."

A total of nine airplanes made up the funeral cortege. In addition to the planes loaned by Lake Mead Air and Sky West, there were several privately owned aircraft and a Park Service airplane. Earl Leseburg, with the casket, took off first. When Leseburg reached Tuweep Valley he overflew the dirt airstrip and went down into the Grand Canyon at Toroweap Overlook, flying between the walls of the canyon and skimming over the river. In a symbolic tribute to Riffey's love of the canyon, Leseburg took him on one last tour.

Riffey's friends carrying the casket from the truck to the grave.

My mother and I were passengers in the nine-passenger aircraft from Sky West. By the time our plane landed, the casket had been taken off and placed in the back of Riffey's personal pickup

18

truck, and six pallbearers sat on the sides of the truck bed, three on each side, ready to lift the casket out when it reached the burial site. I'm certain Riffey would have approved this simple, no-nonsense method of transporting his body.

Mr. and Mrs. Howard Ferris of Peoria, Arizona, who had been camped in their motorhome at Tuweep when Riffey died, used their motorhome to transport people from the airstrip to the burial site located about a quarter mile south of the ranger station.

When my mother and I arrived at the gravesite, the casket had already been lifted out of the pickup and Meribeth was issuing orders to turn the casket around. Contrary to usual custom, Meribeth insisted that Riffey must be placed facing west, overlooking the valley.

As the pallbearers struggled to turn the casket one of them slipped and fell into the hole. The unfortunate man was quickly pulled out and the casket lowered.

Since there were no prepared remarks for the actual burial, Meribeth improvised by leading everyone in singing Kum Ba Yah. No one felt like singing. I remember hoping each verse would be the last, but dutifully following Meribeth's lead into yet another verse. Riffey's nephew Jim said recently, "I thought that Meribeth would never get through Kum Ba Yah." I suspect that the song was Meribeth's way of delaying the inevitable—the filling of the grave.

When the song ended, the pallbearers picked up shovels and went to work. The sound of dirt and gravel hitting the top of the casket was loud, final and unforgettable. I took my mother's hand and together we turned away. The whish-ka-chunk; whish-ka-chunk echoed in my head and stabbed into the pit of my stomach as we walked down the hill toward the Ferris's motorhome.

An official report made by Deputy Sam Barlow from the Mohave County Sheriff's Office in Colorado City, Arizona, states that Riffey was buried on July 12, 1980 at 6:09 p.m. Art Gallenson remembers when he left the valley after the burial the sun was starting to set. He flew over the gravesite and he said, "Rick and Teresa and Edie and God knows how many others were still there. It felt like the end of the day. From the air you could feel it."

Tryntje Seymour, who had been staying at the ranger station when Riffey died, stayed on after the funeral to help Meri-

During the grave-side ceremony.

beth pack and get ready to move. The Ferrises also stayed in their motorhome and helped. Art Gallenson and Dan Merrill returned several days later and, together with Tryntje and Howard Ferris, chose a rock from the nearby hillside for a headstone.

Using Waltzing Matilda, Riffey's name for the front-end loader, the four helpers moved a heavy boulder to the grave. And it was there when Richard Phelan, a writer for *Sports Illustrated* visited the grave a few months later, prompting him to write: "The gravestone isn't granite, and it hasn't been carved or polished. It's a rock from the hillside near his house, chosen for its square, satisfactory shape and set upright in the ground."[1]

20

Several years later Meribeth replaced this simple headstone with a granite marker. Etched into the new gravestone is a panoramic view of the valley. Under Riffey's name are the words:

A Man Who Could Spend A Lifetime On The Rim
And Not Waste A Minute
Tuweep Ranger From 1942 to 1980
Good Samaritan, Gentle Friend, Teller of Tall Tales

Every year since his death Riffey's friends have gathered in Tuweep to remember him with stories and in Riffey's own words to have a drink "for men over forty and women of any age."

There have been a number of rangers stationed at Tuweep since Riffey's death. (I won't call them replacements, because no one could replace Riffey.) Seasonal employees, Tom Conner followed by Sonja Hoie, were the first to take over this outpost. The next ranger was Michael Ebersole, a permanent employee who recalls that he was often the beneficiary of the good will generated by Riffey. After Mike came Ed Cummins and wife Cathy Alger, followed by Liz and Clair Roberts, John J. Miller, and currently Jim and Maria Wessel. Each, in his or her own way, has continued Riffey's legacy of friendly service. Mike Ebersole, who sent me this list, wrote, "I still look back on it as the best job I ever had in the National Park Service."

Meribeth had purchased land a mile north of the ranger station and planned a cabin as a place where she and Riffey could live after he retired from the Park Service. Unwilling to give up the dream after he died, she built the house and returned to Tuweep each summer. There she entertained Riffey's many friends and held annual reunions until her death in April of 1993.

Alta Hansen inherited the Tuweep house when Meribeth died, and she continued the custom of get-togethers in Riffey's memory.

On April 21, 2001, the informal reunions became a planned event. Tuweep Rangers, Liz and Clair Roberts, invited anyone who had memories of John Riffey to attend the John Riffey Memorial and Tall Tales Rendezvous. Fifty-two people braved the day's snow flurries, gathered around the grave, told stories about how Riffey had helped them and laughed as they remembered his jokes and one-liners.

But it didn't end there. People continue to come. They park beside the road, walk the short distance through shin-high brush to stand or sit beside his grave. Rocks, just right for sitting, have been stacked beside the grave along with a metal box containing a book where anyone can write his or her remembrance. The book contains stories of Riffey's helpfulness and comments on his wisdom, spirit and dedication.

Recently I had the privilege of attending yet another wake-like gathering. The reunion was held in the little house a mile north of the ranger station, which is now owned by my niece, Sharon Carter. Both Alta Hansen and Sharon have kept the spirit of Riffey's hospitality alive.

The wake which started on July 12, 1980 in my mother's living room will, I'm sure, continue for as long as there are people who remember the last old-time ranger.

Chapter 2
Becoming a Ranger

Whenever Riffey's friends gathered together, the conversation always turned to memories of things he said and did. Inevitably I would hear, "Someone should write a book about Riffey." And I would think, "Yes, someone should." But it was my son, Chuck, who looked me square in the eye and said, "*You* should write a book about Riffey. *You* knew him longer than anyone." This is true, at least, longer than anyone still living.

In an effort to preserve Riffey's memory Liz and Claire Roberts, the Tuweep rangers, hosted a Tall Tales Rendezvous at Riffey's gravesite in April of 2001. Liz taped the stories told that day and compiled them—along with articles written by Riffey's friends—in a booklet, *John Riffey Memorial Tall Tale Rendezvous.*

That booklet gave me a starting point and Chuck provided the motivation. But if I were going to write a biography I would need to do research, a lot of research. I had only been ten years old when I met Riffey and he had been thirty-one. Almost half of his life happened before I knew him.

Fortunately a Park Service employee, Julie Russell, interviewed Riffey on May 16, 1980, a little more than a month before he died. From this interview I learned that Riffey was born in Durango, Colorado, lived on a cattle farm at a place called Thompson Park and went to school in Mancos, Colorado.

I sent for Riffey's employment records located in the Civilian Personnel Records Center in St. Louis, Missouri, and a month later a hefty packet of records arrived in the mail. Now I had dates and facts.

Next my husband and I traveled to Durango and Mancos, Colorado, to see where Riffey had lived and gone to school. I knew that Riffey had attended Fort Lewis College, but I soon learned the Fort Lewis of Riffey's day is more than ten miles from its present location. Old Fort Lewis's buildings, at Hesperus, Colorado, had been turned into dairy barns for the new school's agricultural department and then later abandoned. However, I was able to obtain Riffey's school records.

My next stop was Mancos, Colorado. Mancos is a small town in farming and ranching country. It doesn't appear to have changed much in the eighty years since Riffey lived there. The school Riffey attended is on Main Street, and a nearby store owner proudly informed me that it is the oldest school building in Colorado still being used as a school.

I also met with Riffey's nephew Jim who lives at Cortez, Colorado. From Jim I learned that Riffey's father, John Wesley Riffey, came from Ohio and the family settled at Thompson's Park when he was 4 years old. Riffey's mother, Elizabeth Hauert, was born in Germany and came to this country when she was nine years old and her family settled at Thompson's Park. His mother and father were married on November 30, 1905 and soon after they moved to the La Plata Mountains where John Wesley was employed as a millwright and carpenter. They had four children. The first, a girl, died soon after birth. The second, Jim Riffey's father, was named Albert Arnold. John Hauert was the third child. Esther was the fourth. In 1911, the same year that John Hauert was born, the family moved to Mancos. John Riffey built the two-story house that they lived in, and Jim told me his grandfather also donated his carpenter skills to help less fortunate families in the community. At the same time they either leased or owned a 600-acre ranch south of Mancos. This property was known as the Alamo Ranch and was once owned by the Wetherills, who are credited with discovering Mesa Verde.

Jim provided me with family pictures and directions to Riffey's

24

boyhood home in Mancos. This house is a two-story frame building located three short blocks from the school.

A contemporary of Hauert, Herman Wagner, now in his nineties and a lifelong resident of Mancos, still remembers Elizabeth's hospitality. She always fed her children's friends great cookies. There are few photographs of that period. School yearbooks were victims of the Great Depression.

The Riffey home today doesn't look too different from when John Riffey Sr. built it in 1911.

I returned home and started writing. The first question I addressed was: how did Riffey become a ranger?

People who remember him as the helpful, wise and dedicated ranger may imagine that the Park Service welcomed him on board with open arms. It didn't happen that way. Becoming a ranger is not easy. It isn't easy now and it was especially hard during the years of the Great Depression.

Added to the fact that securing employment with the National Park Service is difficult, is also the fact that Riffey, a normal teenager, was not dedicated to this goal. Even though it's hard to believe, John Riffey wasn't always the smart, mature ranger that in later years everyone knew and loved.

He was once a teenager with most of the ups and downs experienced by normal adolescents. The summer of 1929 between his junior and senior high school years must have been a real high for John Hauert Riffey. That summer he worked as an assistant electrician for the Sunnyside Mining and Milling Co. at Silverton, Colorado—his first job and he was earning $130 per month! This was a lot of money for a boy not yet out of high school.

The population of Mancos is still around the 800 mark it was at in the 1920s. The high school has expanded from its original footprint but its core hasn't changed since John was a student.
Photo courtesy of Tom Martin.

But on October 29, 1929, the stock market crashed sending shock waves through America's economy. At first people in Colorado, far away from Wall Street's financial center, shrugged off the market crash as being no concern of theirs. But over the next few months, banks failed and people's savings disappeared. Customers stopped buying and businesses were forced to lower prices, reduce wages and lay off workers.

By the summer of 1930, when Riffey (called Hauert to distinguish him from his father also named John) graduated from high school, the Sunnyside Mining and Milling Co. was no longer hiring assistant electricians. In fact, no one was hiring the recent high school graduates.

However, C.W. Everett, a rancher near Mancos, contracted with John Riffey (the father) to remodel his ranch home. Mr. Riffey then hired Mr. Everett's fifteen-year-old son, Mark, and his own son as carpenters' helpers. He paid Hauert $100 a month.

That fall the father secured a job at Fort Lewis College in Hesperus as a carpenter and Hauert enrolled as a freshman. During the week father and son lived at Hesperus, but on weekends they drove to their home in Mancos.

Over the next three years Hauert Riffey's school and employment records reveal a young man adrift or, at least, less than dedicated to a goal. At that point he was not a perfect student working steadily toward the goal of a Park Service career. However, in reviewing his grades I've reached the conclusion that like many freshmen, he was enjoying campus life and not spending much time studying. The summer following his freshman year Riffey worked at Fort Lewis College with his father as a truck driver and landscaper. In the fall he did not go back to school.

I have carefully reviewed all documents pertaining to Riffey's employment and education and have discovered a blank spot. I cannot find any record of his activities during the winter of 1931–32. My best guess is that in filling out employment applications he "fudged" a little, allowing anyone reviewing the applications to assume he returned to school at the end of the summer in 1931. However, there is no school record for this period. He probably continued to work at Fort Lewis as a truck driver and landscaper that winter.

In July 1932 he went to work for the Bureau of Public Roads

as a rodman/chainman for a road surveyor and earned $115 per month. When this job ended in December 1932 he was faced with two choices: find another job or go back to school. It was now the height of the Depression and unskilled laborers were—to use a cliché—a glut on the market.

He needed a skill. Probably at the urging of his parents, he traveled to Long Beach, California, and enrolled at the Long Beach Business College where he studied bookkeeping and typing. It is very likely that a distant relative and close friend of his mother's, Adelaide Green, prompted this action. Mrs. Green lived in San Diego and corresponded regularly with Riffey's mother. What is known is that he lived with an elderly woman in Long Beach, ran errands and did light housekeeping in exchange for his board and room while he went to school.

At the end of six months he may not have known what he wanted to do with his life, but he had reached some decisions about what he didn't want to do. He didn't want to work in an office or, as he put it in an interview years later, "in a cage," and he didn't want to live in a crowded metropolitan area.

He returned to Colorado, joined the CCCs (Civilian Conservation Corps) and worked from June to October at Mesa Verde Park. His duties were: recreation area construction, tourist information and clerical work. He worked with old-time rangers who greeted park visitors, helped them enjoy their National Park experience and—when the need arose—could patrol the back country on horseback, fight a forest fire or build a trail. At last he had found what he wanted to do, and his life became directed toward the goal of becoming a Forest or Park Service Ranger.

He made a plan. He would go back to school and upon graduation with a degree in Forestry he would become a ranger. Even if he had known of the obstacles that lay between this dream and achieving his final goal, he undoubtedly would not have been deterred.

The first step toward becoming a ranger was to get a college degree. In the fall of 1933, Riffey returned to Fort Lewis College as a student and the records show a dramatic improvement in his grades.

The Riffey family moved to Hesperus, because his father had continued to work at the college as a carpenter, and living there was more convenient. However, the family home in Mancos was maintained as a weekend residence.

At the same time Riffey enrolled as a sophomore, his best friend, Mark Everett, registered as a freshman. In 1980 after Riffey's death Mark Everett wrote a letter to Riffey's nephew, telling about this period of their lives:

> The summer of 1933 I worked at the Fort Lewis College farm at Hesperus, Colorado. At that time Hauert's father was the college carpenter and on weekends he would drive to Mancos to spend time with his family. I was always invited to make the trip with him.
>
> That fall the Riffeys moved to Fort Lewis so that both Hauert and Esther could attend college there. I continued to work on the farm as the dairyman....and attending school as a freshman.
>
> Two years later both Hauert and I transferred to Colorado State College at Fort Collins, Colorado. We both were studying Forestry. Hauert right away purchased a very expensive slip stick (slide rule) with a good leather case. It was always hanging from his belt and he used it in nearly all class work. He was more proficient with it than any of the registered engineering students.
>
> We did most all things together. We roomed together, we slept together, we studied together, we ate at the same table, we walked to class together, we took the same classes, we had the same professors and were together in all things—except grades. Hauert made good grades while I only managed to get B's. At school he was known only as Riffey and everyone at the school knew Riffey and the kid that was always

29

with him. I think perhaps all teachers and professors have pets and Riffey was without doubt always respected and the teacher's pet. Many times I took advantage of his favored status to gain some favors. I was just not above sharing his good name in a political way.

Hauert got his degree a year earlier than I. He graduated with his B.S. Degree in Forestry in 1937 and I received mine in 1938.

It was while going to school at Fort Collins that Riffey met Laura Smith. Laura and her sister Ellen were also attending Colorado State College. Riffey became acquainted with Laura when a group from the Durango area got together at a school social. She belonged to a home economics sorority and in an interview two months before he died Riffey recalled that "she asked me to go to one of the dances that they had and I did and … somehow or another that's the way it went."

Shortly after Riffey asked Laura to marry him she contracted polio. She was in a coma for several days and when she began to recover her doctor told her that she would never walk again. Not wanting to be a burden, she offered to release Riffey from their engagement. But he declined this offer. He was certain the doctor was wrong and even if she couldn't walk he still wanted to marry her. People who have known both Riffey and Laura are not surprised by his decision to stick by her.

Riffey graduated with a B.S. degree in Forestry on January 22, 1937. At this time there were few job openings for forestry majors, but he was hired for temporary seasonal work with the Forest Service. He worked in ponderosa forests along the front range of the Rocky Mountains marking, chopping down and burning bark beetle-infested trees. It was not the career he'd hoped for, but it was a job at a time when jobs were hard to find, and he thought it would lead to permanent employment as a forest ranger.

At that time Laura was living with her parents. Determined to prove wrong the doctors who'd said she would never regain the use of her left leg, she spent many hours each day in a swimming pool exercising and strengthening her muscles. By summer when she was able to walk with the aid of a cane, she returned to Fort Collins where she worked and took classes in home economics.

On July 18, 1937, Riffey married Laura at her parents' home in Colorado Springs. At first they lived in a small house trailer in Fort Collins. Later they moved to Aurora, a suburb of Denver. Both Laura and Riffey worked, and with careful management of their money, they enjoyed a period of financial smooth sailing.

Even though Riffey's jobs with the Forest Service were temporary, when each job ended he managed to secure another appointment. But in October 1938 government funds for seasonal temporary work ran out. Several years later on his application for employment as a National Park Ranger, Riffey listed his reason for leaving the Forest Service as, "Termination of work & funds."

From October 1938 to June 1939 Riffey was without steady employment. Years later Laura told me that she and Riffey had faced some very lean times. She said she always kept a twenty dollar bill hidden in her purse and this rainy day fund saved them more than once.

Before his work terminated and for months afterward Riffey sent out dozens of job applications. I imagine this as a very stressful time when he did odd jobs, filled out job applications and waited each day for the arrival of the mailman with the news that someone, somewhere had hired him.

I'm certain Riffey was referring to this time in his life, when he answered the question, "Did you know what you wanted to do?" by saying, "You did what you could because that was during the Depression, and I felt what I really wanted was to be a forest ranger."

In June of 1939 he went to work as "a management trainee" at Montgomery Ward in Denver. Not fooled by the fancy job title he later stated that he was "a glorified stock clerk on roller skates."

However, Riffey had not lost sight of his goal. Because both he and Laura believed in education as the means of attaining their dreams, he once again enrolled at Colorado State University. Starting in January 1940 he took classes to fulfill the requirement for a teacher's certificate in vocational agriculture. His aim was twofold: to secure employment as a teacher and to further his education in a field that would lead to his ultimate goal as a forest or park ranger.

He continued to work at Montgomery Ward while going to school and did not leave this employment until September 1940, when he became a fulltime student.

In August 1941 he was hired to teach vocational agriculture at Gilcrest High School in Colorado and Laura was hired as a home economics teacher.

Riffey continued to take civil service examinations and send out applications to the Department of the Interior seeking a position as either a National Park Ranger or Forest Service Ranger. It had been five years since his graduation from Colorado State University with a B.S. degree in Forestry and he still had not attained his goal.

And then it happened. I like to imagine a hot summer day in July. I see Riffey busy mowing the lawn or trimming the hedge in front of their home. He sees the postman, stops what he's doing, walks out to meet him. When the mailman hands him a letter from the Department of the Interior, his heart begins to beat a little faster. He's almost afraid to open it, dreading another disappointment.

Of course, it probably didn't happen this way. But in any case it was a day for celebrating, because this time it wasn't a disappointment. The letter offered him a position as National Park Ranger at Grand Canyon National Monument, Arizona. The appointment was for "the duration of the war and six months thereafter unless sooner terminated." Salary $1,860 per year.

Even though this was his dream come true, Riffey hesitated.

His and Laura's combined salaries at Gilcrest High School were almost twice what he would make as a beginning ranger. And where would they live? The notice said it was a distance of 72 miles to the nearest town that provided services.

But Laura urged Riffey to take the job, because she knew it was what he really wanted to do. She said, "You can always go back to teaching if you don't like it."

Chapter 3
A Place Called Tuweep

If John Riffey had been assigned to a different area, say Yellowstone or Yosemite or any of the many places considered tourist attractions, he would not have been "the last old-time ranger." He would have been caught up in and swept along by the changes within the Park Service—changes to accommodate the pressures of increased visitation, tight budgets, crime and pollution. He would have been remembered as simply a good ranger—dedicated, helpful and thoughtful. He would probably also have been remembered for his intelligence and as somewhat of a maverick, but he would not have been called "a legend in the National Park Service."

But Riffey was assigned to the Grand Canyon National Monument at a place called Tuweep and that made all the difference .

So, where is Tuweep? Or is it Toroweap?

The original Paiute name of the valley was Toroweap. However, the cowboys and sheepmen who first came to this region incorrectly pronounced the word Tuweep. The Park Service with its insistence on political correctness refers to the valley as Toroweap. The locals, who have never given a hoot for political correctness, call it Tuweep, but grudgingly "allow as how" the rim might be called Toroweap Overlook. Since I'm a local, I have always called it Tuweep and I'm too old to change.

Anyway, if you travel south from Fredonia, Arizona on a dirt road marked BLM Road #109, after sixty-one dusty or muddy miles (depending on the weather) you will arrive at Tuweep Valley. I could describe the valley as being approximately eighteen miles in length, two to three miles wide and sloping gently toward the rim of the Grand Canyon where it ends in a vertical 3,000-foot drop-off. But Tuweep is more than its width and length; it is a remote, lonesome, spacious valley located in the heart of a vast high desert—the Arizona Strip.

People who live there like to say it is the wettest, driest, hottest, coldest place in the world. That's a slight exaggeration, but when it rains it can be very, very wet and when it doesn't rain— which is most of the time—it is very, very dry. It can be a very hot place in the summer with temperatures reaching 100° Fahrenheit. In the winter it can be a very cold place. A temperature of 0° Fahrenheit has been recorded.

Picture, if you will, a treeless prairie valley near the center of an unoccupied wilderness, a place so quiet you can hear a crow's wings swish-swish as it flies overhead, and you will have some idea of Tuweep.

The isolation of this area is due to the illogical way lawmakers drew the state boundary. In 1850 Congress established the 37th parallel as the southern boundary of Utah. Therefore, when the Territory of Arizona was created in 1863 its northern boundary was already fixed. This resulted in a big chunk of Arizona (the Arizona Strip) being cut off from the rest of the state by a formidable barrier—the Grand Canyon.

With an area of more than 8,000 square miles and a population of fewer than 1,000 hardy souls, the Arizona Strip did not have enough people to become a county by itself, so this region was divided into two counties (Mohave and Coconino) with boundaries extending across the Colorado River. Flagstaff was named the county seat of Coconino County and Kingman the county seat of Mohave County.

Politically tied to Arizona, yet economically tied to Utah, the people living on the Strip pay taxes for services to Arizona, but buy their groceries in Utah. Consequently, Arizona lawmakers view this area as being of little or no importance. The Arizona

Strip is the state's stepchild and is provided with few services and poorly maintained roads.

The geologic actions that formed Tuweep Valley are relatively recent. The main features of the Grand Canyon were already in place when, 1.2 million years ago, volcanic eruptions dammed the Colorado River less than a half mile below the present mouth of Tuweep Valley.

Part of this volcanic action (more than sixty volcanoes) formed the Pine Mountain Range to the west of Tuweep. Lava from Mt. Trumbull in the Pine Mountain Range and Vulcan's Throne near the canyon rim, flowed down into the Grand Canyon and effectively dammed the river. A lake formed behind this dam and volcanic ash, and water-borne sediments were deposited over a period of hundreds of thousands of years to a depth of 1,400 feet. Eventually the water broke over this natural dam and slowly (again over hundreds of thousands of years) cut the river's channel through this barrier. This action was repeated and these forces of volcanism and erosion produced a side canyon filled with the sediment of a now nonexistent lake—Tuweep Valley.

All that remains of the lava flow that dammed the river are a few igneous ledges, a loose black cinder cascade on the north wall of the river channel and one huge black boulder sticking up out of the water. This lava cascade can be ascended by physically fit hikers and is called the Lava Falls Trail. This "trail" is the steepest and shortest route from the rim to the river. John Riffey is quoted as saying, "They say that slope sits at the maximum angle of repose, but sometimes it doesn't repose."

At the base of this cinder slide is Lava Falls Rapid, the most dangerous rapid on the river. At first it was thought that the rapid was created by water flowing over the remains of the lava dam. However, recently geologists have determined that huge mud flows deposited rocks and boulders here, making a debris dam and creating the rapid.

Even though Tuweep Valley was once, hundreds of thousands

of years ago, a lake, it is now a very dry place and due to this lack of water only a few people have ever made it their home.

The first people to live in Tuweep Valley were the Anasazi. From about 600 or 700 A.D. to around 1150 A.D. a few Anasazis, probably never more than two hundred, lived in an area of Tuweep known as The Cove. Dr. Richard R. Thompson, from Southern Utah State College excavated part of this site. Because there are no springs in this area Dr. Thompson and his students theorized that the people living in The Cove collected rain water in small solid rock pools that resemble bath tubs.

Some writers have stated that in 1776 two Franciscan padres, Silvestre Velez de Escalante and Francisco Dominguez, searching for a place to ford the Colorado River were the first white men in Tuweep Valley. However, there is no creditable evidence to support this idea. It is much more likely that the padres bypassed Tuweep and Mormon pioneers were actually the first to explore the area. The writers who claim members of the Escalante/Dominguez group reached Tuweep in 1776 cite as evidence a white cross painted on the lava rock wall near a pool of water in the foothills of Mt. Trumbull on the west side of Tuweep. However, Major John Wesley Powell and Captain Clarence Dutton, two early explorers, make no mention of this cross which leads to the conclusion that it wasn't there when they explored the Tuweep area.

Major John Wesley Powell traversed the region north of the Colorado River in 1870 searching for three boat crewmen who had left his river expedition the year before. Powell and his men camped near the pool of water, which they named Witches' Pocket because Powell's Indian guides believed evil spirits, *innupin*, lived there.

In 1875 Captain Clarence Dutton became a member of Powell's survey party, and in 1879 Congress sent Dutton to the Grand Canyon to continue and expand Powell's survey. His observations were published in 1882 in the *Tertiary History of the Grand Canyon District*. Dutton, who was a keen observer, wrote a beautiful, detailed description of Tuweep Valley. His party also camped at Witches' Pocket, and he describes the pool and its surroundings in precise detail but makes no mention of the white cross.

Mormons, who settled in what is now southern Utah, explored Tuweep Valley in the late 1850s and early '60s and were probably the first white men in the area.

Later in the mid-1870s when timber was cut from Mt. Trumbull for use in building a temple in St. George, one of the timber cutters, Marc Schmutz, took special note of nearby Tuweep Valley. When the country was opened for homesteading, Schmutz advised his two sons, Marcel and John, to file claims. The Schmutz brothers were the first homesteaders in Tuweep Valley, filing claims in 1914.

Next came the Kent families: "Grandma and Grandpa" Kent with sons Walter and Vaughn; and daughters Mabel, Helen and Ruth. They filed on five homesteads in 1927. The Homestead Act required that the land be lived on and improved. Two of the Kent claims were abandoned before the necessary improvements (a house, a fence and tilled acreage) were made.

Mattie and Bud Kent with their son Amos at their homestead c.1931.

39

Several other families homesteaded about this same time: Bill and Edna Cunningham, Bob Sullivan and the Grahams. In 1931 my family, the Craigs, took up two homesteads near Tuweep on the north side of Mt. Trumbull.

Suddenly Tuweep was a growing community and the residents petitioned for a post office. Since the original Paiute name of the valley was incorrectly pronounced Tuweep by locals (and unaware of the correct pronunciation or spelling) the petition listed the name as Tuweep. This resulted in the establishment of a post office on June 9, 1929, with the official name of Tuweep. The first post office was at the upper Kent homestead in the northern end of the valley, but was later moved from homestead to homestead and ended up eight miles from its original location before it was abandoned in 1950.

Tuweep Valley would be a perfect place for farming and ranching except for one major drawback—there is no water. Even the Witches' Pocket used by Indians and early explorers could not be depended on in drought years. But because early homesteaders desperately needed water they believed stories of ancient people living in the valley who irrigated their crops with water now hidden in the limestone walls of the valley.

Marcel Schmutz told Riffey the following story:

> *During the spring of 1925 I was in Tuweep Valley hunting horses and late in the evening was coming by the mouth of Brady Canyon and saw a campfire up in the canyon. When I came closer I saw three men around the fire, looked like Indians but were white men. They were Brady Inglestead, Frank Heaton and another fellow. I camped with them that night and they told me the following story.*
>
> *They were digging for water up there and 4 hours out of 24 they could hear water flowing back in the rock. In a hill running east and west they could hear it running in a westerly direction. They thought the Indians had dammed it off, since there were over-100-year-old Indian houses (ru-*

ins) in the valley. They figured the Indians had watered the valley with it, then hid it when they left.

They figured to run a tunnel in and catch it where they could hear the water running. It didn't run at set times but just any time about 4 hours a day. They ran a tunnel in about 25 feet, didn't hit water and finally gave up for lack of money and ambition to go any deeper.

Some years later Walter (Bud) Kent, an early homesteader, had a dream that in ancient times Indians had lived in Tuweep. In his dream Indians irrigated their farms with water from a spring in the hillside. Other tribes wanted their land and invaded. They drove off the invaders twice, but knew there would be a third invasion and they would be defeated. So they sealed the water up into the cliff on the east side of the valley and fled.

Mattie Kent believed her husband had had a divine revelation. She and her sister-in-law, Mabel Sullivan, worked six days a week all one summer with a sledgehammer, a drill and dynamite. Swinging a 10-pound hammer is hard work, but these two women were determined to find the much-needed water.

They followed a tiny seep, hoping to uncover a hidden spring. At the end of the summer they gave up, and since the seep would only furnish enough water for a turtle dove, it was named Turtle Dove Spring.

Preying on the ranchers' need for water, a man living in Fredonia brought a Mexican water witcher to the Arizona Strip in 1956. The Mexican could not speak English but his slick-talking accomplice charged $300 for a well location. The local conman said the Mexican never failed, but if water was not found the $300 would be refunded. Two ranchers on the Arizona Strip paid and drilled wells. Water was not found and neither were the man from Fredonia with the refunds or the Mexican water witcher.

The valley's settlers—the Anasazi, homesteaders and ranchers—all needed water to survive. However, it was the National Park Service, interested only in preserving the natural beauty of the area and not depending on a water source, that became an enduring presence.

The National Park Service's interest in what they called Toroweap Valley was sparked in 1929 when E.T. Scoyen, superintendent of Zion National Park, visited the area. Scoyen was impressed by the scenic beauty of Toroweap Overlook and suggested adding it to the National Park system. However, no action was taken until 1930 when President Hoover added the lower Grand Canyon to the tract withdrawn for the creation of Hoover Dam.

In 1932 Roger Toll, superintendent at Yellowstone, and others visited Toroweap to assess recreational opportunities. Because of the area's isolation this group recommended creating a national monument rather than an extension of Grand Canyon National

The ranger's house-cum-station was built near the entrance to the Monument facing west.

Park. This report, together with recommendations by Miner Tillotson and Horace Albright, was sent to President Hoover resulting in 426.79 square miles being proclaimed as Grand Canyon National Monument on December 22, 1932.

Now there was a need for a ranger station. This need occurred during the Great Depression when billions of dollars had been allocated to the Public Works Administration (PWA) to be spent on the construction of public projects as a means of providing employment for the nation's unemployed. Because there was a need and money was available the Olds Brothers of Winslow, Arizona, were awarded a contract to build a house of native rock, a combination barn/garage of the same material and a water catchment system. The house was constructed near the base of the 1,300-foot eastern wall of the valley and six miles from the canyon rim.

During this same time period PWA funds were provided for the construction of a fence to enclose the Tuweep District of the Grand Canyon National Monument and a dam to create a lake. The fence, which separates the Monument from adjoining grazing lands, still stands, but the dam broke the first day the lake filled.

For some years after the creation of Grand Canyon National Monument, maps showed a small lake at the lower end of the valley and, when interviewed shortly before he died, Riffey recalled tourists arriving with fishing poles asking directions to Tuweep Lake. Unfortunately, or perhaps fortunately, there is no lake and Tuweep remains as dry as it was before the Park Service intervened.

A rare rainstorm fills the ephemeral lake at Tuweep in 1940.

Bill and Gertrude Bowen.

Except for an occasional ranger from the South Rim the ranger station remained vacant until October 1940, when Bill Bowen and his wife Gertrude arrived. Bill Bowen was the first Tuweep ranger.

During the two years that the Bowens lived at Tuweep Gertrude became pregnant. When it came time for her baby to be born Bill and Gertrude rented a house in St. George near the hospital. Tragically the baby died soon after birth, and Gertrude blamed the lack of doctors (only one was on duty) and poor medical facilities for the baby's death. Gertrude concluded this story in her interview with Cathy Alger on March 15, 1995, by saying, "That broke me. I'd had enough of Tuweep." When Bill Bowen was offered a chance to transfer to the South Rim he quickly accepted, paving the way for Riffey's appointment.

Riffey waited a long time for his Park Service appointment, but he was rewarded with a place, which allowed him to develop his potential to the maximum. Unhampered by rules and restrictions he expanded his expertise in every area. Riffey was the right man for Tuweep and Tuweep was the right place for Riffey.

Chapter 4
Riffey Comes to Tuweep

Upon receiving notice of employment with the National Park Service Riffey and Laura began making plans for the move. They knew the assignment was for Grand Canyon National Monument and were told the location of the ranger station was Tuweep, Arizona. But what kind of place was Tuweep?

An information sheet sent to them listed the nearest town "which must be depended on for essential services" as Kanab, Utah. The fact sheet said Kanab was seventy-two miles from park headquarters.

Concerning the ranger's house the only information provided stated, "There is one residence with barn, garage and small shop building." What kind of house? Riffey and Laura had heard of rangers being asked to live in remodeled sheds or old historic buildings. Even though the Riffeys had no knowledge of this, in a book about his experiences in Yellowstone, a seasonal ranger wrote that he and his wife lived in a remodeled outhouse.

The Riffeys had a trailer house from their college days at Fort Collins. If the Park Service accommodations were too primitive, they planned to live in this trailer house.

The first Grand Canyon National Monument ranger, Bill Bowen, and his wife Gertrude, probably met Riffey and Laura at the South Rim and escorted them to Tuweep. The Riffeys had gone to school with Bill and his wife at Colorado State University at Fort Collins so they were already well acquainted.

Even before they reached the ranger station in Tuweep, Riffey and Laura realized the road conditions made the idea of a trailer house impractical. The road was nothing but rocks and ruts and every few miles as they passed from one rancher's range to another's they had to stop to open and close gates. It took five hours to drive from Fredonia to Tuweep and with a trailer the trip would have been much longer. In fact, Riffey figured with a trailer they would have spent most of their time digging out of the deep washes they had to cross.

The land was over-grazed and the cattle they saw along the road were skinny with long legs and little bodies. Riffey called them "high-wheeled cows," and he began to have second thoughts about his decision to come to such an inhospitable place.

After sixty-five miles of dust and desolation the ranger station came as a pleasant surprise. The five-room house, a combination residence and office, was a picturesque rock cabin nestled at the foot of a 1,300-foot cliff. It was new—less than ten years old—and built for comfort. Large front room windows framed a perfect view of the valley, which suddenly didn't look so desolate.

The view from behind the ranger house overlooking Tuweep valley.

The house was modern with running water in the bathroom and kitchen. Even though there is less than seven inches of rain each year in Tuweep, a rainfall catchment provided adequate household water. This water system consisted of a low flat roof made of galvanize metal (the catchment), two concrete 4,400 gallon cisterns and a pipe to the house. The catchment and cisterns were located on the hillside well above the house allowing gravity to provide water pressure.

There was no electricity, but propane tanks supplied gas for lights throughout the house and there was even a small propane refrigerator. The kitchen stove was a combination gas/wood burner. Water pipes next to the fire box provided hot water for dish washing and bathing.

Laura and Riffey fell in love with the house.

The Riffeys stayed with the Bowens for two weeks before taking over on their own. During that time Bill and Gertrude introduced them to the people living in the valley and up on Mt. Trumbull, which flanks the west side of the valley.

Tuweep, which had once been the home address for five Kent families, two Cunningham families, Mr. and Mrs. Graham and occasional cowboys, now had only two permanent families. The harsh, lonesome life of homesteading combined with availability of good paying jobs in the cities had decimated the Tuweep population.

The two remaining Tuweep families were both Kents. Walter (Bud) and Mattie Kent lived a mile and a half from the ranger station. Hugh Kent (Bud and Mattie's son) and his family lived eight miles away on the original Grandpa and Grandma Kent homestead.

The Tuweep post office was a mile and a half from the ranger station and Mattie was the postmistress. Bill and Gertrude introduced Riffey and Laura to the delightful local custom of gathering each Tuesday at the Kents' home while Mattie sorted the once-a-week mail delivery at the drop-leaf desk in her living room. Each family came with their mail sack which contained their outgoing letters and visited in the cool shade of the front arbor while Mattie filled their sack with incoming mail. On cold winter days, of course, everyone crowded into Mattie's tiny living room.

Waiting for the mail to be sorted was a sociable time.

On nearby Mt. Trumbull there were three families: Bob Sullivan, a bachelor; Bob Marshal and his wife; and Al Craig with his wife, two daughters and his mother. Also there was a sawmill operated by the owner and one or two workers on Mt. Trumbull.

Laura was fascinated by the people they met, and she began to think of them as characters for a book.

Mattie and Bud Kent were the closest neighbors. Bud, who was always promoting get-rich-quick schemes, was often away on trips, but Mattie kept the home fires burning. Everyone liked Mattie and she was described by Gertrude Bowen as a "wonderful Christian woman." Some people called her a religious fanatic, because she had a small church built about a mile from her house. She undoubtedly had the idea "if you build it they will come." However, they didn't come; undeterred Mattie went every Sunday to church all by herself.

Bob Sullivan, a bachelor, was a farmer from Arkansas. He

homesteaded on the south side of Mt. Trumbull. He had married one of the Kent daughters, the widowed Mabel Kent Hoffpanir, and started building a lovely two-story Victorian style home for his bride and her two children, Francis and Ruth. However, Mabel's religion came between her and Bob. Mabel, like her sister-in-law Mattie, was a member of a small conservative religious sect. Unable to convert Bob to her beliefs she viewed him as an unrepentant sinner. When they separated the house construction stopped. The inside of the house was never finished, and according to those who saw it, was never cleaned.

Bob Marshall and his wife Floy lived on the west side of Mt. Trumbull. Bob was an excellent musician. He had played guitar, banjo or fiddle professionally in a country/western band. He came to the Arizona Strip to get away from the temptations of alcohol which threatened to ruin his life. He lived alone most of the time while his wife supported his homesteading endeavor by working as a linotypist for a major newspaper in Los Angeles.

This brings us to my family, the Craigs. Al Craig was a former garage owner from Redondo Beach, California. Seeking adventure he homesteaded on the north side of Mt. Trumbull in 1931. His mother, Almeda Craig, known as Grandma Craig, also took up land. Almeda moved onto the ranch in the spring of 1931, but Al, Mary and their two daughters didn't become permanent residents until 1938.

When Bill and Gertrude introduced the Riffeys to Grandma Craig she was 74 years old. They didn't meet Al's wife that fall because Mary and the girls were living in St. George, Utah during the school term.

After meeting the people living in Tuweep and nearby Mt. Trumbull, Riffey focused on his duties at the Monument which were range management—protecting Park Service land from disastrous over-grazing.

Bill Bowen explained that on an average the Park land would support about ten head of cows or horses per section (one square mile). But one rancher in years past had grazed more than 1,000 head on what was then considered free range. The Park Service issued grazing permits limiting the number of cattle and it was the ranger's job to enforce a restricted use of the land.

Bowen told Riffey about the resentment against the Park Service that had existed in Tuweep before he and Gertrude arrived. Some ranchers had smeared cow manure on the walls of the house as a message to rangers that they weren't wanted. The mess had been cleaned up before the Bowens arrived, but he had heard about it.

To counter this hostility Bowen explained that he had instituted a policy of listening to grievances, talking over problems and trying to get along with the stockmen. Years later Riffey said, "He (Bill) could sit on the (corral) fence and talk." By taking the Park Service message to the ranchers in friendly conversations on the stockmen's turf Bill generated a lot of goodwill.

Riffey saw the wisdom of Bill's methods and made it his policy too. Riffey worked with the ranchers and made his management decisions in the form of suggestions. Stockmen soon figured out that it was better to be regulated by someone who understood their problems and who would try to get along with them, than to buck the system.

Even though Riffey made an effort to get along with the ranchers, he was capable of enforcing decisions. One story, which may or may not be true, is about a disagreement between two permittees (ranchers holding grazing permits within the National Park). One rancher's stock continually strayed onto the other rancher's range. Finally the Park Service decided to allow a fence to be built between the two permit holders. Riffey met with the ranchers and explained this decision. The man whose stock always strayed off his allotment objected to the fence and is quoted as saying if a fence were built it would be over his dead body. According to the story, Riffey walked away without saying a word. The belligerent rancher called out, "Where are you going?" Riffey answered, "To get my gun." The fence was built without bloodshed, and while this story may not be true, it illustrates Riffey's ability to use humor to defuse hostility.

As well as introducing Riffey to the seventeen permittees, Bill Bowen took him to see the Covington mine located below the rim of the canyon at the top of the Redwall Limestone. Henry Covington's mine was not being worked at this time, but it was viewed by the Park Service as a potential problem.

Bowen remembered this incident in an interview with Cathy Alger in 1995, because of a close encounter with a rattlesnake. Bowen told about showing Riffey the mine and described how he was down on his hands and knees looking into the mine while Riffey stood behind him. When Bowen started to move his right hand, Riffey said, "Don't put that hand down again, Bill." He looked where he'd been going to put his hand and there was a coiled red rattlesnake. The rattlesnake was allowed to go on about his business, but Henry Covington was not. (More about this later.)

After meeting and visiting with the seventeen permittees Riffey's next priority was to get ready for winter. Wood, coal and food had to be stockpiled. Riffey and Laura made several trips to Kanab in the Park Service pickup for groceries and coal. Because of road conditions a trip to town took two days; they always stayed in town over night.

Wood was cut and hauled from nearby Mt. Trumbull. Riffey got a wood permit from the Forest Service and spent several weeks getting in the winter's supply.

Supervision of tourists did not figure into Riffey's work day, because the rare tourists that found their way to Toroweap Overlook were appreciative and considerate of the environment. The year before Riffey arrived only nineteen tourists visited the Monument during the spring and summer months and none during fall and winter. Nineteen a day are not uncommon now.

Sometime during that first year Superintendent Harold C.

Bryant from the South Rim paid a visit to the new ranger. The Superintendent probably wanted to see how Riffey was doing, and maybe he also enjoyed getting away from the hectic schedule of his office.

Dr. Bryant and his wife camped in Riffey's garage, which Riffey called the Waldorf Astoria. It definitely wasn't a five star hotel, but the Bryants were used to camping and undoubtedly enjoyed their trip to Tuweep. Dr. Bryant had started his career as a zoologist at the University of California at Berkeley and his first love was teaching about nature and the environment. Riffey claimed he learned a lot by following Dr. Bryant around and listening carefully to what he said.

Riffey and his boss had a good working relationship. Years later Riffey said his range management decisions were always given full support by the Superintendent and Chief Ranger at the South Rim. Riffey liked his boss, Dr. Bryant, and he liked his job. Both Laura and Riffey felt they had found a perfect place to live and work.

Chapter 5
I Remember Mr. and Mrs. Riffey

I met Mr. and Mrs. Riffey in May 1943, when it was time to move our cattle from winter to summer range. (I say Mr. and Mrs. Riffey because I was only ten years old and was taught to address my elders as such.) Our winter range was a tributary of the Grand Canyon called Son of a Bitch Canyon. My mother called it S.B. Canyon and on current Park Service maps it is labeled 150 Mile Canyon. But back then official documents, even our tax notices, called it Son of a Bitch.

My dad, Al Craig, was one of the seventeen permittees with grazing rights in the Park, and Mr. Riffey and his wife were going along to count the cattle as we brought them out of the canyon. Dad, with a flair for the theatrical, called the gathering of our small herd a roundup and planned a week-long camp-out.

On the appointed day, my mother and I, with camp supplies loaded in the back of our yellow Model A Ford, met the ranger and his wife at the forks of the road in Upper Tuweep Valley. Dad and a hired hand were traveling to the canyon rim on horseback.

Since I had never met Mr. and Mrs. Riffey I tried to imagine what they would look like. I thought the ranger's wife would look something like Mrs. Bowen, the former ranger's wife, who was trim, young and pretty. However, when the Riffeys drove up I saw they bore no resemblance to their predecessors. Mr. Riffey was tall and thin. He looked like a basketball player, and during the campfire conversation that evening I learned that he had played basketball in high school and junior college. He wore blue jeans, plaid shirt and a straw cowboy hat, which then as in later years was well broken-in. Mrs. Riffey wore jodhpurs, a long-sleeved shirt and wide-brimmed felt hat, and was about as shapely as a sack of potatoes. But she had a friendly smile.

We traveled with the Riffeys to the rim of S.B. Canyon, set up camp and waited several hours for my dad to arrive with the horses.

View from the rim looking at SB Canyon. Photo courtesy of Tom Martin.

My recollection of the camp activities is hazy, but I clearly remember the after-dinner campfire. Rolled-up bedrolls were arranged around the fire for seats. Since Mrs. Riffey had had polio and needed something more comfortable to sit on, they had canvas fold-up chairs.

As we sat around the campfire I learned a few things about the Riffeys. (I now wish I had listened better and remembered more.) Soon after dark a few mosquitoes began to buzz around and Mr. Riffey sang a silly song about the mosquitoes. Mrs. Riffey explained that he had been a member of the Glee Club in college.

Tongues of flame curled up from the campfire, and each time

my dad stirred the logs, sparks sailed up and out into the dark night. The grown-ups talked and I listened. My dad told about getting cows to go down the treacherous S.B. trail by coaxing the lead cow along with a bucket of cottonseed cake. He said where one cow would go the others would follow.

The conversation moved from subject to subject. My mother told about living in Redondo Beach, California, at the time of the 1933 Long Beach earthquake. This earthquake occurred on March 10, 1933, at 5:55 p.m. and measured 6.25 on the Richter scale. One hundred and twenty people were killed, and there was over 50 million dollars in property damage.

Mr. Riffey said he'd been living with an elderly woman in Long Beach at that time, attending Long Beach Business College. He remembered when the earthquake hit he'd thought an airplane had crashed into an upper floor of their apartment building.

The fire died down, and we rolled out our bedrolls. Mr. and Mrs. Riffey slept on an air mattress in a tent, but my family slept out in the open on the ground (which didn't seem as hard to me then as it does now.)

The next day we went down into the canyon. My memory of this trip is somewhat foggy, but fortunately I have a letter my mother wrote telling about this adventure. My mother was a great letter writer and two people—her mother and a college sorority sister—saved her letters and returned them years later. The letter, detailing the canyon campout, was written to her sorority sister and is dated February 9, 1944—nine months after the event.

My mother wrote:

> Last spring Al could get no help to bring the cattle out so held them there until May 15ᵗʰ when Jean's school was out and we went with him. It is the ranger's duty to count the stock when it comes out but as he had never been into S.B. Canyon he and his wife asked if they might go with us. So we were quite a party. Al was a little worried about Mrs. Riffey as she has had infantile

paralysis and her left leg is not so strong. Al took some ex-
tra horses from the ranch for them and Jean and I rode to
the rim with them in their pickup. It is 28 mi. from the
ranch to the rim so Al was most all day coming with the
horses. We camped on the rim that night.

The trail is too steep and narrow to ride so next
morning we women started down while the men were
packing the horses. We took about 1½ hours while the
men and horses came down in 30 minutes. Then it was
7 mi. into camp but as most of our horses were already in
the canyon we all walked except Mrs. Riffey. Al calls his
main Camp the "Hotel." I think it is a long ago Indian
dwelling. There is a great overhanging rock in the canyon
wall that forms a protection from storm and all but the
morning sun.

My dad, a practical joker, always introduced first time visitors
to the "Hotel" to the Igaroties. When no one was looking Dad
would use the heel of his hand and the tips of his fingers to make
small bare-foot tracks in the soft sand in the camp. Then he would
draw the visitor's attention to the tracks by saying something like,
"Looks like those doggoned Igaroties have been here again."

When Dad showed Mr. Riffey the tracks, he immediately
speculated that the Igaroties had made off with his lost gloves.
People who knew Riffey in later years will remember that the Igaroties were also said to be at the ranger station in Tuweep and were
always blamed for misplaced items and mechanical failures.

My dad was the creator of the Igaroty myth and this is just
one of the many instances where my dad and Riffey played off
each other. Whenever one of them made a joke, the other one
enlarged on it.

Also my dad gave places and things quirky names, such as
calling his camp the "Hotel." This is another practice that was
adopted and enlarged on by Riffey. For example, since there was
no air conditioning at the ranger station the Riffeys liked to camp

out on hot summer nights at a secluded spot near the canyon rim. They called their camping place, "the south bedroom."

Mrs. Riffey went along with these original names and even added to their vocabulary with a few misnomers and mispronunciations of her own.

Returning to my mother's letter:

> .... *We spent three days just sight seeing and if you like that type of scenery there is none that excels it any place in the Grand Canyon. Then the actual business began. We were all day sweeping the benches and panels for cattle.*

Mother's letter tells about the difficulties of forcing the cattle up the steep S.B. trail and about the campout on the rim that night.

Her letter ends with this paragraph:

> *It was two days from there to the ranch so everyone was up at dawn the next morning. The Riffeys could have skipped home in their pickup in 3 or 4 hours but were enjoying themselves so poked along with the herd. He (Riffey) enjoyed riding so she (Mrs. Riffey) would drive the pickup and he would relieve Jean a while and then me a while.*

That trip to S.B. Canyon began a friendship between the Riffeys and the Craigs that lasted almost forty years. Mrs. Riffey claimed me as their "adopted daughter," and they treated me to a couple of nice trips and some good advice.

When I was about thirteen years old they took me with them to the North Rim one day when Mr. Riffey had business there. This was my first visit to the Grand Canyon Lodge and the only way to describe my reaction is to say I was awestruck. I clearly remember dinner in the dining room that night—not what we ate—but what I saw. Our table was next to a window that looked out over the canyon and while we ate someone played an organ.

I returned to this magical place a few years ago. The dining room was crowded, my husband and I were not seated by a window and there was no organ music. However, even if we had been seated by the window, even if there had been organ music, it would not have been the same as when viewed through the eyes of a child raised on an Arizona Strip homestead.

When I was fifteen years old the Riffeys made a special trip to Ogden, Utah, to take my mother and me to rodeo queen tryouts. My dad was too busy and anyway he couldn't be bothered with such foolishness, but the Riffeys always had time for me. I didn't win, but I had a good time.

However, the real advantage of being an "adopted daughter" was the excellent advice given to me when I was eighteen years old during my last summer at home. I had graduated from Dixie Junior College in St. George, Utah and was making plans to attend the University of California at Berkeley. I chose University of California because it had been my mother's school, and my mother had written to one of her sorority sisters still living in that area and made arrangements for me to join her sorority.

That's when Mrs. Riffey invited me to stay at the ranger station for a week. I thought I'd been invited to help with house cleaning, but soon learned the real reason for the invitation. She and Mr. Riffey wanted to talk to me.

The first morning, as Mrs. Riffey and I sat at the breakfast table and drank our orange juice, she asked about my plans for college. I told her I'd be living in a sorority house. I can still hear Mrs. Riffey's words: "You don't want to join a sorority. You can't afford it and your folks can't afford it."

I'd been working, earning money since I was thirteen years old, and I certainly knew the meaning of the words, "can't afford it." But I had never thought about what sorority living would cost. At that moment Mr. Riffey came in from the kitchen with a plate of mudgrips (waffles) and said, "Listen to what Laura is telling you."

I listened. The Riffeys advised me to go to the student employment office and ask for a list of people who offered room and board to a student in exchange for a few hours work each week. I followed this advice and I have never regretted it.

There have been many "adopted granddaughters and grandsons" over the years, but I believe I had the honor of being their only "adopted daughter."

Chapter 6
Active Duty and Ranger Duty

A little more than a year after being assigned to Grand Canyon National Monument Riffey was drafted. The Park Service issued him a furlough for military service, and he was inducted in the army on October 9, 1943, in Salt Lake City, and after basic training assigned to the 9201 Medical Detachment where he served on a troop-carrying Liberty Ship.

Because the ship's home port was Brooklyn Harbor, Laura stayed with a relative in the New York area while he was in service. Neither Riffey nor Laura liked the big city and Riffey's nephew remembers that his uncle "did not speak very fondly of New Yorkers." Riffey said that when he told people his only neighbor in Tuweep lived 1½ miles away and that he had to drive 72 miles for groceries he was not believed. He always claimed this was when he started telling tall tales, because no one believed him when he told the truth, yet accepted his whoppers as true facts. It seemed most New Yorkers knew very little about the West and what they did know (or thought they knew) came from wild-west movies and dime novels.

In remembering her experiences Laura scoffed at her aunt's insistence that she wear hat and gloves for social engagements and recalled shocking her aunt by hanging her undergarments on the line to dry without placing them inside a pillow case.

Riffey served as a medical technician and ran a dispensary on a hospital ship that made two trips to various overseas ports in Africa, Italy, Sicily and France. He saw the carnage of war and hated it.

61

He received an honorable discharge on November 1, 1945, at Ft. Logan, Colorado after serving two years: 1 year 5 months in the United States and 7 months in Foreign Service.

After his discharge Riffey contacted the National Park Service at Grand Canyon and in accordance with the Selective Service and Training Act was returned to his former position on January 14, 1946. He was given two within-grade promotions and his annual salary was increased to $2,920.68. This doesn't seem like much money now, but when you consider that his rent for the house in Tuweep was only $12.50 a month it wasn't too bad.

During the two months before returning to Tuweep, Riffey and Laura visited their families in Colorado. Riffey had stayed in close contact with his parents in Mancos and visited them after his discharge from the service. He also visited his brother Arnold who had moved to Denver during the war to work in construction at Lowry Air Force Base. Riffey's nephew Jim remembers very little about this visit except that his uncle had a new car—a Nash, which Riffey called the Nash Can.

Jim says his uncle stayed in closer touch with his sister Esther, who was nearer his age than with his brother, Arnold, who was several years older than Riffey.

Esther's husband, Harry Fink, was an infantry soldier in the European Theatre during the war. After the war Esther and Harry lived in Albuquerque, New Mexico, and Riffey and Laura probably visited them also.

When Riffey and Laura returned to Tuweep they were happy to find there had been very little change during their absence. There was one less family living in Tuweep. Bud and Mattie Kent's son and family had moved away. But the new sawmill owner had brought his wife to live with him on the mountain, so the population had not changed, and everyone still gathered every mail day at the Kent's homestead and visited while Mattie sorted the mail.

Few tourists visited the Toroweap Overlook and Riffey's job classification was still range management. But what did he actually do?

His first job was to finish the work started at Saddle Horse Spring by his wartime replacement Ed Laws. While Riffey was in the army Ed Laws had developed Saddle Horse Spring, a small seep under the rim of the canyon, because more water was needed for his horse (in those days the Park Service furnished the Tuweep ranger with a saddle horse) and the retired mules (mules too old to carry people in and out of the Grand Canyon).

Ed Laws had enlarged the Saddle Horse Spring and brought in a pump and pipe. However, Riffey arrived before Laws had completed the project, and he handed it off to him. Riffey laid the pipe and then made a procurement run to the North Rim for a thousand gallon tank and a water trough.

After solving the water problem Riffey's next big project was road building. The six miles from the ranger station to the rim were almost impassable. Locals in pickup trucks could creep in and out of washes and up over big boulders, but tourists in passenger cars either got stuck on high centers or damaged their vehicles or both. Riffey gave the few people who arrived at the ranger station in passenger cars a ride to the rim in the Park Service pickup.

To make the Toroweap Overlook more accessible Riffey hauled gravel, filled ruts and worked on the worst places in the road with pick and shovel. Always creative and resourceful, he invented and built a road drag out of old log-wagon wheel rims which he found in Al Craig's scrap pile. This piece of equipment, called Jig-along Josie, cut down high spots in the road, deposited the dirt in ruts and could be pulled behind the Park Service pickup. His diagram and directions for making the road drag were reported in a Park Service publication, and he was awarded a $15 prize for it. Eventually the Park Service furnished him with a grader and the loan of a dump truck.

When the county began installing cattle guards—a great improvement over opening and closing gates—Riffey built one at the entrance to the Monument. He liked to tell the story about the mule, Yuma, who watched as he built it out of 2 × 6s. When the job was finished, Yuma carefully placed his hooves on the wooden bars and walked across. Yuma then trotted down the outside of the fence and tried to encourage the other mules to try it. When none of the others would come over, Yuma gave up; he crossed back over the cattle guard and never tried it again.

An important service provided by Riffey was the delivery of messages. The Park Service radio was the only way to get emergency messages to ranchers in the Tuweep/Mt. Trumbull area. If someone in town became ill, or there was a death, or some other emergency; the message was telephoned to Park Headquarters at the South Rim. The dispatcher at the South Rim then radioed Riffey, who delivered the message. This system of relayed communications some times resulted in garbled information. Sometimes the rancher receiving the message couldn't tell whether Aunt Mary—or was it Ann Mary—was dead or seriously ill. But they were, at least, alerted that there was an emergency.

About once a week Riffey and Laura drove up on Mt. Trumbull to visit Bob Sullivan, Bob Marshall, and my grandmother who was often alone on our ranch. In the event of an accident or illness these homesteaders, widely separated and without telephone communication, would have no way to signal for help. The Riffeys' visits were his and Laura's way of making sure everyone was okay.

A great deal of Riffey's time was spent fixing things. Because the ranger station was too far from town to make calling a repairman practical, Riffey was his own repair service. One piece of equipment that often needed to be repaired was the electric generator.

Some time during the years after World War II the Park Service wired the ranger station for electricity and installed an electric generator in a shed between the house and the garage. This first generator was an Onan and because it was always in need of repairs Riffey christened it Oh-No. After a few years Oh-No was replaced by a more reliable Witty Generator. The new generator, called Sparky, was also replaced, and over the years there were several Sparkies. One of these replacements was a twin cylinder Nordberg powered Cato Generator called Nasty Nora Kate because of her habit of spitting sparks. Nasty Nora started a fire in the cheat grass and would have burned down the ranger station if Riffey hadn't spotted the blaze in time and put it out before it spread.

His early training with his father as a carpenter's helper enabled him to make household repairs, and his good friend, Al Craig, with mechanical know-how and a shop full of tools, aided him in making mechanical repairs. Al and Riffey could fix almost anything that broke.

Since he could not run to the store to buy parts, Riffey improvised. In 1969 a reporter for the *Los Angeles Times* told of Riffey's going through Craig's scrap pile to find a piece of angle iron to be used as a shock absorber bracket on his Park Service pickup.

Another time Art Gallenson remembers seeing Riffey replace a worn-out starter bushing on Pogo, his personal airplane, with a piece of copper water pipe. The pipe was a fraction too small and the starter would not turn over. Even after the pipe had been squirted with WD40, the starter still would not turn. That's when Riffey ran out of patience. He put the copper pipe in a vice and hooked a heavy-duty gear drill to the starter. Riffey rarely used swear words, but as Art recalls, Riffey said, "I think this will make that son of a bitch turn." And it did.

Art was also there when Pogo came to Boulder City airport for an annual inspection a year later. He remembers the surprised mechanic who found a copper tube in Pogo's starter instead of a bushing.

In recognition of his "creative" repairs, a Park Service recommendation for a quality increase in salary states, "He maintains a small machine shop in which he manufactures some needed parts and overhauls others." Riffey's philosophy was that if someone was smart enough to make it, he was smart enough to fix it.

In the summer, when there were frequent thunder storms, detection and suppression of wildfires became his responsibility. He hiked to these fires and packed along a fire shovel, a Pulaski and a canteen of water. In the late 1960s when his arthritis made hiking difficult Riffey bought a two-wheel all-terrain vehicle called a Tote Goat to ride. In Riffey's vernacular the Tote Goat was called a mule.

Riffey rides his mule.

Usually the lightning strikes were on nearby Mt. Trumbull. This was Forest Service land, but it didn't matter where the fires were, Riffey responded. If only one tree was burning, he watched it and let it burn. Riffey noted in an interview shortly before he died, that in the years since this has become Park Service policy, but he did it because it made sense.

Riffey hiked to fires, he hiked down into S.B. Canyon because that was the only way to get into that canyon, and he even hiked the treacherous Lave Falls Trail when a guide was needed, but it was not something he generally did for pleasure. However, Superintendent John McLaughlin liked to hike, so when McLaughlin came for a visit the two of them explored the Monument together.

In the fall a good part of each day was devoted to getting ready for winter. Wood, coal and canned food had to be stockpiled. There was no pantry or space for food storage in the ranger station. The first ranger, Bill Bowen, solved the problem by digging a hole in the garage and putting canned goods in it. His wife, Gertrude, told about this in an oral history interview. She said, "We stuck them (cans) down in the ground and the moisture loosened the paper covers on the cans, so we never knew what we were going to eat! We'd get a can and whatever it was, we ate it." Faced with this same problem Riffey dug into a hill behind the house and made a food cellar.

Even during ordinary winters keeping warm was serious business. In 1948 it became the number one priority. It began snowing on February 4th, and the Riffeys, who had planned to go to the South Rim for a few days, found themselves snowbound. Snow storms, one after the other, kept them snowed in for six weeks, and Riffey's only contact with the outside world was his morning radio report to the South Rim.

During this time, daily activities were limited to cooking, cleaning, carrying in wood and coal, carrying out ashes and reading. With a good supply of books and magazines Riffey and Laura spent many hours reading. They subscribed to: *National Wildlife, National Geographic, Audubon, Natural History, US News and World Report, Newsweek, Scientific American, Reader's Digest, Arizona Highways* and *Desert Magazine*. Plus they had a well stocked library.

One of Riffey's favorite books was *The Complete Works of William Shakespeare*. And his favorite play was *The Tempest*. He could quote Shakespeare—sometimes inaccurately, but interestingly—and may have memorized these passages during the winter of 1948 when he couldn't get out.

However, except for the days when weather kept him housebound, Riffey was always active. His job title was range management, but it could have been jack-of-all-trades. And as the sole representative of the Park Service in Tuweep, he did everything in his power to enhance and maintain the image of rangers as public servants. If someone needed a ride to the rim, he gave them a ride. If their car was stuck in a mud hole, he gave them a tow. If a hiker ran out of water, he'd find Riffey waiting for him at the head of the trail with a canteen. If a rancher's cow became trapped in a cattle guard, he got it out.

Beyond responding to needs, Riffey and Laura were thoughtful neighbors. I found an example of the Riffeys' neighborliness noted in my grandmother's diary. On May 12, 1946 (Mothers' Day), she wrote:

"Mrs. Riffey brought Mrs. Kent up & cooked dinner for us. We were the only mothers in the valley. Gee, but it was good."

Gale Burak, a retired seasonal ranger, described this thoughtfulness as a natural gift. When Gale Burak learned that I was writing a book about Riffey she wrote to tell me about Riffey's *"ease of manner, delightful warmth and sense of humor and an awareness of the feelings of others that are all part of the charm of such gifted people."*

Riffey viewed this thoughtfulness as simply his job. For Riffey being a good neighbor was part of being a good ranger.

Chapter 7
An Old-Time Ranger

Early day rangers were rugged individuals who did their jobs without a lot of rules and regulations. In fact, in 1877 only seven rules governed the actions of the men hired to protect Yellowstone National Park. But as the Park Service grew, it became, as one Yellowstone ranger put it many years later, "an inflexible …bureaucracy." However, isolation allowed Riffey to continue in the tradition of the old-time rangers.

There are many differences between Riffey, an old-time park ranger, and most present day rangers. One big difference, Riffey was a generalist; present day rangers are specialists. In the Park Service today there are, to name a few categories, law enforcement rangers, naturalists, pilots and maintenance personnel. Riffey preformed all of these services and more.

Another difference was Riffey was not afraid to lend a helping hand to park visitors. Due to the growing propensity of the public to sue, Park Service employees in the 1960s and `70s were told something to this effect, "Thou shalt not help," because the Park Service might be held liable. Riffey understood the logic behind these directives, but he realized there was a difference between the hordes of tourists who swarmed the South and North Rims of the Grand Canyon and the few hardy individuals who braved sixty-five miles of dirt road to view the canyon from the Toroweap Overlook.

Other parks had visitors—often rude, even criminal visitors—the Monument had guests. Riffey, as host, extended genuine hospitality to all who came to Tuweep. He helped people—tourists, ranchers, anyone needing help. He reasoned, why radio for a tow truck when he could hook on to a stuck car and pull it out of a mud hole in a few minutes at no cost? And as far as I know no one ever sued him or the Park Service as a result of his services.

Yet another difference between Riffey and the modern ranger was his sense of humor. Unfortunately, many of today's rangers are so intent on following the rules that they have lost their sense of humor. There is something about putting on a uniform, pinning on a badge and strapping on a gun that makes everything serious business. If you take your job too seriously, you can't report a "trace" of rain as a "six-inch rain storm," as Riffey often did in his morning radio reports to the South Rim, and when questioned explained that you measured six inches between the drops.

And even though Riffey knew both the common and scientific names of plants in the valley, he enjoyed making people smile by identifying wild flowers as Pink, Yellow or Blue Nearoda (growing near the road) or Pink, Yellow or Blue Faroda (growing far from the road). He made no effort to impress visitors with his knowledge. However, if someone wanted real information, and was not simply making conversation, he could give accurate answers.

The emphasis on rules and procedures has resulted in an agency that is cumbersome and slow to act. For example, some time in the 1970s Riffey received a radio message to be on the watch out for two men in a pickup truck who were armed and dangerous. The men and their vehicle were described and Riffey was instructed to let park headquarters know immediately if he saw them.

A short time later Riffey spotted the men driving toward the canyon rim. He radioed this information to the South Rim and suggested that a road block could be set up. Then he waited for instructions. He waited and waited. Three days later, after the criminals were long gone, the dispatcher asked him where he wanted the road block.

So how did the National Park Service, which had once been perceived by the public as an organization of rugged, helpful protectors, become the bureaucracy that it is today?

The answer is too many people and too much crime. After World War II there were more people, buying more cars and taking more vacations. In 1942, the first year of the war, there were 132,584 visitors to the Grand Canyon. Ten years later, after the war, the number had increased to 736,159. Multiply this increase by the number of parks in our nation and you will have some idea of the tremendous pressure being put on the park system. As the population in the parks grew, the job became too much for a few men. The Park Service was forced to expand, and the once small, simple organization became large and complex.

However, Riffey in his isolated area with a relatively small increase in visitation was able to continue doing his job the same way he'd always done it. There was no need for change.

Many of today's rangers would like to go back to good old days when there were only seven rules governing their actions. Sadly this is not possible. For better or worse the Park Service has become a bureaucracy.

One of the characteristics of a bureaucracy is conformity, and to ensure conformity, the practice of moving rangers from park to park became standard in the early 1950s. Therefore it came as no surprise to Riffey when his employer began pressuring him to take a transfer promotion. Riffey turned down these offers. He felt Tuweep was the ideal place to work. Laura's health had improved in Tuweep and his twinges of arthritis (first noticed during his time on ships during the war) had disappeared. He liked being his own boss and being able to help people. They had many friends among the Tuweep/Trumbull ranchers and even more friends in Fredonia. Desire for money and power were minor considerations when weighted against health, happiness and good friends. In short Tuweep was a good place to work, so why go anywhere else?

However, the Park Service could exert enormous pressure on

a nonconformist, and Riffey began to feel that he had two choices: transfer or quit.

In the summer of 1953 my mother learned that the Riffeys had purchased a building site in Fredonia, and Laura had applied for a teaching position at Fredonia High School. Mother questioned Laura. Were they planning to move to Fredonia? Weren't they happy in Tuweep?

Laura explained that they were very happy in Tuweep, but there were problems with the Park Service and Riffey might be forced to quit. She would not elaborate on the problems, but I now know Riffey was under extreme pressure to transfer to another park. This information comes from writer, Richard Phelan, who stated in an article for *Sports Illustrated* that in the 1950s Riffey had been told he must either accept a transfer or be fired. Phelan quoted Riffey as saying something to the effect, "All right, fire me."[1]

Riffey wasn't trying to outmaneuver or undermine his employer, but knowing he might soon be forced to quit, he and Laura made plans. When he lost his job, they would build a house in Fredonia and he would either teach at the high school or go to work for the Forest Service.

In preparation for what they felt was inevitable Laura accepted a position as a teacher at Fredonia High School and Riffey built temporary living quarters for her. The "house" was a one-room metal shed with a concrete floor. It had windows and a door and was wired for electricity but had no bathroom. Since at that time many homes in Fredonia had privies, this was not considered unusual. They furnished it with a bed, a stove, table and chairs. Its only saving grace was its proximity to the school—1½ blocks.

Riffey continued to live and work at the ranger station while Laura lived and worked in town. When the road wasn't too mud-

---

[1] Reprinted courtesy of *Sports Illustrated*: from "On the Scene" by Richard Phelan, July 29, 1985. Copyright © 1985. Time Inc. All rights reserved.

dy or the snow too deep Laura joined her husband in Tuweep on weekends and holidays.

This was a real sacrifice on her part, but one she was willing to make, because she was always Riffey's number one advisor and supporter.

Push never came to shove and Riffey was allowed to remain at Grand Canyon National Monument. Laura quit her teaching job after one year, and the Riffeys never built a real house in Fredonia because, of course, the National Park Service was his career choice and Tuweep was their home. Not only was he not fired, but because he did everything and did it well, he received outstanding performance ratings.

Over the years Riffey became the subject of numerous magazine and newspaper articles. He was even featured in the July 1978 issue of *National Geographic* in a story about the Grand Canyon. Suddenly Park Service officials realized they had a real treasure—a ranger in the old-time tradition.

However, it can truthfully be said that if it weren't for Laura, Riffey never would have become "the last old-time ranger."

Chapter 8
Pogo

No Riffey biography would be complete without a chapter about Riffey's personal airplane, Pogo. Actually there were two Pogos. The first was an Aeronca that had crashed and been extensively repaired. Riffey purchased this airplane in 1954 and a few years later replaced it with a Piper Super Cub.

He said he got the idea of owning an airplane and flying from his nephew, Jim, who had bought an airplane right after graduating from high school and was enthusiastic about flying. One day when Riffey was visiting, his nephew took him up in his airplane. As Riffey watched his nephew at the controls, he started thinking maybe he could learn to fly.

When he mentioned this idea to Laura, she was in full agreement. She had always hated the long trips to town, over rough, washed-out roads. An airplane she agreed would be the perfect way to travel. And it would certainly make the fire patrols required by the Park Service much simpler.

It is interesting to note that headquarters at the South Rim had sent Riffey a directive requiring him to drive to Hancock Knoll, climb a tree and look for fires each day during the fire season. Obviously the person sending this notice had never been to the Arizona Strip. Someone at headquarters had simply looked at a map and thought something to this effect, "Here's a high spot and it's only about seven miles from the ranger station. The ranger could drive out there each day to look for fires." To get to Hancock Knoll Riffey would actually have to drive about twenty-seven miles over some very rough terrain. It would take at least a half day. Because it didn't make sense, Riffey ignored this directive. But it pointed up the need for an airplane.

There was an unused airstrip near the ranger station. Sometime in the late 1920s or early 1930s Bud Kent had made a landing strip on a section of leased state land next to his homestead. One of Bud's many money-making ideas had been to turn his property into a resort-type guest ranch. To make his ranch accessible to potential investors and guests he bulldozed a runway. He even managed to entice a couple of prospective backers to fly in for a look at his ranch. However, they flew away without offering the much-needed cash.

This unused airstrip was adjacent to the Monument and only a half mile from the ranger station. Riffey bladed off the new growth of salt brush and cactus, and the airstrip was ready for use.

Next, he built a shed for his airplane out of scrap lumber. This hangar had an open front with sides made of vertically placed boards. It wasn't much of a hangar, but it protected the plane from weather and curious cows that nosed about looking for something to eat or a place to scratch an itch. A few years later he put an electric fence around the shed to keep cattle out.

When people asked him how he learned to fly Riffey would say, "Pogo taught me," or "I followed the instruction book," or "I wore out four instructors before I got my license." But the truth is, that because he had agreed to buy a plane if he could learn to fly, an instructor came to Tuweep and stayed at the ranger station until Riffey was able to make his solo flight.

After learning the fundamentals he confined his flying to the Tuweep/Trumbull area checking for fires and looking for signs of trouble, such as stalled vehicles or cattle trapped behind a drift fence. Rancher Al Craig made an airstrip on his homestead so going to the Craig ranch became a quick hop, instead of a 22-mile drive. After about a year, when he had gained confidence, Riffey began making trips to St. George and Kanab, Utah.

When an associate editor of *National Geographic*, W. E. Garrett, came to Tuweep, Riffey offered to give him an aerial tour of the canyon. Garrett, who was writing an article about the Grand Canyon, figured this would be a great way to get some unusual photographs. Riffey tied Pogo's window up and Garrett attached a camera with remote control to the wing. In this way he was able to get a picture of Riffey inside the plane with the canyon showing in the background. This picture appeared in the July 1978 issue of *National Geographic*.

Riffey in the Maintenance Section of Tuweep International Airport.

Everyone who was given a ride in Pogo has a story about this experience. These rides always started with Riffey removing boxes of mouse poison from the wings as he explained that mice had been known to build nests in the wings and he hoped they hadn't "chewed up something important." Next the fabric covering the wings was inspected for damage and sealant applied to any rips. By this time Riffey's guest would also be looking Pogo over for signs of damage. If a bulge in the fabric was pointed out, Riffey commented, "Guess Pogo's getting arthritis, just like me."

Riffey's stories as he checked out the plane were geared to make the passenger feel a little nervous, unless of course, his guest was already having doubts. I remember Riffey made no jokes before giving my sister a ride.

As he checked the spark plugs he would tell about the time a loose spark plug caused the engine to cut out briefly while he was flying over the canyon. When asked, "What happened?" he would say, "It was all right; my hair was already gray."

Next he would turn the propeller and explain, "I'm winding the rubber bands that make Pogo fly." Then add, "Know what the propeller is for?" And answer his own question, "It's to keep the pilot cool, because when the propeller stops turning the pilot begins to sweat."

After they were in the air some of his younger passengers remember he would pull the stick out, hand it to them and say, "Here you fly for a while." Of course, Riffey was actually in control using foot pedals.

Foreign visitors were always given a warm welcome and many

Riffey about to take off with passenger Sue Nigh.

were invited for a ride in Pogo. I'm certain no foreigner ever returned home complaining about the rude, inhospitable behavior of Americans after meeting Riffey. Therefore, when two Germans who had chartered a plane in Las Vegas landed at Tuweep because one of them had become air sick, they were given a typical Riffey welcome.

The two men, a writer and photographer, were affiliated with an airplane magazine in Germany. They were immediately attracted to Pogo and were looking the little airplane over when Riffey drove up. Riffey, of course, invited them up to the ranger station, and when he learned of their interest in flying, gave them an air tour of the Grand Canyon.

A few months later an article with pictures of Pogo and the Grand Canyon appeared in a German aviation magazine. The German writer sent Riffey a copy of this article and after Riffey's death the article was given to his nephew, Jim Riffey. Neither Jim nor I could read it, but my German friend Karl Grill translated it for me.

I found the German writer's interpretation of this visit interesting and somewhat amusing. The title of the article was a John Riffey quote: "I Watch Out that No One Steals the Grand Canyon!" The writer described the primitive hangar and the electric fence around it that he said was necessary because "otherwise livestock would come up and nip on Pogo." He also commented on the wind, dust and the bumpy landing strip. And, of course, he mentioned the removal of mouse poison before take-off.

After describing the beauty of the canyon viewed from Pogo's cockpit the writer stated that Riffey had approximately 1200 hours of flying time without a "mishap." As did everyone who rode with Riffey, this writer found him to be a very careful pilot.

Besides making trips to town easier and sharing his joy of flying with friends, Pogo was used for fire patrol, rescues and ambulance service. At first Riffey flew fire patrols on his own initiative and used his own fuel. Looking for fires in Pogo certainly made more sense than driving to Hancock Knoll and climbing a tree. After spotting a smoke from the air, Riffey would fly over the Craig ranch and drop a note directing Al Craig, who was the Forest Service fire warden, to the fire.

This system wasn't very satisfactory. Riffey, still learning to fly, kept Pogo at a healthy altitude and Al didn't always get the messages, at least not in time to go to the fire. Sometimes Al got the note a year later when he was out on a hillside getting in the winter's wood supply.

It wasn't long until the Park Service, the Forest Service and the Bureau of Land Management, the three agencies responsible for fire control in the Tuweep/Trumbull area, saw the wisdom of the air patrol. (See appendix for Joint Citation for Superior Performance.) The Forest Service provided Riffey and Al with radios for better communication and the three agencies shared the cost of fuel. After that, when Riffey flew over the Craig ranch, he picked up the radio mike and said, "This is Fly Boy to Ground Hog. Come in, Ground Hog."

Mary Craig remembered, "He (Riffey) knew the area pretty good, so he'd tell Al where the fire was or where the smoke was." Riffey would return to the ranger station and get the Park Service pickup and fire fighting equipment. Then he and Al would meet at a designated point close to the fire.

It was also Riffey's job to enforce no hunting regulations. During deer season when poaching was most likely to occur, he patrolled an area of 200,000 acres in Pogo. Assuming people were law abiding until they proved otherwise, he gave warnings before issuing citations. When he spotted hunters from the air on the Monument, he buzzed over them and dropped a note which said, "You are in the National Park and hunting is illegal here. I will be back in two hours. If you are still here I will have to give you a ticket." Occasionally this warning was ignored and Riffey was forced to issue citations. During the 1960 hunting season he wrote six "violation notices" for hunting in the Monument.

From time to time Riffey was required to attend a meeting at Park Headquarters on the South Rim. Riffey always said that he didn't mind going to the South Rim, but "Pogo wouldn't go." However, when necessary Pogo would go and a 50-mile hop in Pogo was much preferred to the 300-mile drive. Former Assistant Chief Ranger Joe Rumburg wrote, "By John's use of the plane and the air strip we had on the South Rim, John could much more conveniently attend various meetings."

Pogo also aided Riffey in rescue missions. One of the earliest of these rescues was in 1959. A group of river runners was testing the ability of jet boats to go up stream on the Colorado River. To prepare for this trip several men made the trip down the river to cache fuel. At Lava Falls, Bill Austin, a member of the group doing the ground work for the up-river run, broke his leg. With a man in need of immediate medical attention, the river runners wrote a big SOS in the sand and waited for help.

Riffey, alerted by the Park Service to watch for these boaters, flew over, saw the SOS and relayed their message to South Rim headquarters. A helicopter from Luke Air Force Base flew into the canyon and rescued Austin.

Another time Ray Schmutz remembers that his brother Stan and a hired man were cutting stays for a fence near Tuweep. Stan accidentally cut a deep gash in his foot. The hired man drove Stan to Riffey's place and Pogo performed ambulance service.

This was not the only time Pogo was called upon to transport an injured or ill person to the doctor in St. George. All the ranchers knew they could count on Riffey and Pogo in the event of an emergency.

Once Pogo came to my father's aid when, in my dad's opinion, the situation was serious, but definitely not life threatening. During the winter of 1967 my mother was staying with me in Henderson, Nevada, while she recovered from hip surgery and my father, Al Craig, and a companion were staying at the ranch. Sometime in December they became snowbound for seventeen days. Al and Riffey had both purchased C.B. radios and had a regular scheduled time to talk to each other, so even though snowbound they had daily radio contact.

When Riffey asked Al if he needed anything from town, my dad told him they had run out of two staples—coffee and Bull Durham. Imagine, if you will, two old cowboys huddled close to the stove trying to keep warm with no coffee to drink and no tobacco! Riffey realized this was a real emergency. He cleared the snow from the airstrip (it was not as deep in Tuweep as up on the mountain) and he and Pogo flew off on a mission of mercy. The day before Christmas Riffey flew over the Craig ranch and dropped the emergency rations plus two T-bone steaks.

Occasionally Riffey was asked to search for lost people. This was rare because all the ranchers and even most tourists who came to the Monument were familiar with the country. Usually, he simply checked on travelers to see if help was needed. After a thunderstorm while looking for fires, he also watched the roads to see if anyone was stuck in a mud hole. If he spotted anyone in trouble he returned in his pickup to help them.

When he knew hikers were expected to be coming up from the river on the Lava Falls Trail he would check on them from the air and then return to the head of the trail in his pickup with water. Many a hiker remembers those canteens of water.

During the late 1950s and early '60s Pogo was almost the only airplane landing at the Tuweep airstrip, but in the late '60s this changed. River boat companies began advertising 5-day and 3-day river trips, in addition to the regular 8-day trip. People who purchased a 5-day package were picked up in the canyon by helicopter and brought to Tuweep. From there they were flown in fixed wing aircraft to Page, Arizona or Las Vegas, Nevada.

The tiny Tuweep airstrip became a busy place, especially on weekends. Sometimes as many as 150 people would be helicoptered up out of the canyon in one day. If these people had to wait for the airplanes to take them to Las Vegas or Page, Riffey would drive down from the ranger station, visit with them and offer them a drink of water. In this way Riffey met people from all over the world.

He decided with all this international traffic, his little airport had gained international status, so he made a sign.

Some time after 1980, new Park Service rules restricting flights into the canyon made the option of leaving the river at Lava

Luckily the airstrip was outside the park. The sign did not conform to NPS standards.

Falls no longer feasible, and the "Tuweep International Airport" fell into disuse. In 2005 the Federal Aviation Authority closed the airstrip.

On another sad note, shortly before his death Riffey became aware of his physical limitations. He may have even known of his heart problems. Sensing that he was an unsafe pilot he refused to let anyone fly with him. Tryntje Seymour, who had always enjoyed flying in Pogo when she was in Tuweep, remembers that Riffey wouldn't let her fly with him that last year.

Riffey sold Pogo before he died.

And what happened to Pogo?

Rose Houk wrote a note placed in a metal box beside Riffey's grave: "Pogo was happy and well with Phil Shoemaker when we met him in Alaska in 1987."

This note prompted me to write to Phil Shoemaker. He answered that he'd made a deal to buy Pogo before Riffey died, but he'd had possession of the airplane for only a short time. When

Riffey died, Phil was unable to complete the deal and Pogo was sold to someone else. He wrote, "Over the years I kept track of Pogo and attempted to buy it from its various owners. The last one was in North Dakota but I'm afraid it may now be wrecked, (or hopefully is being restored), as it is no longer registered with the FAA."

I know airplanes don't last forever, but I like to think that the little airplane that served Riffey for so many years is being restored and will soon be happy and well again.

Chapter 9
Laura's Illness

After Riffey and Laura were engaged, but before they were wed, Laura contracted polio. She recovered from this illness, but never regained her former good health. Then in the late 1950s she began suffering extreme pain and realized that something was terribly wrong. Riffey flew her to a clinic in Cottonwood, Arizona, and the diagnosis was not good. She had bone cancer.

For more than a year after this diagnosis Laura was able to attend to her personal needs and even perform simple household tasks, but she was never free from pain. It was during this time that an incident occurred which shows a seldom-witnessed facet of Riffey's personality. There are many stories of Riffey's cheerful good humor, but few people ever saw him when he was angry.

Riffey always said that sixty-five miles of dirt road acted as a filter, and that only good people made it to the ranger station, but one day a not-so-good person avoided the dirt-road filter by flying into Tuweep.

Riffey was busy working on some machinery in the garage, so when the airplane landed Laura drove down to the airstrip. The pilot who had been hired to bring this man to Tuweep—obviously anxious to be rid of his passenger—flew off leaving Laura to deal with a disorderly drunk who tried to hand her a hundred dollar bill and ordered her to drive him to the Craig ranch.

Unimpressed by his money and deeply offended by his behavior Laura gave him a ride to the ranger station and turned him over to Riffey, who then drove him to the Craig ranch. The man, somewhat sobered by the time they arrived at the Craig's, got out of the pickup, offered an apology and reached out to shake Riffey's hand. My mother remembered that Riffey refused the offered hand by putting his hands behind his back and said, "Your apology is not accepted and you are not welcome at the ranger station."

My mother knew their visitor had committed an unforgivable offense, but it wasn't until several weeks later while visiting with Laura that she learned of his rude, obnoxious behavior. Riffey, who was tolerant of personal differences and even deviant behavior, brooked no disrespect toward his wife especially when she was sick.

My mother often stayed with Laura when Riffey's duties took him away from the ranger station and because Laura knew she didn't have long to live, she asked Mother to help her sort through her personal belongings. Good clothes were packaged to be mailed to her sister in Denver. Other items she either gave to my mother or donated to charity. Next she made lists, instructions and recipe cards for Riffey. She also told my mother that Riffey was too young to be left without a wife and that she was encouraging him to remarry when she was gone.

One of Laura's favorite pastimes had been bird watching, and she had kept a record of the birds in Tuweep. (This record, "Tuweep Bird Observations, 1947 -1950" is filed in the Grand Canyon Archives at the South Rim.) Even when she became bedfast she enjoyed listening to the birds. Mother recalled that Laura often lay with eyes closed and appeared to be asleep, but from time to time would open her eyes and say, "Did you hear that?" And she would identify the sound as a Gambel's Quail, a Canyon Wren or some other bird.

Then one night in September 1962, when Riffey made his eight o'clock radio contact with the Craigs, he asked my mother and father to come to the ranger station the next morning to help him load Laura into Pogo. Laura, too sick to resist, had finally agreed to return to the Cottonwood Clinic. When my parents arrived in Tuweep the next morning it was apparent that Laura was dying, but they managed to keep a stiff upper lip by pretending she was going for a miracle medical treatment.

Laura in happier times.

87

Riffey had modified Pogo's seats to accommodate a make-shift stretcher, and in an effort to lighten the tension my dad made jokes about flying as they wrestled the stretcher into the airplane. Laura, who had appeared to be in a coma, opened her eyes, looked at Riffey and said, "Don't pay any attention to him; he's just a cowboy."

A few weeks later Riffey returned alone.

Laura was buried in the Denver area where Riffey had purchased two burial plots—one for each of them.

Chapter 10
Change

For years there was very little change in Riffey's life. He lived and worked in the same place, did the same things and enjoyed the same friends. Then, in the space of a few years, everything changed. The years immediately prior to 1960 and the years following were times of major changes, both in his personal life and in his ranger career. The most devastating change was Laura's death. Without her at his side nothing would ever be the same for him.

In addition to Laura's death there were also the deaths of both of his parents and a nephew with whom he'd formed a close bond. Riffey's father had died in 1951, his mother passed away in 1959 and after Laura's death, for the first time in his life, he was without close family.

Both Riffey and Laura had kept in contact with their families. Every summer during the late 1940s and early 1950s Laura's sister, Ellen, and her two children, Bill and Lyn, had been house guests.

After Bill and Lyn grew older and no longer came for summer visits, Riffey's nephew Johnny Fink began spending his summers at Tuweep. Riffey had corresponded regularly with his sister Esther, so when her son Johnny became a rebellious teenager, Riffey offered to ease the tension between parents and son by inviting Johnny to spend his vacations at the ranger station.

Johnny spent every summer in Tuweep until military service took him to Viet Nam as a helicopter pilot where he was killed when his helicopter crashed while trying to rescue a downed fighter pilot. During the summers when Johnny lived at the ranger station a close relationship formed between uncle and nephew. When Johnny was killed Riffey felt as if he'd lost a son.

In addition to the loss of family Riffey also lost his closest neighbors, the Kents, when Mattie and Bud sold their livestock and moved to California. Mattie's Post Office closed in 1950 ending the weekly get-togethers on mail day. During the 1950s and into the early `60s Bud and Mattie returned from time to time for extended visits. However, they lived in a trail house that they brought with them and never moved back into their old home. The Schmutzs continued to graze cattle in the valley but had always lived in St. George. So, after Laura's death Tuweep became a very lonely place.

Riffey's many friends tried to help him adjust to life without Laura. My parents, Al and Mary Craig, talked to him every night at eight o'clock on the C.B. radio, and Al found numerous excuses to drive to the Monument. Riffey ate dinner with the Craigs two or three times each week. Mary knew that if Riffey drove up on the mountain for any reason she could count on his staying for dinner, or if Al and Riffey went to Fredonia together, he would stay for dinner before going home when they returned.

Pops Durant, a friend from Cedar City whom Riffey had met at the Kents, stayed with Riffey for several weeks at a time during that first winter after Laura's death. Pops has been credited with showing his host the difference between a "schoolboy" bourbon-and-seven and a "schoolgirl" size drink. A "schoolgirl"—a double—was definitely Pop's preference. During school vacations Pops brought his daughter and her two friends with him. The girls became the first of Riffey's many adopted granddaughters.

During this time of change and adjustment in Riffey's personal life there was also a major change in his professional life. The Grand Canyon National Monument was changing from a grazing area with occasional tourists into a tourist area with only a few grazing permittees.

In 1942 when Riffey first came to Tuweep there were seventeen permittees on the Monument and by 1980 there were only two. Since grazing permits in National Parks could not be sold or transferred, the number of permittees declined as ranchers either died or sold out. For example, my father, one of the permittees, sold his cattle and stopped grazing S.B. Canyon in 1957.

During this same time period visitation at the Toroweap Overlook increased from twenty per year to twice that many in a week. With this decline in permittees and the increase in tourism it is plain to see that Riffey's duties shifted from grazing management to outdoor recreation management.

Several factors contributed to this increase in visitation; one was Colorado River traffic. In 1938 Norman Nevills began carrying paying passengers down the Colorado. However, it wasn't until after World War II that the idea of commercial river boat trips really caught on. Riffey took several of these early river trips and estimated that fewer than 200 people had preceded him on this adventure.

In 1954 there were only a handful of commercial river runners piloting a few paying passengers down the river. But by 1980, using inflatable war-surplus rafts, these companies were carrying an estimated 16 to 17, 000 people through the canyon each year. Although the Lava Falls Trail can be more aptly called a route, it is one of the few places where the river is relatively close to the rim and Riffey began to see occasional hikers either joining or leaving a river party.

Later in the 1970s helicopters were used to bring boat passengers out of the canyon at this point. The helicopters landed at the Tuweep Airstrip, and sometimes as many as 150 people a day made the transfer to fixed wing aircraft there.

Experienced hikers could hire Earl Leseberg, a commercial flyer, to take them to Tuweep to begin a hiking/floating trip down the river. Riffey always offered these adventurers a ride to the rim and sometimes gave them a good breakfast before they started down the Lava Falls Trail.

Another factor that contributed to the increase in visitation was the attention Riffey and Toroweap Overlook received in newspaper and magazine articles during the '60s. However, Riffey didn't think very many people came to the Monument as a result of having read about it. He said, when interviewed by Julie Russell in 1980, that once in awhile someone would tell him they had read an article about Toroweap. But it was his opinion that the power of the press was not all that effective, especially when there were no paved roads to back up these travel adventure stories.

So while the river, the airstrip and articles in newspapers and magazines contributed to the Monument visitation, it was better vehicles and better roads that caused the real increase in tourists.

In the 1960s car companies began making vehicles designed both for unpaved roads and for passenger comfort. These more rugged automobiles were the forerunners of the Ford Bronco and the Chevy Blazer that made their début in the late '60s.

At the same time Mohave County, Arizona, hired a fulltime grader operator, Dale Finicum, to improve and maintain the roads on the Arizona Strip. Visitors could now drive to Toroweap Overlook in relative comfort in about three hours.

And as if all these changes were not enough there was still yet one more change in this decade of change.

For more than twenty years the Park Service had been telling Henry Covington that his mining claim located near Toroweap Overlook, at the top of the Redwall formation, was null and void. But Covington, who believed the mine was legally his, had continued to sneak into the Monument to do the yearly $100 of assessment work in order to maintain his claim. The Park Service wished that Covington would just give up and go away. Henry Covington just wished the Park Service would quit harassing him. But with neither side pushing the issue, the situation had remained at a stalemate.

In 1959, when Henry Covington hired three men with a

bulldozer to build a road to the canyon rim above his mine, the Park Service could no longer ignore him. Covington was charged with trespassing and damaging the Park, and a hearing was held in United States District Court at Prescott, Arizona, on August 3, 1960.

The transcript of the 1960 court proceeding is rather confusing, but as near as I can tell the mine was originally located by Jim R. Henry in 1921 and was called the Little Chicken Mine. Henry Covington filed on the claim in 1929 and called it Shepherd's Folly.

According to Riffey, Covington had a partner, Brady Inglestead, nicknamed Windy Jim, who later filed on the claim in his name only and called it Warbuck No. 1. A windlass was built at the top of the Esplanade Sandstone to haul the ore from the mine in a sling up and over the five-hundred-foot cliff. Between 20 and 40 tons of ore containing silver, zinc and lead was shipped to Pueblo, Colorado some time during the 1920s. At some point Windy Jim was arrested and hauled off to Texas where he was wanted for some shenanigans.

Covington stated at the hearing that he relocated the Shepherd's Folly as the Ram in 1938. But it gets even more confusing because according to Covington's testimony there were two other claims, the Silver Fox and Sly, that were contiguous to the first claim which was known at various times as the Happy Hunting Ground, the Red Fox and the Golden Slide.

The lawyer for the Park Service wanted not only to prove trespassing and damage but also that Covington's claim was null and void. The lawyer tried unsuccessfully to prove the claim was non-mineral and also that Covington had located the claim after 1932 when the land was withdrawn for the creation of Grand Canyon National Monument. However, Covington was able to show that the mine was mineral and had been located before 1932.

Next the lawyer attempted to prove Covington had not done his yearly assessment work. Riffey's loyalty was with the Park Service, but he felt a certain amount of sympathy for Covington. Riffey called the proceedings a kangaroo trial. When interviewed by Julie Russell, Riffey said that when the lawyer tried to pin Covington down on the exact dates of his assessment work Covington would look over at him as if he expected Riffey to answer for him. The court record shows that twice Covington actually appealed to Riffey for confirmation of the dates. At one point when asked when he did his assessment work he answered, "I can't remember exactly the year. Mr. Riffey might remember, I don't." Of course, Riffey, as a witness for the prosecution, could not answer.

The results of this hearing were that the Park Service's decision declaring the claim to be null and void was invalid yet Cov-

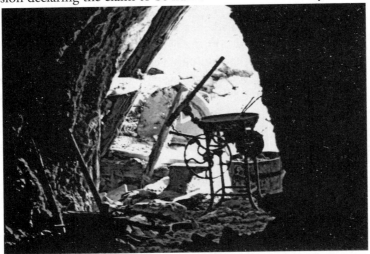

From the outside, the mine did not look like much but inside there was some equipment in use. Photo courtesy of E. Burbank.

ington was fined $1,000 for trespassing and damaging the park.

Even though Henry Covington made his point, that he did have a valid mining claim, he never worked the mine. Sometime before 1970 Covington died, and the mining claim was declared null and void by administrative decision, subject to appeal by

Covington's heirs. On February 17, 1972 the case was marked closed.

The mining claim that represented Covington's dreams of wealth is now no more than an insignificant scratch at the top of the Redwall, testimony to the fact that man's hopes, dreams and problems disappear, but the Grand Canyon lasts forever.

For most people the changes in the 1960s, the loss of family and neighbors, the decline of ranchers and the influx of tourists, would have been an emotional rollercoaster ride. But I like to think that Riffey needed only to stand on the rim at Toroweap Overlook and view the vast canyon—maybe even remember how Covington's problem, which had seemed so important to both Covington and the Park Service, had simply disappeared—to regain his emotional stability. Perhaps, this was why he said in an interview with Julie Russell shortly before he died, "I never let very much of anything disturb me for a very long time."

Chapter 11
The Extra Mile

Everyone who knew Riffey has a story about how he helped them, but he didn't just help people, he put himself out to be helpful. He went the extra mile.

At first it was the ranchers who were beneficiaries of this helpfulness. Permittees were allowed a certain number of cows or horses on the Monument, and it was Riffey's job to count the livestock as it entered or left. Riffey did more than count; he camped out with the ranchers and helped with the cattle drives. Ranchers, who had resented the intrusion of the Park Service, suddenly saw it in a new light.

River runners were the next group to enjoy his helpfulness. In the late 1940s and early 1950s a handful of daring young men— P.T. Reilly, Doc Marston, Norm Nevills and a few others—began boating down the Colorado River. Riffey was asked to watch for these river runners, and to make sure they got through the treacherous Lava Falls Rapid. At first Riffey watched from the rim with binoculars. But he wanted a closer look, so the next time a boat party came through, he hiked down the Lava Falls Trail and met them. This led to his being invited to accompany them on river trips. Soon all river runners knew if they got in trouble they had a friend up on the rim at Toroweap Overlook, which brings me to a story told by Dave Mortenson about his father, V.R. (Brick) Mortenson.

Brick Mortenson, who had started running the river in 1955, was a boatman in the P.T. Reilly party. In those days, before Glen Canyon Dam, the spring runoff (side streams dumping into the river) could make the river wild and dangerous. Now the Glen Canyon Dam releases between 5,000 and 30,000 cubic feet of water per second (cfs), but in 1957 when this adventure began the river topped out at 125,000 cfs.

Because of the high water and dangerous conditions the Reilly party stopped their trip at Bright Angel Creek and left their boats at the river gauging station. In May of 1958, they returned to complete the trip. However, the river was once again running wild. Near Mile 140 Brick's boat flipped over. The boat was lost and Brick almost drowned.

When they reached Lava Falls Rapid they had only two boats for six people. According to Dave's story, told in the *John Riffey Memorial Tall Tale Rendezvous* booklet, "Lining the boats in Lava looked very risky and running it was totally out of the question. They knew it would be safer to hike out and go to John Riffey's place for help."

They cached some of their supplies, prepared to carry some things up the Lava Falls Trail and turned their remaining two boats loose. Would the boats make it to Lake Mead? They could only hope.

Brick was the first to make it to the rim and start walking the six miles to the ranger station. When he was about halfway there he met Riffey driving toward the rim. Riffey picked up Brick and then drove on to the rim and gathered up the others and their gear.

Riffey loaned these stranded boaters his personal pickup, allowing them to drive to Temple Bar on Lake Mead, (a distance of more than two hundred miles) where they had left their own vehicles. A search of Lake Mead turned up two of their boats and the third was found by hikers a few years later.

Dave Mortenson concluded this story: "From Riffey's perspective it was probably all in a day's work. But without the knowledge of John Riffey above at the Toroweap Ranger Station this river party probably would have attempted to continue on with only two boats. Had they had another flip, which was highly possible, they would probably have lost more than another boat." Although typical of Riffey's helpfulness, this was more than "all in a day's work"—this was going the extra mile.

In May 1951, photographer and river runner, Martin Litton, and his wife came to Tuweep intent on hiking down the Lava Falls Trail. He remembered Riffey's greeting when they drove up was, "Well, you managed to get yourselves lost, huh?" Upon learning that they weren't lost, Riffey invited them into his home.

In a telephone conversation with Litton I learned that he and his wife spent several nights as house guests and were made to feel welcome by both Riffey and Laura. Riffey gave them directions, (there is no real trail so directions are important) but he did not try to dissuade them from their proposed hike.

They made it down to the river without any trouble and camped for several days. However, coming back up the trail loaded with sleeping bags, cameras and a tripod was a different story.

Litton said, "We started to come back up. Now you need, not two hands to come up from the river, you need three or four hands. You're working all the time, and the land is coming down as you go up. ... you reach out, and try to pull yourself up by a rock, and the rock comes off and goes, and you're lucky it doesn't take you with it, as it goes to the river."

Riffey had told them to stash canteens along the trail on their way down, and Litton remembered, "The only thing that kept us going up, was the thought of that next canteen." Riffey met them at the top of this trail and, according to Litton, was "draped with canteens."

One trip up the Lava Falls Trail was enough for Litton. After this experience he vowed to never again hike *up* this trail. Therefore, some time later when he returned as a guide for a group of ladies joining a river expedition at Lava Falls, he hitched a ride with the boat party to Whitmore Wash where Riffey had agreed to meet him. The hike out at that point was shorter and easier, and

Litton could ride back to his vehicle at the ranger station in the 4-wheel-drive van that Riffey called the Monster.

Since Whitmore Wash is less than thirty miles from the ranger station, this doesn't sound like anything more than Riffey's usual helpfulness. But the route to Whitmore (which cannot be called a road) parallels the canyon and winds through deep washes. In many places one can walk faster than one can drive. It took Riffey ten hours to drive to Whitmore and back.

Litton, acting as a guide, made this trip down the Lava Falls Trail several times, and each time Riffey met him at Whitmore Wash. As usual, Riffey was ready to go the extra mile, even over an almost nonexistent trail.

In 1958 Riffey went well beyond the call of duty to help a Las Vegas-based flight school recover one of their airplanes, which had landed in S.B. Canyon. A student pilot on his solo flight lost his way, ran out of gas and landed in S. B., a tributary of the Grand Canyon. The pilot didn't know where he was, but it is very likely he called it by its proper name. He hiked along the Esplanade and after three days reached Toroweap Overlook.

The pilot was safe, but the rental plane was still down in the canyon. Riffey, my father and a mechanic/pilot from Las Vegas hiked down into S.B., camped for several days and repaired the plane's landing gear. When the mechanic deemed the airplane ready to fly, they cleared a short runway down the side of the hill. This runway ended in a drop-off. They tied the plane down; the pilot got in, revved up the engine and, on a given signal, Al and Riffey cut the ropes. When the plane reached the end of the runway, it was either fly or fall. The plane flew.

During the 1960s when Riffey's duties changed from range management to recreation management, park visitors became the main beneficiaries of his extra mile of service. Most visitors to the Monument were familiar with the terrain, and Riffey was seldom called on to search for lost hikers. But in 1969 two groups of students from Northern Arizona University hiked into the canyon from opposite directions intending to meet in Tuckup Canyon. Susan Varin, Jim Sears and John Wehrman hiked into the canyon from the south while at the same time George Billingsly and Jan Jensen came in from the north side at Tuckup Canyon. The plan was for Varin, Sears and Wehrman to float across the river on air mattresses and meet Billingsly and Jensen in Tuckup Canyon. That was the plan, but things don't always go according to plan.

Somehow the two groups missed their rendezvous. Billingsly and Jensen hiked out of the canyon, alerted authorities of Mohave County at Kingman, Arizona about the missing hikers and then drove to Tuweep to ask for help. They explained the situation to Riffey. Even though a search of the area was already in progress, Billingsly wanted to fly over Tuckup to look for his friends. He stated in his journal, "I wanted to get over to Tuckup so bad I was willing to walk over there since I couldn't get any one to go." According to Billingsly, "He (Riffey) said 'hop in the plane and we'll go look.'"

However, while Billingsly and Riffey were flying in Pogo over the Tuckup Trail the missing hikers were found by another searcher on the road to the Craig Ranch.

Another time, Myron G. Best, a geology professor from Brigham Young University, was "the beneficiary of John's good-natured assistance and kindness." A note written by Professor Best in a book at Riffey's gravesite tells how in April 1979, he and a group of Geology 101 students were caught in an April snowstorm at the Toroweap Overlook. They decided to abandon the field trip. But after loading their camping equipment into the school van they discovered the vehicle would only go in reverse. The professor backed the van the six miles from the rim to the ranger station and told Riffey of his problem.

Professor Best's tribute to Riffey reads in part:

"After trying quick fixes, such as adding more transmission fluid, all to no avail, John simply said in a matter-of-fact way 'Well, hop in the (crew-cab) pickup, and I'll drive you into

Kanab.' It was a bit of a challenge getting us all on two bench seats, but with some creative squeezing and stacking of bodies we were on our way." Every few miles Riffey stopped to let everyone get out and run around to restore blood circulation. Once again Riffey had gone the extra mile (or in this case 72 miles) to help park visitors.

Best ends this story with: "On our next April field trip the next class of Geology 101 students, hearing of the Good Samaritan, offered to bake a batch of chocolate chip cookies for John. But alas, he was gone."

With the increase in visitation Riffey's duties now included picking up roadside trash, emptying garbage cans and, if the visitor was interested, explaining the geology of the canyon. At the same time he continued to fly fire patrols, fight fires, repair and service Park Service vehicles and write reports (even though no one seems to remember seeing him do this, he did write monthly reports.) He accepted the additional tasks of recreation management without changing his friendly, helpful way of accommodating people.

Because he didn't wear his uniform, campers at the rim sometimes mistook him for a park maintenance man. Riffey told of one camper who asked him if he ever saw the old ranger who lived in the cabin up the road.

Riffey enjoyed meeting people and always had time to chat with the visitors, both serious students of nature or, in his opinion, misguided youth. He liked to tell about a young man camped on the rim, who said he was a student at a university. He named a college Riffey had never heard of and said he was studying the Grand Canyon. Interested and ready to offer information, Riffey asked about the curriculum. The young fellow explained that he could study whatever he wanted and when he felt he had covered the subject he would be given college credit for it—no textbooks, no final exam. Amused by this approach to education, Riffey said, "You must be very mature. I'm sixty years old, and I don't think

I'm mature enough for that kind of education."

The Park Service would have had to hire three people to replace Riffey. In recognition of his extra miles of service the Forest Service and the Park Service jointly presented him with a Superior Performance Award in 1965 at a special ceremony. It is worth noting here that Riffey was in full dress uniform for this presentation. Several years before, Riffey's superior, Superintendent McLaughlin, had been reprimanded by the Director of the National Park Service because when the Director visited Tuweep, Riffey was not in uniform. McLaughlin defended Riffey by pointing out that rangers couldn't fight fires, fix fences or dig ditches in uniform. The uniforms cost too much and the rangers didn't make that much money. Afterward, McLaughlin told Riffey about this reprimand and said in the future he would let him know when he might expect official visitors, and he had better get the uniform out.

Another incident regarding uniforms occurred in 1968 when all rangers were issued a new badge to replace the traditional arrowhead badge. The new badge was unpopular with rangers and two years later it was recalled. Riffey returned his badge still in its plastic wrapper.

On June 28, 1970, Riffey received the Department of the Interior's Meritorious Service Award. This award, the Department's second highest award, was signed by Walter J. Hickel, Secretary of the Interior on December 31, 1969. Riffey graciously accepted the award and even posed for a picture with Superintendent Robert Lovegren. However, a visitor's thank you carried as much weight with Riffey as a piece of paper signed by the Secretary of the Interior.

Riffey helped everyone but never felt he was doing anything out of the ordinary. He helped ranchers, rescued hikers and boaters and welcomed park visitors as if they were his best friends. When asked if the increase in Toroweap Overlook visitation bothered him, he answered with a typical understatement, "It hasn't bothered me to any great extent. ..... I like people."

The ranger's house looked less barren and more welcoming than it had when John and Laura first moved in.

Chapter 12
Meribeth and the Bird Girls

Dr. Meribeth Mitchell came to Tuweep in the spring of 1964 on a field trip with a group of students from the University of Utah. Meribeth, a professor of biology at Western Washington University, was on sabbatical leave and taking classes at the University of Utah in Salt Lake City.

Whenever Riffey was asked how he met Meribeth he would say, "She came to the valley hunting flowers and I stole her shoes." But that is, of course, not what happened. In fact, no one seems to know exactly what happened, but it is a pretty good guess that Meribeth "set her cap" for the Tuweep ranger the first time she met him. At any rate, after that first encounter she returned with a friend, camped on the rim and became better acquainted with Riffey.

In my mother's diary the first mention of Meribeth is on November 13, 1964. Mother said Dr. Mitchell, Riffey and another couple came for dinner. My mother wrote that, "Dr. Mitchell (Meribeth) seemed to particularly enjoy the evening."

Some people I've interviewed have said they were surprised when Riffey announced his intention to marry Meribeth, but I'm sure the announcement came as no surprise to my mother, who noted in her diary that Dr. Mitchell arrived at the ranger station for Christmas and stayed through New Year's Day.

The courtship was not all one sided. Riffey spent Valentine's weekend in Salt Lake City with Meribeth.

Incidentally, he bought a Dodge crew-cab pickup in Cedar City on his way home. Because the new vehicle was like a car with front and back seats, but had a truck bed, it was christened in the words of a song from the '40s, "Alexander the Swoose—half swan and half goose."

After completing her classes at the University, Meribeth came to Tuweep with a truck load of furniture, and my mother and father were called on to help unload it. Mother recalled that clearly there was not room in the small house for both Meribeth's things and Riffey's. My mother suspected that Meribeth's furniture had been recently purchased with the purpose of replacing the first wife's furniture.

A buffet was brought into the house, and a buffet was taken out of the house. A chair came in, a chair went out. A bookcase came in, a bookcase went out. But when Meribeth's small dining table came in, Riffey objected, saying it was too small. Mother remembered that Meribeth asked, "How many people do you expect?" Riffey answered, "Just as many as I can get." That settled it. Riffey's big table stayed in the dining area, and Meribeth's table found a place in the office.

Riffey and Meribeth were married in a Catholic Church in Cedar City on Riffey's 54th birthday, August 28, 1965. Meribeth was a devout Catholic and Riffey was, to use his word, "unchurched." However, he was tolerant of other's beliefs and wishes, so if Meribeth wanted to be married by a priest in a Catholic Church he had no objection.

After the wedding the couple entertained their friends with a wedding dinner at a private home in Leeds, Utah, that catered to small parties.

Riffey was probably attracted to Meribeth, at least in the beginning, because she reminded him of Laura. While neither of these women could be called fat, both had large, well-padded bodies. They wore their hair short and favored comfortable clothes rather than the latest styles; and both had friendly smiles. They even shared the same interest in birds. Meribeth's special area of expertise was ornithology, and she was an Audubon bird bander.

106

Meribeth seemed to enjoy desert living after the rainy Northwest.

Meribeth was more than ten years younger than Riffey, but they shared many similar interests. Probably the one characteristic that made the marriage work was the fact that they both liked people and enjoyed entertaining guests. Before marrying, Meribeth's idea of entertaining was dining out at a nice restaurant. However, there were no restaurants in Tuweep so she bought cookbooks and learned to make delicious company dinners.

Meribeth wanted to continue teaching part time at Western Washington University and apparently Riffey had no objection to this, as long as she didn't expect him to move to Bellingham, Washington. Riffey did spend a couple of his vacations in Washington, but he didn't like being away from Tuweep and his arthritis flared up in the damp climate.

Meribeth worked out a schedule with the university which allowed her to spend half of each year in Tuweep. She taught two quarters and did research projects in Tuweep during the rest of the year. For her research on birds and their habitats she needed student assistants—hence the "bird girls."

My niece, Sharon Empey Carter, was Meribeth's first assistant. Sharon was spending the summer with her grandparents, Al and Mary Craig, in 1967 when Meribeth offered her a job. Sharon drove down the mountain each Monday and spent the week helping Meribeth stake out 50 acre plots in various types of habitat and keep a record of the numbers and kinds of birds found in the plots.

Fun outings were mixed with work projects, and they some-

Meribeth using herself for scale of this penstemon. She contributed to many scientific reports on plants and birds of the Grand Canyon and Kaibab Plateau.

times had picnics at Jacobs Lake while studying birds and plants on the Kaibab National Forest where Meribeth had a special use permit. Sharon was starting college at University of Nevada, Reno that fall, and she remembers that Meribeth took a motherly interest in her, advising her on everything about campus life from classes to clothes.

Sharon returned to work with Meribeth the next summer. After that there were a series of "bird girls," all claimed as granddaughters, great granddaughters or even great, great, granddaughters by Riffey.

Riffey always referred to Meribeth's research projects as counting "dickey birds." One day Al Craig and Riffey decided to spice up the bird count in Meribeth's 50 acre plots with artificial birds purchased at a craft store. Al and Riffey thought this was a very funny joke. Meribeth was not amused.

Every year Riffey had more park visitors and fewer neighbors. My parents moved to St. George, Utah, in 1971 where my father died in '72. After the Craigs left, Riffey's only and closest neighbor was Pat Bundy, 32 miles away. However, Meribeth and her "bird girls" kept Riffey from becoming lonely.

In 1975 the Grand Canyon National Monument became part of the Grand Canyon National Park and the Monument became known as the Tuweep District. Riffey's official title changed from supervisory park ranger to area manager.

Because my mother yearned for her home, but couldn't live there by herself, my two boys and I spent the summers from '75 to '78 with her on the mountain, and I became well acquainted with the last three bird girls: Tryntje Seymour, Mary Allen and Robin Hunter.

Tryntje Seymour came to work in 1976. Meribeth met Tryntje on a school sponsored nine-day raft trip in the Grand Canyon where Meribeth was doing natural history interpretation. Tryntje was an eager student volunteer on the trip, and Meribeth was impressed by her willingness to help with camp chores and the loading and unloading of two big plant presses.

At the end of the trip Meribeth invited the boat crew and students to come to Tuweep for a party on the rim. It would be three days before the student group reached Tuweep, but Tryntje was given a special invitation to fly with Meribeth back to the ranger station and help prepare for the party.

When I interviewed Tryntje she said, "I was pretty wide eyed, because I was born and raised in New York City." She explained, "John (after Riffey married Meribeth her friends started calling him John) pulled every practical joke in the book on me. And I fell for them so well; I think that's the reason they asked me to come back out."

Tryntje worked for Meribeth each summer for five years. During this time there were also two other "bird girls," Mary Allen and Robin Hunter.

Mary Allen came to Tuweep in 1975 with Dr. Richard Thompson, an archeologist from Southern Utah State University in Cedar City. Dr. Thompson camped with a group of his students at a place south and west of the ranger station called The Cove where they excavated ruins that were rich in arrow points and pottery.

Riffey, always interested in scientific studies, drove up to The Cove to check on the group two or three times a week. He brought them water from Nixon Spring, repaired their vehicles and graded

109

the roughest parts of the road to The Cove. Of course, the teacher and students were invited to the ranger station for cookies and

Robin Hunter and Riffey churning ice cream.

coffee. Everyone who came to Tuweep was invited in for Riffey's "fresh baked" cookies that came in a cellophane package labeled "Dad's."

Mary was recruited from among the students doing the archeology dig. She said, "I was enjoying the social life at the ranger station and, you know, she (Meribeth) just kind of approached me and said, 'What do you think about coming out here and helping out with birds?'"

Tryntje and Mary both came to work for Meribeth in 1976. They claimed they had the best room in the house—the screened-in porch. They slept on bunk beds and used orange crates for a dresser.

In 1978 Robin Hunter joined Tryntje and Mary as a "bird girl." Robin started off with her own quarters, "The Waldorf Astoria," otherwise known as the garage. Robin didn't like being alone and separated from the others, so Tryntje and Mary invited her to join them on the porch. The three girls roomed together in a space not much bigger than a good-sized clothes closet.

These girls all remembered Riffey's special names for things: racing slicks were pancakes; mud grips were waffles; and flannel cakes were pancakes with a round piece of cotton cloth cooked inside. As a Tuweep initiation, each girl was served a flannel cake as part of her first breakfast. They each remembered being embarrassed when they couldn't cut the pan cake into a bite-size piece, and then enjoying the joke when Riffey removed their plates and served them regular "racing slicks."

Incidentally, the flannel cake breakfast was one of the many things Riffey learned from my dad, Al Craig. I remember, even before Riffey came to Tuweep, that visitors were always served flannel cakes on their first morning at our ranch.

Riffey always introduced the girls as his adopted great, great granddaughters, with one notable exception. Sometimes river boat passengers had to wait for fixed-wing aircraft at the "Tuweep International Airport" after being brought up from the river by helicopter. As a joke the pilots would tell these tourists that there was an old guy who lived in the house nearby who was a polygamist. When Riffey drove up to offer water and information about the valley, these tourists would see three young girls in his pickup. Mary Allen remembered the strange looks they got and stranger questions they were asked. Rather than ask what it was like to be a polygamist wife, they were asked how they liked living in Tuweep and if they ever got to go to town. Riffey would go along with the joke, introducing Tryntje, Mary and Robin as his wives.

In the summer there were always a lot of people at the ranger station. As Riffey explained to an interviewer, "Somehow or another, I can't really understand it, but when you get a bunch of

111

those good looking girls, you have boys."

People liked Riffey and they came back again and again, not just to see the beautiful scenery, but to visit with their friend. And everyone was greeted as a friend. Riffey didn't judge a person by his income, intelligence or years of education. The biker who rode up on his Harley was greeted as warmly as the banker in his "Texas Cadillac."

One of those who returned again and again was Art Gallenson. Art met Riffey in 1963 when he and two college friends stopped by the ranger station on their way to the rim. Art became one of Riffey's best friends and has provided me with many interesting stories about Riffey. Art says the Tuweep Ranger Station, "was not just a ranger station; it was a happening."

I have accounts of these "happenings" or social occasions from two sources. Both Art Gallenson and Edie Eilander have described a memorable Thanksgiving. Edie, a rural Colorado school teacher and writer, first came to Tuweep in 1971. Remembering Thanksgiving in 1978 she wrote, "...a group of 'granddaughters,' as he liked to call us, gathered at Tuweep to share Thanksgiving dinner with Riffey. It was a wonderful time, filled with stories and laughter, warmth and turkey, (and) fourteen pumpkin pies."

Art also remembered this Thanksgiving. Among the twenty-six guests were two medical doctors, Dr. Wallen and Dr. Janis, who had come to the party with a banjo and a guitar. Art recalls Riffey's saying, "When we got our doctors going, the roof would jump up and down."

In the summertime there were Grand Canyon river boat crew parties with between twenty-five and thirty people enjoying Riffey's special hospitality. Guests were sometimes entertained on the flagstone terrace in front of the house, and other times the party was on the rim of the canyon. Beef tenderloin fillets and homemade ice cream (two of Meribeth's culinary successes) were always part of the menu. Overnight guests stayed in either the Waldorf Astoria (garage) or the Hyatt Regency (the fire cache) and both were often at full occupancy.

Art remembers one of these summertime shindigs was a combination crew party and birthday party for Pat Bundy, an eighty-three-year-old homesteader who lived on the other side of the mountain and was Riffey's only permanent neighbor.

When Pat arrived for the party, he was driving his battered Jeep with springs poking out of the seat cushions. Wanting to be helpful, Art started to tie the springs down. Riffey stopped

Dear Lord. We thank you.
Photo courtesy of Gene I. Wendt

him saying, "Don't do that! If the springs don't poke him, Pat will fall asleep and kill himself."

Always helpful, Art became the bartender for this celebration. He mixed Riffey a "school-boy" bourbon-and-seven and then knowing Pat to be a Mormon, offered him a choice of lemonade or soda. Pat nodded at Riffey's drink and said, "I believe I'll have one of those." At the ranger station you could be yourself—no pretending. You could drink liquor, lemonade or soda; all were acceptable.

My niece Sharon Carter summed it up this way, "He accepted people as they were. He tended to bring out the best in them." Riffey's guests were made to feel part of his family by being introduced as

113

his great, great granddaughters or grandsons and also by being allowed to help with everyday tasks. Edie Eilender, Mary Allen and Art Gallenson all recall being asked to drive Big Scratchy, the road grader.

Edie described this experience in an article titled, "Ranger John Riffey, A Lifetime of Solitude on the North Rim at Tuweep." She wrote, "Riffey announced to the Park Service crew (the current house guests) at breakfast that the conditions were right for grading the road. And that he and I were going to do it. I looked up, my cereal spoon in hand. What? Me, grade the road? But soon we were rumbling along, me behind the wheel of the grader and

Edie Eilander, Riffey and Marvyl Wendt by the picture window.
Photo courtesy of Gene I. Wendt.

Riffey, beside me, giving instructions. Not only did I learn how to drive Scratchy, John's name for the grader, and to move dirt from one side of the road to the other, I learned how to tell the difference between a marsh hawk and a red-tail."

In the mid 1970s, a young couple from Tennessee joined the

114

Tuweep family. Rick and Teresa were touring the country in an old army bus. They came to Toroweap Overlook for a short visit and stayed for the whole winter. Originally headed for southeast Texas, they met Riffey, lost track of time and forgot all about the sunny beaches of Texas.

As cold weather approached Rick and Teresa realized they had a problem. An old bus converted into living quarters was great for summer camping, but it was not made for cold weather. Riffey came up with a solution to their problem. Since my mother's house on Mt. Trumbull was vacant, he suggested that they could make arrangements with her to live in it during the winter to protect it from the ravages of weather and vandalism.

Rick and Teresa moved into the Craigs' house and enjoyed being Riffey's great, great, great grandchildren so much that they came back again the next winter.

During the 1970s there were many great, great, great grandchildren. Two that I haven't already mentioned were Helen Habgood, who was also a bird girl, and Bob Dye, one of the river boatmen.

Riffey's guests were always treated to genuine generous hospitality and even though he had problems and concerns, he never let them show. Sometimes he was lonely, especially after Laura died. But when asked about it he said, "You do get lonely occasionally. There's nobody who wouldn't." And when asked what he did when he got lonely he answered, "Go to work; that always cures it."

However, there would have been many lonely days for Riffey after Laura died, if he hadn't married Meribeth, who recruited young girls for assistants, who in turn attracted young boys. In the summertime, Meribeth and the bird girls and all the great, great grandchildren turned the ranger station into a social center.

Supervising photographers Ted Phillips and Ted Cate at Toroweap Point, looking eastward into the gorge. October 1953.

Chapter 13
Stuck in the Mud

No matter what route one chooses, going to Tuweep, means driving on a dirt road. In dry weather, these roads are miles and miles of wheel-ruts and dust. In wet weather, these same roads turn into miles and miles of wheel-ruts and mud.

Therefore, many stories about Riffey involve being stuck in the mud. The occasional torrential summer rain storms and winter snow melt made getting stuck a real possibility. In fact, old-timers had words of caution for newcomers. In the monsoon season the advice was, "Get over the road before noon," because the summer thunder storms came in the afternoons and evenings. In the winter when snow melt caused the problem the advice was, "Wait for the freeze."

Locals always travel with tire chains, a shovel and a canteen of water. The chains, of course, are to be put on before getting stuck. But even with chains, vehicles still get bogged down in the mud. Arizona Strip mud is the slickest, gummiest and deepest in the world—just ask anyone who ever got mired down in one of the many loblollies that booby-trap the road.

When you become stuck you push, shovel and chop sagebrush. Sagebrush laid in the ruts sometimes, but not always, gives enough traction to get your vehicle unstuck. If pushing, shoveling and chopping sagebrush fail, if you are hopelessly stuck, you either settle down to wait for help or else grab your canteen and walk for help.

The first Tuweep Ranger, Bill Bowen and his wife Gertrude, had only been at the ranger station a few months when they had their mud initiation. Coming back to the ranger station after a week at the South Rim they got stuck near June Tank.

In an interview conducted by Cathy Alger, Bill Bowen described this experience. "...up there by June Tank was one of the places where the road went wherever it looked like you could go. When the ruts got too deep, they moved over and went somewhere else. And I got in there and it was raining and snowing and I couldn't find anything better to do than try to straddle the last rut. I was going just fine except I slipped into it. And, of course, with two-wheel drive you didn't have any great surge of power then, so we slept out there that night."

The next day Bill and Gertrude, who was six months pregnant, walked nine miles to the Kent upper place. Bud Kent drove them in his truck the remaining ten miles to the ranger station. On March 11, 1941, Bill submitted a travel voucher for this trip to Park Headquarters. His letter with the voucher told about his experience. He received compensation for vehicle miles traveled but only sympathy for their long walk.

Riffey's mud experiences usually (but not always) involved getting hapless travelers unstuck. My dad liked to tell how he and Riffey pulled some "damn fool hunter" out of a mud hole. That "damn fool" was Senator Berry Goldwater, who ran for president. After that incident, that particular mud hole was called Goldwater Gulch.

The places where travelers were likely to get stuck besides Goldwater Gulch were: (to name a few) Bony Hollow Wash, Hack Canyon, Clayhole and John's Bog. On the road up the mountain to the Craig Ranch there was a bad spot called the Knuckle. Snow melt in the winter caused the problems at the Knuckle, and many a time my dad had to walk the five miles from the Knuckle to our homestead.

Riffey's experience at the Knuckle came one cold night in January 1970. My dad's health was failing and Riffey had been asked to bring my sister, Margaret Empey, to the ranch to help with chores, and Pat Bundy had also hitched a ride to his homestead on the other side of the mountain. Late that night they got stuck on the Knuckle. Not wanting to wake my mother and dad up in the middle of the night, Riffey, Margaret and Pat spent the night wrapped in a sleeping bag and old quilts in the cab of the truck. At daybreak the next morning, Riffey walked to the Craig Ranch, drove Al's tractor back to the Knuckle and pulled the truck out of the mud.

A few years later when Rick and Teresa Wynn were staying at the Craig Ranch a woman who had been visiting them got stuck going down the Knuckle. Somehow it didn't occur to this woman to leave her VW van and walk back to the ranch. Six days later, Riffey came along. At this point in the story someone would always ask, "Was she starving?" And Riffey would answer, "She was a vegetarian, and by the time I got there, she did have the place pretty well grazed down."

Then there was John's Bog adjacent to the John Schmutz homestead in Tuweep. This was the mother of all mud holes. When it rained, Riffey always flew over John's Bog to see if anyone was stuck.

Some of Riffey's friends recall that they met him when they became stuck in John's Bog. Tony Williams recounted this experience at the John Riffey Memorial Tall Tales Rendezvous. According to Tony he met Riffey on his second trip to the rim in 1971. He didn't actually get stuck, because he says he had "sense enough to stop before the bog, and after walking it, decided to walk to the rim." He hadn't gone far when he was met by Riffey in a mud-covered government truck. Riffey gave Tony a ride to the rim and then invited him for dinner that night.

Tony concluded this story by saying that after that he visited Riffey at the ranger station every summer staying for several days, sometimes as long as a week. He became part of the Tuweep family—a great, great grandson.

Not everyone who got stuck in John's Bog became Riffey's

friend. Even though Riffey was usually careful and considerate of the vehicle when giving a tow, there was one time when he was not careful.

Late one summer evening after a thunder storm Riffey and his guests at the ranger station saw a yellow glow in the sky. Fire! Quickly they got in the Park Service fire-pumper truck and drove up the valley. When they got to John's Bog they found a late model car stuck in the mud and John Schmutz's barn was a smoldering heap of ashes and charcoal.

The owner of the car explained that after getting stuck he and his girl friend had built a fire in the barn to keep warm. The young man seemed to think this was very funny, and he was more concerned about his vehicle than the burned barn. When John Schmutz's son, Ray, told me about this he described the young couple as irresponsible and reckless and, while he didn't say so, alcohol may have been involved.

Riffey was disgusted by their lack of concern for another's property and when he was asked to give them a pull, he gave them a real pull! Ray told me, "Because they got a sideways pull to get them out and bent something ...they were unhappy. But he (Riffey) didn't care. He was pretty disgusted."

This story reminded Ray Schmutz of another irresponsible (actually criminal) young couple that he found stuck in the mud. Ray and his ranch hand, Tex Moore, gave this couple a ride to their camp in Tuweep and then got in touch with Riffey. When Riffey radioed a description of the couple and their vehicle to South Rim, he learned that they were wanted for theft. They had been traveling across the country stealing stuff as they went. However, their crime spree came to an end in a mud hole on the Arizona Strip.

Riffey's personal pickup was named Alexander, the Swoose. It was half car and half pickup. However, in spite of being "half swan and half goose," Riffey learned it couldn't swim.

Soon after Riffey and Meribeth married they were coming

home from town after a rain storm. At Hack Canyon, another infamous mud hole, they found the road flooded. According to Riffey, Meribeth said, "You better not drive off in there!" But Riffey decided to assert himself, let his new bride know he knew what he was doing.

This was neither the time nor the place to be assertive. The force of the water carried them downstream a few feet before leaving them wedged into the bank. They were not hurt and the truck was not damaged, but they spent a cold, wet night stuck in Hack Canyon wash before help came along. Riffey always smiled when he told this story and insisted it was all Meribeth's fault because she told him not to drive into the wash.

Locals do get stuck, but it is visitors, unaware of the mud hazards, who most often become victims. One time some of my parent's friends from California stopped in St. George to ask directions to the Craig Ranch. After giving directions their informant asked if they had chains, a shovel and a canteen. When he learned that they had none of these items, he shook his head and said, "No shovel, no canteen, no chains; no brains."

The unprepared traveler is foolish, because getting stuck is an accepted part of living on the Arizona Strip. And nowadays Riffey won't come to your rescue.

Chapter 14
The Magic Window

It is a ranger's duty to preserve and protect our National Parks. Riffey carried this mandate one step further. He preserved, protected and enjoyed his park. He enjoyed the scenery, the desert vegetation and the animals—especially the animals. He didn't need household pets, because right outside his front window he had quail, ground squirrels, rabbits and even an occasional bobcat, skunk or coyote.

Everyone who visited Riffey remembers this front window and the view. Mary Allen, one of the bird girls, called it, "the magic window," because when sitting at the dining table one could look out at a small shallow pool surrounded by salt bushes and cactus and watch a never-ending wildlife show.

Sometimes the show featured a mother quail cautiously checking out the territory before giving the signal for her brood to join her for a morning drink. And one could always count on the ground squirrels to perform. Their routine consisted of quick dashes, sudden stops and playful sit-ups. Occasionally, a melodrama was enacted, when a predator, such as a bobcat or coyote, came sneaking onto the stage, not wanting a drink but looking for a meal. This villain was always foiled. The animals would disappear, the stage would become empty, and Mr. Bobcat would saunter over to the pool pretending he only wanted a drink.

Judy Elsley, a young woman from England who spent two months as Riffey's guest in 1980, remembered in an article titled, "Getting Comfortable: A Woman in the West," that she always threw a cupful of grain in front of the window so that she and

Riffey could watch the Gambel's Quail while they ate breakfast. Judy didn't call it a "magic window," but I'm sure she would agree that that is what it was.

My niece, Sharon Carter, remembers how she and her two sons sat by this window one evening. She said, "We were graced by the presence of a ringtail cat, running around the window looking in and, if you moved, he'd duck and hide." Ringtail cats are rarely seen, but in the 1970s one made regular appearances at the "magic window," and was given the name of Misty the Ringtail.

All of Meribeth's student helpers have told me of their fond memories of the wildlife at the ranger station. In addition to the "magic window" they talk about the screened-in-porch—"the best room in the house," according to Tryntje Seymour. Tryntje remembers sleeping on the porch and hearing a mocking bird or a coyote chorus at night. Tryntje also remembered how a humming bird flew into the screen around the porch and got its beak stuck. She described for me how Riffey carefully, gently pushed its beak back out, letting the humming bird fly away.

Both Meribeth and Riffey rescued and nurtured sick or wounded animals, and these animals were given names. There was: Pelican Pete, Robert the Reject, L.P., Lazarus the Lizard and Geraldine the Dumbest Eagle in the West.

Pelican Pete was rescued from a pond in upper Tuweep where he'd landed exhausted, suffering from a damaged wing. Meribeth with the help of the Cusick family from Fredonia drove the pelican up onto the bank of the pond. Then Meribeth, wearing welding gloves, caught him. She put the pelican in a gunny sack and took him to the ranger station to recuperate.

After a few days when Pelican Pete had regained his strength, but was still unable to fly, she released him at Nixon Spring. The fish in the pond at the spring would provide him with meals while he convalesced. Someone (maybe Riffey) put up a sign by the pond that said, "Don't Shoot Pelican Pete."

Robert the Reject is remembered by many of Riffey's visitors.

Some predator had tried to make a meal of this ground squirrel, but he'd managed to get away. Badly mangled, but still active he was named Robert the Reject and lived in a cage Riffey bought for him. Eventually when Riffey thought he could make it on his own, he was turned loose to join his brothers, sisters and cousins by the dozens in front of the magic window.

Robert the Reject. Photo courtesy of George I. Wendt.

L.P. was a baby ground squirrel that had somehow been gassed. Meribeth fed him with an eyedropper and nursed him back to health.

One fall day Riffey found Lazarus the Lizard—cold and stiff—looking more dead than alive. But when Riffey put him behind the wood burning stove, like his biblical namesake, he came back to life. Lazarus spent that winter in the house.

Geraldine, the Dumbest Eagle in the West, was rescued by Meribeth. Geraldine had been abandoned by her mother, and even though she was perfectly healthy, she would not fly. Meribeth tried to teach her to fly by putting her on the garage roof and then dragging a piece of meat on a rope across the roof. Geraldine would hop after the meat, but when Meribeth pulled it off the roof Geraldine would not fly after it. In fact, rather than fly, Geraldine descended by way of the ladder, hopping from rung to rung. Eventually the eagle did learn to fly, but she continued to hang around the ranger station hoping for a handout.

However, most of the wildlife at the ranger station remained in its natural habitat. The few that needed care were the exception, not the rule.

All animals were welcome at the shallow pool in Riffey's front yard with one exception. When a rattle snake slithered up to the pool hoping to make a meal on a ground squirrel or quail, Riffey caught him with a hook on a long pole and put him in a gunny sack. Sack and snake were then put in the refrigerator. When the snake became too cold to move, Riffey took him in an ice chest to a new hunting ground, far away from the ranger station.

A few months ago I visited the new ranger and his wife at the Tuweep ranger station. Sadly I noted that the cement pool has disappeared. (I suppose the Park Service has some rule about not feeding and watering wild animals.)

The young ranger and his wife invited my husband, my niece and me to dinner. The meal was delicious and the conversation lively. Riffey would have liked that. But the dining table no longer sits in front of the "magic window" and, of course, the magic is gone.

Chapter 15
The Last Winter

Judy Elsley, an English woman, spent two months with Riffey during the winter of his last year. She described this experience in an article titled, "A Winter with Riffey" published by Jumping Cholla Press, Tucson, AZ, 1997, and reprinted in *John Riffey Memorial Tall Tale Rendezvous*, booklet compiled and published by Liz Roberts. Because Judy Elsley's article is definitive, I have with her permission, used it as a major source for information about Riffey's last winter.

Judy met Riffey through her uncle, who in the 1960s planned a tour of the U.S. for her and her English parents. The itinerary included Riffey and Toroweap Overlook. Judy's uncle had read an article about the Tuweep ranger in the *New York Times* and had written to Riffey asking if he might visit him. Riffey, of course, said yes.

Some years after that initial visit Judy's uncle returned with his niece for another visit. Judy visited Riffey several more times and, for a brief time, became one of Meribeth's bird girls. While at the ranger station she fell in love with a man she met there and in 1979 moved to the United States. Judy lived with the boyfriend for a few months until he left her. That's when she turned to Riffey for help. She arrived on his doorstep in November 1979 and she says, Riffey "rolled out the hideaway bed in his office and made room for me."

A letter Riffey wrote that winter to his long-time friend, Mark Everett, would indicate that he too may have been feeling abandoned. In a letter dated 1/20/80, Riffey wrote: "Meribeth is back teaching. Seems to be over her last year's cancer bout and doing fine. Also had to have a foot operation recently and that is coming along OK too. Kept her from coming down here for Xmas. Had a turkey all ready and no one showed up to eat it. Still living on scraps. Good thing I like turkey!"

When I interviewed Mary Allen she remembered that Riffey had also invited her to come to the ranger station for Christmas. However, circumstances prevented her from accepting the invitation.

On Christmas morning Judy and Riffey were all by themselves and probably feeling lonely. As an antidote for loneliness Riffey suggested that they take a special tour of the canyon in Pogo. Judy wrote, "It was a sunny windless morning with just a skiff of clouds. Instead of flying over the canyon as we often did, we dropped into it—strictly against Park Service regulations. We flew about 600 feet above the green water, the steep red walls sheer on either side of us."

In addition to this account of their Christmas adventure Judy gave a detailed description of a typical day at the ranger station that winter.

The day started at 6:30 when Judy was awakened by the electric juicer. Breakfast began with orange juice, "one eye opener" and coffee, "the other eye opener." In addition to the mudgrips and racing slicks which the bird girls remembered, they also had gruel (oatmeal) served with toast with axle grease (butter) and plum jelly, which might actually be apricot or raspberry jelly.

After breakfast the day was filled with activities. Judy went with him to check stock tanks and break ice for cattle; to check on tourists and offer help if needed and to empty the garbage cans at the rim. At the rim they always took time to look down into the canyon to enjoy the view or, as Riffey would say, to make sure the Indians hadn't stolen it.

Sometimes Riffey would disappear into his workshop. According to Judy, "There was always something to be fixed. The breakdowns were all the fault of Witch Hazel and her horde of little egeroties. .... They specialized in dead batteries that winter."

Ten o'clock was coffee-break time. Coffee was served with cookies that Riffey claimed to have baked that morning, as he shook them out of the cellophane wrapper. Lunch consisted of do-it-yourself sandwiches. The afternoon break was "time to get drunk." Riffey, who believed in moderation, did not get drunk, but he did enjoy a bourbon-and-seven served with Carters (peanuts). And the dinner menu—regardless of what was actually served—was always announced as "beef steaks smothered in pork chops."

One day in January, Judy remembered, former Superintendent Merle Stitt accompanied by other Park Service officials flew into Tuweep to present Riffey with a "ruby pin to mark forty years of faithful service for the government of the United States." The Park Service "brass" wore full dress uniforms. Riffey as usual was wearing denim jeans and a plaid shirt, and as Judy remembers, the pants were stained with grease.

Riffey graciously accepted the pin with some comment about the way time flies and then, as Phil Shoemaker, the Park Service pilot, recalls "said he would be sure and put it right next to his 20 year and 30 year pins." Phil remembers that Riffey walked into his office and, as he passed him, he winked and said under his breath, "if I can find them." Judy wrote of this event that he then served his guests coffee and cookies "that he had baked himself just that morning."

During that winter Judy did not note anything unusual in Riffey's behavior, but, in retrospect, she realized he'd known his body wasn't going to last much longer. He talked half-heartedly about retirement, but Judy also remembered he said, "A place good enough to work and live, is good enough to die," and "Don't call the helicopter till you know I'm dead."

And Judy was probably the last person to be given a ride in

Pogo. Even though Riffey never mentioned it, he'd almost certainly had dizzy spells and warning signs of an impending heart attack. He continued to fly for another couple of months, but refused to take anyone with him.

Superintendent Stitt, on his last day before retiring, presented Riffey with his ruby pin. Within seven months they had both died.

In the spring, Meribeth returned as usual to continue her bird research. Because the BLM was no longer funding this project, only one assistant, Tryntje Seymour, was hired.

Tryntje had always enjoyed flying with Riffey, so when he flew on fire patrol she asked if she could go with him. Instead of saying, "come along" as he had in the past, he simply refused to take her with him. She didn't understand his refusal then, but now realizes he knew of his heart condition, and, while he didn't mind leaving this world in Pogo, he didn't want to take anyone with him.

Shortly before his death Riffey sold Pogo to Phil Shoemaker.

Phil, who now lives in Alaska, wrote, "During the time I owned Pogo I flew around the canyon country at every opportunity and on calm, early mornings I loved to fly deep into the inner gorge of the canyon. It was still legal at that time and the small engine of Pogo was quiet. John enjoyed this type of flying and was quite accomplished at it. I am convinced John knew he was ill, which is why he suddenly decided to quit flying, but I was a flight instructor and was able to talk John into taking one last early morning flight with me in the back and him again at the controls of Pogo. So from John's last views both Pogo and I were happy."

Even though Riffey had been given a special dispensation that allowed him to remain in his position for as long as he could perform his duties, officials at the South Rim realized they might soon be losing the "last old-time ranger." In the interest of preserving his history and the history of Tuweep, Julie Russell, a Park Service employee was sent to interview him.

The interview began on May 16th and was continued the next day. Julie's questions covered subjects from Riffey's birth and life to his knowledge of Tuweep. Riffey refrained from his usual tall tales, but the document contains a couple of errors caused either by Riffey's not remembering a detail or by inaccurate transcription of the tape.

Riffey never told anyone—not Judy Elsley, not Phil Shoemaker, not Julie Russell—of his forewarnings of a heart attack. Yet it is almost certain that Riffey knew his days in Tuweep were drawing to an end.

Chapter 16
The Last Day

On July 9, 1980, Riffey drove to Nixon Spring on Mount Trumbull to fill the water tanks on the Park Service truck used for fire fighting. Howard Ferris, who was camping next to the ranger station with his wife and son, went with Riffey.

The Ferrises had been vacationing in Tuweep for almost twenty years. They spent two weeks every summer enjoying the peace and quiet of the canyon and two weeks every fall deer hunting on Mount Trumbull. During these visits Riffey and the Ferrises had become good friends. So in 1980 when they arrived in Tuweep, instead of camping near the rim, they parked their motorhome next to the ranger station.

According to Howard Ferris, after they got to the spring, Riffey told him what to do with the hoses. Since normally Riffey would not have needed help, he probably wasn't feeling well that morning.

When the tank was full they started back down the mountain. Twice Riffey cut corners short and one time they almost went into a ditch. Riffey said his eyes were playing tricks on him and asked Howard to drive. He stopped the vehicle, and they changed seats.

Shortly before arriving at the ranger station they met Mrs. Ferris and Meribeth walking. They stopped, and the women got in. By the time they reached the station it was obvious that Riffey was not well and he had to be helped into the house. Meribeth wanted to call the South Rim for a doctor, but Riffey absolutely refused. He kept insisting that his condition was not serious and he would be alright in a few minutes.

Finally he said, "We're going to have to go to St. George."

Since he would not let Meribeth call the South Rim for a helicopter, they decided to transport him in the Ferrises' motorhome. The Ferrises' son, Robert, had cerebral palsy and was confined to a wheelchair, so they used his wheelchair to get Riffey into the motorhome.

They helped Riffey onto the bed and started for town. After a short distance Riffey said he needed to use the bathroom. They stopped and helped him into the bathroom, but Riffey said, "Nothing works." Then he passed out. Howard and Meribeth laid him on a sleeping bag on the floor in the hall and they started on for town.

Riffey died shortly after they crossed Clayhole Wash.

Mrs. Ferris wrote, "We stopped to compose ourselves, then went on to the sheriff's office in Colorado City." It was nearly six o'clock when they reached the office of Deputy Sheriff Sam Barlow in Colorado City. Barlow examined the body and confirmed that Riffey was, in fact, dead. It was decided not to move him to an ambulance, and he was taken on to the Spillsbury-Graff Mortuary in St. George in the Ferrises' motorhome.

Mr. and Mrs. Ray Schmutz, my mother and Tony Heaton came to the mortuary that night to help Meribeth make the necessary arrangements. Since it was late the Ferrises and Meribeth spent the night at my mother's home in St. George.

The next morning Meribeth and the Ferrises drove back to the ranger station to get Riffey's (seldom worn) uniform and to inform the Park Service of his death. When the Superintendent at the South Rim heard this news, he immediately suggested that Riffey could be buried in Tuweep.

Art Gallenson, upon learning of Riffey's death flew to Tuweep and he helped Meribeth select a suitable site for the grave. They chose a place a short distance from the ranger station near the road to the rim. The gravesite is on a hillside and, according to Art, a place where Riffey could oversee the valley.

Riffey, a man who often quoted Shakespeare, saying "What fools these mortals be," was no fool. He lived life on his own terms, and he died on his own terms. When Riffey died he had 540 hours of annual leave and 3,600 hours of sick leave. He had taken no annual or sick leave during the year of his death. He didn't take days off because like early day rangers, being a ranger was his way of life, not an eight hour a day job.

A plaque at the 1907 Logging Ranger Station in Glacier Park states, "The first park rangers were chosen for their self-sufficiency and knowledge of the backcountry." This plaque describes in detail the characteristics of an old-time ranger, stating that he was a capable outdoorsman and a jack-of-all-trades.

Riffey was a capable outdoorsman and a jack-of-all-trades, and his death put a period at the end of a tradition that had already disappeared.

He was the last old-time ranger.

Riffey at Boysag Point, September 1979. Photo courtesy of Anthony Williams.

Appendix

Superior Performance Award

John H. Riffey

Without regard to personal sacrifice or inconvenience, you have been performing duties for a number of years for both the National Park Service and the U. S. Forest Service without additional compensation or official recognition. We are sure that you have always felt it to be your overall responsibility to protect the public lands and timber, preserve law and order and maintain facilities, regardless of whether it is under the jurisdiction of the National Park Service or the U.S. Forest Service.

For many years you have been the only park employee stationed at Grand Canyon National Monument. This is a very isolated area, which makes the duties of protection, conservation, maintenance of facilities, law enforcement, interpretation and visitor services extremely diffficult. You have the remarkable ability of talking the language of ranchers and other local residents. They respect you and look to you for advice and assistance. As a result of these desirable relations, both services have had the benefit of the local residents' cooperation and help in many matters, including fire suppression. Many compliments have been received from the U.S. Forest Service, and the Bureau of Land Management, for early detection and suppression of fires on their lands. In expressing the appreciation of your efforts on behalf of the U.S. Forest Service, Mr. F. M. Hodgin, Kaibab National Forest Supervisor, recalls that for the 23 years you have been stationed at Grand Canyon National Monument you have voluntarily taken charge of the fire control job on the 17,500 acres of National Forest land at Mt. Trumbull. In addition to your full-time job of administration at Grand Canyon National Monument, you made discovery, first attack, complete mop-up and suppression, and if necessary, recruitment of local fire fight-

137

ers for all fires in this locality. In addition, you kept the time on these fire fighters and turned it in to the District Forest Ranger in Fredonia for payment. Occasionally several fires would start from the same storm which necessitated your rounding up several of the other local ranchers for fire fighting duties. You then coordinated all the fires and of course kept the time for all the fire fighters. Mr. Hodgin has further stated; "I feel that this is the finest example of devotion to duty and cooperation with another government agency that I have seen in my many years in the Forest Service. If not for John's voluntary 'take charge' attitude, it is very possible that the timber on Mt. Trumbull may have been lost to fire".

Over the years you have been able to resolve problems with National Park Service grazing permittees regarding necessary controls without the necessity of legal action. You have accomplished the maintenance of Monument facilities without assistance and in addition to your assigned ranger duties. We know that much of this work is done without consideration of lieu days or after hours. In accomplishing your law enforcement duties, you have been able to furnish the local people with an understanding and appreciation of park and forest policies, thereby causing them to look to you as an authority on legal matters. Due to this close relationship with the local people, you seldom have experienced the need to resort to court action on such matters.

In recognition of your superior performance of duties in Grand Canyon National Park, and the indispensable help and cooperation you have given Kaibab National Forest, we are pleased and honored to present you this joint National Park Service - U.S. Forest Service cash award in the amount of $500.00.

Signed by Howard B. Stricklin, Superintendent Grand Canyon National Park and F. M. Hodgin, Forest Supervisor Kaibab National Forest. September 1965.

Citation for Meritorious Service

John H. Riffey

in recognition of unusual and outstanding service as Park Ranger at Grand Canyon National Monument, Arizona.

Mr. Riffey has established an enviable record in many fields during his tenure as Park Ranger at Grand Canyon National Monument since 1942. At this one-man area he has performed the roles of Park Ranger, Interpreter, Maintenanceman, and Administrator with a skill and dedication seldom equaled in the National Park Service. Since the Monument is isolated and accident potential is high due to sheer cliffs, Mr. Riffey excels in the area of Visitor Protection and Public Safety by alerting each visitor to these hazards and giving aid and assistance when necessary. He takes great pride in the appearance of the area, keeping the roads and trails in exceptionally good condition and the buildings in an excellent state of repair. As a licensed pilot, Mr. Riffey has his own plane and makes numerous flights following summer thunderstorms. In 1960 he spotted and handled eleven forest fires for which the U. S Forest Service commended Mr. Riffey and expressed their appreciation for the fine cooperation between the two Services. To accomplish this, Mr. Riffey, of his own volition, established an understanding with neighboring ranchers, and trained them for forest fire suppression. Also, through his extraordinary knowledge of range practices, he has assisted in bringing about a substantial reduction in grazing and has improved range conditions by advising the ten permittees authorized to graze stock on Monument lands, of better stock grazing practices and assisted them in placing such practices in effect. In recognition of his unique and hightly effective achievements in the fields of cooperation, interpretation, protection and maintenance at Grand Canyon National Monument, Mr. Riffey is granted the Meritorious Service Award of the Department of the Interior.

Signed by Walter J. Hickel Secretay of the Interior
September 1969

Riffeyisms

Alexander the Swoose - half car/half pickup as in half swan/half goose

axle grease - butter or margarine

beef steaks smothered in pork chops - dinner

Beans

     round beans - peas

     square beans - corn

     long beans - green beans

Big Scratchy - the road grader

Canardly - the green truck that can hardly get over the hill

Charlotte - all spiders

Chinaman - an antique road grader pulled by stock or tractor

Copper Penny - Meribeth's vehicle

Demudder compound - bottle of water for cleaning windshields in wet weather

Desdemona - R-5 Caterpillar

Digby - a badger and one of John's trucks

Dobbin - John's gray truck

Faroda, Pink, Blue or Yellow - wildflowers growing far from a road

flannel cake - a pancake with cloth cooked inside as a practical joke

gruel - oatmeal

Francis - Tote-Goat, a two-wheel scooter

George - the barometer

Goldberg whizgizzes - Riffey inventions to make life easier at Tuweep

Hyatt Regency - the fire cache when used as sleeping quarters

idiot stick - shovel

Igaroties (various spellings) - mythical mischevious beings that cause problems at Tuweep

Jig-along Josie - the road drag built from scapped log-wagon wheel rims.

Kansas credit card - a small rubber hose used to siphon gas

Lazarus - a lizard that lived behind the stove

lost - you're at Tuweep

LP - a pet squirrel that got gassed and was nursed back to health

Menihunies - Igaroties after they left Hawaii and were dehydrated crossing the desert

Misty - a ringtail cat that came to the house

Monster - his 4-wheel-drive van

mud grip - a waffle

Nash Can - Nash automobile

Nasty Nora Kate - Cato generator that tried to burn down the ranger station

Nearoda, Pink, Blue or Yellow - wildflowers growing near a road

Oh-No - Onan generator

one eye opener - orange juice

other eye opener - strong coffee

Pat Pending - a prolific Irish inventor, hence his name is on numerous things

Patch - a mule Meribeth rescued from the South Rim

Pegasus - a government truck which wouldn't stay on the road

plum jelly - any flavor jelly or jam

Pogo - his airplane, a Supercub. It makes lots of short hops.

Pogoing - patrolling in Pogo

polyg wagon - a crew cab pickup

politician's storm - thunder and lightning but no rain

racing slick - a pancake

Rancid Roy - a skunk that lived under the current ranger office

Reynard - any fox

Robert the Reject - an orphaned rock squirrel raised by John

Sierra - one of the horses

Something for men past 40 and girls of any age - pre-dinner drinks, usually bourbon and 7-Up

South Bedroom - overlook near the Cove where Laura and John slept on hot summer nights

Sparky - Witty generator

    Arcie - portable generator

    Big Sparky - large generator, required to use broiler

    Little Sparky - smaller generator

Susie - a mule Laura would ride into the canyon

Waldorf Astoria - garage when used as sleeping quarters

Waltzing Matilda - the front end loader

Witch Hazel - source of all mechanical breakdowns, associated with the Igaroties, living with them in the cave under Toroweap Point.

Index

146

About the Author

Jean Luttrell, a retired third grade teacher and freelance writer, is the author of three self-published books and two non-fiction books published by Marlor Press, *Heavy Weather Boating Emergencies* and *Grandma & Grandpa's Big Book of Fun.*

She is a member of Western Writers of America and the Grand Canyon Historical Society. She is a regular speaker for programs at the Arizona Strip Interpretive Association and other historical agencies.

The daughter of homesteaders, she grew up on the remote Arizona Strip. She now lives with her husband in Boulder City, Nevada.